MESSIANIC JUDAISM

MESSIANIC JUDAISM

A MODERN MOVEMENT WITH AN ANCIENT PAST

(A REVISION OF MESSIANIC JEWISH MANIFESTO)

DAVID H. STERN

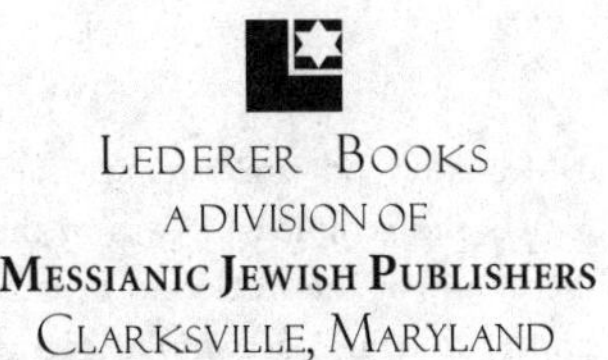

LEDERER BOOKS
A DIVISION OF
MESSIANIC JEWISH PUBLISHERS
CLARKSVILLE, MARYLAND

Printed in the United States of America

10 09 08 07   4321
ISBN 10: 1-880226-33-2
ISBN 13: 978-1-880226-33-9

Library of Congress Control Number 2006940728

Published by
MESSIANIC JEWISH PUBLISHERS
Post Office Box 615
Clarksville, MD 21029, U.S.A.

Distributed by
MESSIANIC JEWISH RESOURCES INTERNATIONAL

Order Line: (800) 410-7367
E-mail: lederer@messianicjewish.net
Website: www.messianicjewish.net

Cover art by Josh Huhn, Design Point, Inc.
Typeset by Barry Segal International, Ltd., Jerusalem, Israel
Printed in the United States of America

The Cover
To convey the fact that Messianic Judaism began in the first century C.E., the picture of Jerusalem depicts the Temple as it was in the days of the Messiah. Many centuries later, the Dome of the Rock was constructed as a holy site in the Moslem religion, and is seen in most similar pictures.

CONTENTS

PREFACE

This book is a partially revised version of my book Messianic Jewish Manifesto, which I developed in 1975 and wrote in 1988. That book was addressed primarily to Messianic Jews, offering elements of ideology, theology and program in a call to action. However, I hoped it would also be informative for others, whether in favor of our movement, opposed, or just curious. The book fulfilled my expectations. Now the time has come to update it.

Most of its facts and ideas are public property, but the presentation, emphases and conclusions are mine. I do not expect complete agreement even from friends, let alone from the movement's detractors. But one need not agree with a book to find it useful.

I combined portions of Chapters III, IV and V with Chapter VIII to form a shorter book, Restoring the Jewishness of the Gospel: A Message for Christians. Its intended readership was primarily Gentile Christians, and its purpose was to present some of this book's ideas more briefly. Whoever reads Manifesto or the present book has no need to read Restoring. Anyone who reads Restoring and has unanswered questions, wants to explore the issues further or is interested in understanding better my point of view is invited to read the present book. Appendix 1 contains a table showing the relationship between the two books in detail.

All the Bible references in the footnotes refer to the Jewish New Testament (JNT), my translation of the New Testament that highlights its essential Jewishness. They can also be found in the Complete Jewish Bible, which combines my version of the Tanakh with the JNT.

Of the many who have contributed to my understanding I wish to acknowledge explicitly the help and friendship of four other Messianic Jewish Israelis: First and foremost, my wife, Martha Stern—Eshet chayil animatzati! ("A woman of valor"—I found one! See Proverbs 31:10-31). The others: Joseph Shulam, founder of the "Roeh Israel" congregation, in which we participate now, the "Netivyah" organization and the "Messianic Midrasha" in Jerusalem; and Shira and Ari Sorko-Ram, in whose congregation we participated when we lived in Ramat-HaSharon. However, I alone am responsible for the book's contents.

I added to the second edition an epilogue called "Aliyah Update 1990" informing the reader of events (which were recent at the time) affecting Messianic Jewish immigration to Israel. To this edition I have added an Appendix called "Update 2006 and Some Thoughts about the Future."

David H. Stern
78 Manahat
96900 Jerusalem, Israel
25 Kislev 5767 (the first day of Chanukah)
Friday, December 15, 2006

CHAPTER I

DESTINY

A. THE HIGH CALLING OF GOD

According to the Tanakh, the goal of the Jewish people is to praise, thank, confess, obey, and make known the living God—in the words of Isaiah, to be a light to the nations.[1] But the Jewish people will never be that light to the nations without shining forth him who is the light of the world, Yeshua the Messiah.[2] Yet the Judaism handed down to us by our rabbis has not prepared us for this.

According to the Tanakh and the New Testament the goal of God's Messianic Community (which Christians call the Church) is to praise, thank, confess, obey and make known the living God—in the words of Yeshua, to make disciples of all nations,[3] so that through him those far from the national life of Israel might be brought near.[4] But the Church will never bring others near to Israel if she does not experience, express and enjoy her intimate involvement with the Jewish people. Yet most Christian teaching has not prepared her for this.

The central theme of this book is that without Messianic Judaism—Judaism which accepts Yeshua (Jesus, "Yeshu")[5] as the Messiah—both the Jewish people and the Church will fail to achieve their proper and glorious goals, goals which are ultimately coextensive.

---

1. Isaiah 49:6.
2. Yochanan [John] 8:12.
3. Mattityahu [Matthew] 28:18-20.
4. Ephesians 2:11-22.
5. The English name Jesus is a transliteration of the Greek Ieesous, which is itself a transliteration of Hebrew Yeshua. Most Israelis pronounce and spell the name as "Yeshu" and think of Yeshu as "the Christian God." But the name is properly spelled with the letter "a" (the Hebrew letter 'ayin) at the end, reflecting the fact that Yosef the husband of Miriam, Yeshua's mother, was instructed, "You are to call him Yeshua because he will save his people from their sins" (Mattityahu 1:21). This explanation explains nothing in English or in Greek; but in Hebrew, where the word yoshia, based on the same root as the name Yeshua, means "he will save," it explains everything.

   As Messianic Jews it is appropriate for us to want the Messiah's name properly spoken, spelled and understood.

This idea is not new. Indeed, it is two thousand years old, but for centuries its social expression remained dormant. However, in the last fifty years a unique constellation of social, historical, political, theological and spiritual factors have brought fresh life to the Messianic Jewish movement, so that it is attracting attention from many quarters, both in the Diaspora and in Israel. I am confident that the Messianic Jewish community will be the vehicle for healing the worst schism in the history of the world, the split between the Christians and the Jews, while helping both to fulfill their God-given callings.

The previous two paragraphs are not mere grandiosities, although one might think so. For of the world's five billion people, over a billion-and-a-half call themselves Christians, with a two-thousand-year history. Moreover, some fifteen million Jews have a four-thousand-year history. Is it possible that at most a few hundred thousand Messianic Jews, struggling to create a movement virtually from nothing, will become the means of dispelling the contradictions, differences, misunderstandings, discord, hate, violence, and refusal to communicate that have marred the relationship between the two separated branches of the one people of God? It is possible, and it will happen.

Why will it? Because God will cause it to happen: Thus says the Lord in the Holy Scriptures—which consist of the Hebrew Bible and the New Testament. God, through the New Covenant given by Yeshua the Jewish Messiah to the house of Israel and the house of Judah, will write the Torah on Jewish hearts; the Church will obey her mandate to proclaim the Gospel throughout the world; the fullness of the Gentiles will come in; and all Israel will be saved.[6]

Thus the destiny of Messianic Judaism is to live out the fact that it is simultaneously 100% Messianic and 100% Jewish, rejecting the "either-or" demanded by many Christians and Jews, and instead, through its very existence and self-expression, bringing reconciliation.[7] It will eventually be centered in Israel, the land God has promised the Jewish people. It will provide the matrix for the growth of true Judaism and true Christianity and for assisting both in fulfilling their rightful aims. It will be the chief means of bringing the Gospel to the Jewish people corporately, as a people.

---

6. Jeremiah 31:30–34; Mattityahu [Matthew] 28:18–20; Romans 11:25–26.
7. See Chapter III, Section G, on Jewish-Christian Relations, especially Section G–8.

But this Messianic Jewish triumph—which will be a victory for everyone, not just for Messianic Jews—will not be due to our power or size, for we are the fewest of all people. Rather, its success will be because, on the one hand, Messianic Judaism is right, an idea whose time has come, a radical solution which is the most natural thing in the world, and, on the other hand, because with God all things are possible.

To the end of forwarding this universal victory, the purposes of this book are to strengthen personal commitment to God and his Messiah, to elucidate what is Messianic Jewish identity, to suggest tasks in the building of the Messianic Jewish community, to present aspects of the Gospel to Jewish people in a Jewish way, to give instruction in overlooked aspects of Jewish evangelism, to increase awareness of the Jewishness of New Testament faith, and to facilitate tolerance and encouragement of the Messianic Jewish community by non-Jewish Christians, non-Messianic Jews and the rest of the world.

B. PLAN OF THE BOOK

1. *For Whom It Is Meant*

When I told the rabbi of the synagogue in which I grew up that I was a Messianic Jew, he said that I was trying to sit on the space between two chairs—nothing there! In a way, this book answers him, yet it is not addressed primarily to him or to non-Messianic Jews in general. Nor is its target audience non-Jewish Christians, many of whom also have doubts about Messianic Judaism. However, both are invited, as are Gentile non-Christians, to read this book alongside the Messianic Jews, for whom this book is meant as a rallying cry, galvanizing the troops to action.

2. *Preview*

Yet I have not even denned what Messianic Judaism is or justified its right to exist; this I will do in Chapter II. In Chapter III I will examine history—Jewish, Christian, Messianic Jewish—and the philosophy of history itself in order to show why Messianic Judaism should, must and does have the central role claimed for it.

The following two chapters deal with theology. Chapter IV is devoted to preliminaries and several substantive matters Messianic Judaism must address, while Chapter V, the longest in the book, is concerned with the key unresolved issue between Judaism and Christianity, the role of the Torah in relation to the New Covenant.

Chapter VI deals with holiness, which is fundamental to any Messianic Jewish vision or program. In Chapter VII, after reviewing where Messianic Judaism stands now, I will paint in broad strokes the outlines of a program for our movement. Finally, in Appendix 11 provide material to aid Messianic Jews in helping non-Jewish Christians play their part in restoring the Jewishness of the Gospel.

C. CHALLENGES

The Messianic Jewish movement is gaining ground, but time is moving on. Many of our pioneers have passed on without glimpsing the fulfillment of its goal, and many more will yet go to be with the Lord without seeing all Israel saved and the Church appreciating what it means to be grafted into a Jewish root and acting accordingly. But those who forward the goal will have the satisfaction of knowing they have participated in what God considers the most important healing in the world. Onward! Surely being a Messianic Jew is the most exciting way to be Jewish!

Lest non-Jewish Christians suppose I think Messianic Jews have a higher status than they in the Kingdom of God, let me say at the outset that all followers of Yeshua are equal. Their salvation is identical, due only to God's grace in providing effective atonement for sin through our Messiah Yeshua. If anything said in this book seems to imply otherwise, it must nevertheless be understood in the light of this assurance. We will see that there is much non-Jewish Christians can do to forward the Messianic Jewish movement, and we encourage and solicit such help from our valued Gentile brothers in the Messiah.

Yet ultimately Messianic Judaism depends on the Jews, because a Messianic Jew is a Jew who believes in Yeshua. Therefore the operative event that forwards Messianic Judaism is more Jewish people coming to Messianic faith. The Jewish reader of this book who does not yet believe that the New Testament and the Tanakh together constitute the words of the living God, and who has not yet accepted Yeshua as his Messiah, Atonement, Savior and Lord will nevertheless find this book a challenge to his received ideas about these things. My hope is that such people will read with an open mind, pray to the God of Abraham, Isaac and Jacob to show them if these things are true, and not fear to commit their lives to Yeshua the Messiah if God answers their prayers in the affirmative.

Finally, those who are neither Jewish nor Christian are invited to consider the truth of what is said here, and to commit their lives to Yeshua (Jesus) the Messiah.

D. THE ORIGINAL TITLE: MESSIANIC JEWISH MANIFESTO

I originally chose the title Messianic Jewish Manifesto for this book because I believed that Messianic Jews needed a clear proclamation of the purpose and direction of the Messianic Jewish movement. By way of explanation I wrote that the word "manifesto" was a variant of "manifest," from Latin manifestus, which means "palpable, clear, plain, apparent, evident." Webster's Third International Dictionary defines "manifest" as: "Capable of being readily and instantly perceived... not hidden or concealed .... Capable of being easily understood or recognized at once by the mind, not obscure, obvious." It defines "manifesto" as: "A public declaration of intentions, motives or views: a public statement of policy or opinion."

I called the book a manifesto because I was declaring an ideology and a program which I hoped would be readily perceived, easily understood by the mind, palpable, clear, plain and obvious, with nothing hidden, concealed or obscure. But I noted that I was writing a special kind of manifesto. The world's most famous document having this literary form is Karl Marx and Friedrich Engels' Communist Manifesto; its effect on twentieth century history is incalculable. The best known Jewish manifesto is Theodor Herzl's The Jewish State, in which the Austrian journalist set forth his ideas on solving "the Jewish problem" by recreating a Jewish homeland; a direct line leads from its publication in 1897 to the creation of the State of Israel fifty years later. However, these men did not try to conform their ideas to the Word of God, and I did require that of myself. Therefore my manifesto involved not only ideology and program, but also theology. I wanted to rally the troops, but only within the framework of God-given truth.

But in 1988, when I was writing the book, the Cold War was the primary fact of world politics, and the Communist Manifesto provided a recognizable backdrop to daily history. Today, fifteen years after the fall of the Soviet empire, that is no longer the case.

Meanwhile, Messianic Judaism is much more widely acknowledged by both Jews and Christians as a social, ideological, and theological force to be reckoned with. Therefore the need now is simply to provide information about the Messianic Jewish movement—who we are, what we want, what we do and why we do it. The book is still a manifesto, but I am giving it a new name, Messianic Judaism—a Modern Movement with an Ancient Past.

In this book I attempt to place before four publics—non-Jewish Christians, traditional and secular Jews, Messianic Jews and "the rest of the world" (non-Christian Gentiles)—a comprehensive picture of what Messianic Judaism is, and where it is headed, in order to replace the negative portrayals frequently found. For there are Christian churches and denominations offended by Messianic Jews and anyone else bringing Jewish people knowledge of the Jewish Messiah and New Testament truth. Other Christians suppose that Messianic Jews advocate non-scriptural doctrines or engage in "Judaizing" or seek to separate themselves from the rest of the Messiah's Body. On the other hand, the Jewish community—which once could ignore, shun or condemn Jews who "converted to Christianity"[8]—is increasingly required to deal seriously with the supposed deceptions and perceived threats posed by the Messianic Jews. We hope, of course, that in the end they will conclude that Messianic Judaism poses neither deceptions nor threats but honesty, reality and promise.

E. MY AUTHORITY TO WRITE THIS BOOK

You may wonder who granted me the authority to write a book explaining what Messianic Judaism is. The answer is: No one. No institution, group, rabbi or pastor appointed me spokesperson. Rather, what I can say is this: I am Jewish (born to Jewish parents and raised with Jewish values and traditions; I am Messianic (a believer in Yeshua; I have been educated at the graduate level in Christian, Jewish and academic institutions; I have thought a lot about the subject; and I had the desire to write this book for many years. Because I am writing on my own, I often use the first-person singular ("I think..."), where others might choose other locutions (e.g., "It is well-known that . . ." and "So we see . . ."), in order to avoid the appearance of claiming magisterial authority. Nor do I claim originality. Many of the same facts and ideas can be

8. See Appendix 1, footnote 5.

found in Daniel Juster's Jewish Roots,[9] rightly described as "the first comprehensive theology for Messianic Judaism," and in books by John Fischer,[10] Arnold Fruchtenbaum,[11] Jacob Jocz,[12] and others. If I have done something original, it is in writing with the purpose of stimulating action toward the goals of our movement. But originality is less important for me than making a systematic contribution to an ongoing discussion.

---

9. Daniel Juster, Jewish Roots (Pacific Palisades, California: Davar Publishing Co., 1986).
10. John Fischer, The Olive Tree Connection (Downers Grove, Illinois: InterVarsity Press, 1983)
11. Arnold Fruchtenbaum, Hebrew Christianity: Its Theology, History and Philosophy (Washington, D.C.: Canon Press, 1974)
12. Jacob Jocz, The Jewish People and Jesus Christ (London: S.P.C.K., 1962).

CHAPTER II
IDENTITY

A. WHY MESSIANIC JUDAISM?

1. *Building a Case*

Why should there be a Messianic Jewish movement at all? What need is there for Messianic Jewish identity? Without constructing the entire case myself, I wish to sketch ways of arguing in favor of Messianic Judaism:

The first four reasons support the idea that Messianic Judaism is *necessary* in the light of Scripture.

- Sha'ul's [Paul's] concept of cultural integrity, which says that the Gospel does not negate cultures but works through them, can be expressed in relation to the Jewish people only through Messianic Judaism.
- Messianic Judaism is implied by any correct theology of the Jews, who are, uniquely among the nations, God's chosen people.
- Messianic Judaism is necessary in order that Gentile Christians have the whole counsel of God.
- Only Messianic Judaism can provide the communal, theological and ideological framework within which currently non-Messianic Judaism can become what it ought to be.

The second group of reasons argue that Messianic Judaism is *useful* in accomplishing certain legitimate goals indicated by Scripture.

- By providing a Jewish environment for Messianic faith, Messianic Judaism is useful in evangelizing Jews.
- It is useful in focussing the Church's attention on the Jewish people, so that Gentile Christians may appreciate their own Jewish roots and have a correct understanding of Jewish tradition.
- It is useful in ministering to Jews who have accepted Yeshua as the Messiah.
- It will be a witness to the world: the healing effect of God's love on Jewish-Christian relations expressed through Messianic Judaism will speak to non-Christian Gentiles.

Besides building a case we must build a positive model of who we are and who we ought to be. This positive model is not altogether abstract. We have not only a glorious future, but also a past history and a present community.[1] We have Yeshua as our perfect example. And we have an ongoing relationship with God—as individuals, as Jews, and as members of the Messiah's Body. This relationship is structured by his Word; and this Word, the Bible, is a given, not subject to the wishes of either Jews or Christians who would rather define us differently. Our history, our community, our future, the Messiah's example and God's Word shape our identity.

2. *Jewish Opposition*

But there is also opposition. Some in the Jewish community would certainly prefer that we not exist as a movement. Given that we do exist, they try to exclude us from their company and sometimes even from their consciousness. Some refuse to acknowledge that we are Jews at all; indeed, this is a common,

1. See Chapter III, Section F, and Chapter VII, Section A.

if ostrich-like, attitude. Or we may be counted as Jews, but only as bad ones. Under such conditions we naturally feel pressure to prove that our Jewishness is both real and good, and that we have a right to be included. Nevertheless, being included and accepted by our brothers in the flesh cannot be our main aim. Only knowing, acting upon and communicating the truth and love of God can fill that role.

3. *Gentile Christian Opposition*

Gentile Christians sometimes subject us to two kinds of treatment which are opposite to each other but both unsatisfactory. Some churches try to assimilate us to Gentile ways, denying our right to express our Jewishness; this is often done under the banner of eliminating "the middle wall of partition" between Jews and Gentiles which has been broken down by Yeshua the Messiah.[2] Other churches regard us as extra-special—either as weird, not quite-Christians, or as super-Christians doubly blessed. In the latter case we are put on display—we are requested to give our "testimony" every other week, and any question about the Old Testament is immediately referred to "our Jewish Christian"—in short, we become the church's token Jew. In either case our Jewishness becomes a *cause celebre,* and—more to the point here—it gets defined not by ourselves but by the Gentiles around us. This tends to dehumanize us, making us into other folks' things instead of our own persons.

Some in the Church argue that Messianic Judaism is wrong. Here are six reasons I have heard, along with my refutations:

a. Separatism: Rebuilding The "Middle Wall Of Partition."

Messianic Judaism is a form of separatism within the Body ruled out by such verses as Galatians 3:28 ("There is neither Jew nor Greek," compare Colossians 3:11) and Ephesians 2:14

2. Ephesians 2:11-22.

(Yeshua "has broken down the middle wall of partition which divided" Jew and Gentile).

> The cited verses mean that Jewish and Gentile individuals are equal before God in regard to salvation from sin, as are men and women. Yet men and women still exist, as do Jews and Gentiles. Each have their own functions, rules and promises in God's economy.[3]

b. No Longer A Jew But A Christian.

A Jew who accepts Yeshua is no longer a Jew but a Christian and should deemphasize his Jewish origins.

> The New Testament Jewish believers like Sha'ul [Paul] and Kefa [Peter] continued to acknowledge and practice their Jewishness.[4] Moreover, the New Testament does not indicate that believers ever called Messianic Jews "Christians."[5]

c. Pride In Jewishness, Invidious Comparison With Gentile Believers.

Messianic Jews may take undue pride in being both natural and born-again members of God's people; they will consider Gentile Christian second-class citizens in the Kingdom of God, and engage in what Moishe Rosen, the former leader of Jews for Jesus, calls "ethnolatry" (idolatous worship of one's own people).

> Pride is indeed a sin, though it is not limited to Messianic Jews. It should always be guarded against, but the risk does not constitute a reason to disallow Messianic Judaism.

---

3. For more on this see Chapter V, Section B.
4. In the case of Sha'ul, see H. L. Ellison, "Paul and the Law, 'All Things To All Men,'" in W. Ward Gasque and Ralph P. Martin, *Apostolic History and the Gospel* (Grand Rapids, Michigan: Wm. B. Eerdmans Publishing Company, 1970), pp. 195-202. Also see Appendix, Section B-2-c, last paragraph.
5. See Section C-4 below.

d. Heretical Overemphasis On Judaism.

Messianic Judaism overemphasizes Jewishness at the expense of New Testament truth and practice, thus becoming a retrograde or heretical form of Christianity, like that of the Ebionites.[6]

> Genuine heresy is to be avoided, but the danger is small. However, in the Diaspora, where a Jew is always under pressure to maintain his Jewishness in a Gentile society, Messianic Jews do risk letting Jewishness replace Yeshua as the focus of congregational life. This danger is greatly diminished in Israel, since there Jewishness can be taken for granted. More on this in Chapter VII.

e. Judaizing.

Messianic Judaism sanctions Judaizing, which is a heresy.

> False. Judaizing means requiring Gentiles to live or behave like Jews (see Galatians 2:11-15); the heresy is insisting they are not saved unless they do so. But encouraging Jews to live as Jews is not Judaizing—how could it be? Remember that Sha'ul did not teach Jews to stop circumcising their sons or to abandon the *Torah.*[7]

f. Artificial, Not Indigenous.

Messianic Judaism is artificial, not truly indigenous, except possibly in the State of Israel.

> This argument could only arise in the Jewish Diaspora; it is a variation of the separatism argument. But God, who intends to preserve the Jews, seems to have done

---

6. On this second-century Jewish-Christian sect which acknowledged Yeshua but not Sha'ul, see Hans-Joachim Schoeps, Jewish Christianity (Philadelphia: Fortress Press, 1964).
7. Acts 16:1-3,21:17-27.

it partly by having them retain their separate religion and customs in the Gentile cultures in which they have lived.

The majority culture need not be Jewish for Messianic Judaism to be indigenous, since normal existence for Jews in Diaspora is as a subculture. The fact that the subculture does not prevail does not make it less real. Therefore, a Jewish form of Messianic faith which arises in a Jewish Diaspora subculture is indigenous.

But I will agree that the most natural place in the world for Messianic Judaism to take root is in Israel, and to this we will return in the last chapter.

B. "MESSIANIC JEW"—DEFINITIONS

1. *Who Is A Jew?*

Defining "Messianic Jew" is not easy. Anyone acquainted with the State of Israel knows that the question, "Who is a Jew?" constantly arises in the politico-religious life of the country,[8] and with no topic is the old quip truer, "Two Jews, three opinions."

According to *halakhah* (Jewish religious law),[9] a Jew is anyone who was born of a Jewish mother or who has converted to Judaism. A current issue in Israel concerns who has the authority to perform conversions which the secular State will recognize. The Orthodox rabbinate claims that only Orthodox rabbis can do it, while the Conservative and Reform movements of course claim the privilege for their rabbis as well.

Meanwhile, it is commonly accepted that the Bible traces Jewishness genetically through the father. According to this

---

8. Baruch Litvin, compiler, and Sidney B. Hoenig, editor, *Jewish Identity: Modern Responsa and Opinions* (New York: Feldheim, 1970) presents views of more than 40 Jewish leaders reflecting the full spectrum of Jewish life from religious to secular on the subject of "who is a Jew."
9. On the meaning *of halakhah,* see Chapter V, footnote 9.

theory, Jewishness came to be traced through the mother at a time of historical turmoil when Jewish women were being sold as concubines to Gentiles, so that there could be doubt whether a child's father was Jewish. However, one can make a case that even in the Bible Jewishness depends on the mother.[10] Some in the Reform movement have cut the Gordian knot by accepting as a Jew anyone with either parent Jewish.

As with most definitions, difficulties arise at the margin. For example, I once spoke in a Pentecostal Holiness church in Oklahoma. Afterwards a lady came up to share what she considered an interesting sidelight about herself, that her mother's mother had been "a Jewess" before "converting to Christianity." The lady's appearance, language and other social traits were the same as those of the Gentile Christian women around her; but *halakhah* says that the granddaughter is Jewish, no matter how she looks or talks.

David Ben-Gurion, Israel's first Prime Minister, said that a Jew is anybody who, given the burdens Jews bear, is willing to call himself one. His witticism shows that there are factors other than parentage which help identify Jewishness: nationhood, peoplehood, ethnicity, culture, sociology, religion, history.

It also points to the subjective side of being Jewish, acknowledging one's Jewishness, as opposed to denying or ignoring it. Should we call anyone whose parents are Jewish a Jew? Or should the term be applied only to those who acknowledge their Jewishness in some fashion? The nearly universal custom is to make no such requirement. But we will return to the subject when defining "Messianic Jew" below, where we will also discuss Gentile Christians who call themselves Jews on the basis of certain New Testament verses.

The issue of "Who is a Jew?" is important for the Messianic Jew wanting to make *aliyah* (immigrate to Israel) under Israel's Law of Return, which grants nearly immediate citizen-

---

10. Israel's former Chief Rabbi Shlomo Goren does this ingeniously in Litvin and Hoenig (*op. cit.* in footnote 8 above), pp. 32-37.

ship and many privileges to any Jew, anywhere in the world, who moves to the Land. For purposes of the Law of Return Israel defines a Jew as "a person who was born of a Jewish mother or has been converted to Judaism, and who is not a member of another religion." The issue yet to be definitively decided in Israel's courts is whether the phrase "and who is not a member of another religion" excludes Messianic Jews. The Supreme Court decided in 1978 that Eileen (Esther) Dorflinger, a believer in Yeshua born of Jewish parents and baptized in a denominational church by an ordained Christian clergyman, although she maintained some aspects of a Jewish cultural lifestyle, could not come to Israel as a Jew under the Law of Return. Another important case, that of Gary and Shirley Beresford, from Zimbabwe and South Africa, was decided against them by the Supreme Court in 1989.[11]

2. *Who Is Messianic?*

Not everyone who is called Messianic or Christian is. In Jewish circles the terms "Gentile" and "Christian" are often used interchangeably. This is confusing. A Gentile is any non-Jew. But a Christian is—well, that's a bit more complicated.

Protestants tend to define "Christian" in terms of belief. Only "genuine believers" are to be counted as Christians. There would be differences over who is a "genuine believer," but something like the following would approach consensus: a person (Jew or Gentile) who has turned from idols or unfaith to serve the living God though Yeshua the Messiah with all his heart and soul and strength, having accepted the truth of the whole Bible—consisting of the *Tanakh* [the "Old Testament"] and the New Covenant Scriptures ("New Testament")—and having acknowledged Yeshua as Israel's Messiah, and as his own atonement for sin and Lord of his life.

Such a definition excludes the "cultural Christian," who may have grown up in a Christian home, gone to church and

---

11. See pages 229-230 and "*Aliyah* Update 1990" on pages 265 ff.

Sunday School, read the Bible and been baptized, but has not been born again,[12] who has not given his heart to live by God's every word. Likewise it excludes the "nominal Christian," who may have concluded intellectually that Yeshua is the Messiah, who may have gone through all the standard rituals and procedures, who may have experienced God's healing, his guidance, and even his presence; but holiness has not entered his life—such "faith without works is dead."[13]

Roman Catholics and the older Eastern denominations, as well as some mainline Protestants, tend to define being Christian in terms of community. This corresponds more to what most Jewish people understand when talking about a person's religion, and it is easy to see why. A person whose parents are Jewish is Jewish. So why shouldn't a person whose parents are Christian be Christian? The answer must finally come from Scripture, and there the definition is in terms of faith. "Men, what must I do to be saved?" asked the Greek jailer in Philippi. "Trust in the Lord Yeshua, and you will be saved. .. ."[14] The Church *is* a community, but only of persons saved by faith, which cannot be inherited from parents.

It remains only to compare the terms "Messianic" and "Christian." "Messianic"comes from Hebrew *mashiach,* which

---

12. Yochanan [John] 3:3. The term "born again," now a cliche in America, originates here. For the meaning in context, see Yochanan 3:1-21.
13. Ya'akov [James] 2:14-26. See also Chapter VI, Section D.
14. Acts 16:30-31. The term "saved" has become a Christian buzzword. But for the individual it means "delivered from guilt, forgiven for sin, brought into the process wherein sin's stranglehold on one's life is being ended." This meaning, hidden to those who live in the fast lane (witness the title of psychiatrist Karl Menninger's book, *Whatever Became of Sin?),* seems to have been known in the ancient world to ordinary people, at least to the Philippian prison guard who asked the question. When the Jewish people gathered at the Temple to celebrate *Shavu'ot* asked essentially the same question, "Kefa [Peter] answered them, 'Turn from sin, return to God, and each of you be immersed on the authority of Yeshua the Messiah into forgiveness of your sins, and you will receive the gift of the *Ruach HaKodesh* [the Holy Spirit]!'" (Acts 2:38, *Jewish New Testament',* see below, footnote 20.)

means "anointed." "Christian" comes from Greek *christos,* which is the New Testament's translation of *mashiach* and means the same thing. Messianic Jews prefer the former for cultural reasons: for most Jews the term "Messianic" creates less cognitive dissonance than "Christian." But a more compelling reason is that in the New Testament the term "Christian," which appears only three times,[15] apparently denotes being a Gentile believer in Yeshua; if this is so, "Jewish Christian" is a contradiction in terms.[16]

3. *Who Is A Messianic Jew?*

So then, who is a Messianic Jew?[17] My first choice for a definition is:

> A person who was born Jewish or converted to Judaism, who is a "genuine believer" in Yeshua, and who acknowledges his Jewishness.

This includes those who call themselves Hebrew Christians (see below). But a narrower definition would exclude them by calling Messianic Jews only those who wish to live a demonstratively Jewish lifestyle, that is, a Messianic life within the framework of *Torah.* (See more on this below.)

A broader definition would also include assimilated Jews who are not interested in, or even are opposed to, acknowledging their Jewishness. We raised this question earlier and said that; this consideration is not part of the definition of "Jew." But perhaps "Messianic Jew" makes different demands. I personally think it is a mistake to confer the term "Messianic Jew" on just any believer in Yeshua whose parents happen to be

15. Acts 11:26,26:28; 1 Kefa [l Peter] 4:16.
16. See Section C-4 below.
17. On how the first-century Jewish believers were regarded by the Jewish community, see Lawrence H. Schiffman, *Who Was A Jew?—Rabbinic and Halakhic Perspectives on the Jewish-Christian Schism* (Hoboken, New Jersey: Ktav Publishing House, 1985).

Jewish. Perhaps, if he has not thought about his Jewishness much, he could be called a "potential" Messianic Jew. But if he is running away from his Jewish identity, calling himself "an ex-Jew" or "a former Jew" or "a Christian and not a Jew," I would ask some consciousness-raising on his part before I would call him a Messianic Jew. One might relate to people in this category with the "Not yet" of Franz Rosenzweig.[18]

There are Gentile Christians who cite verses such as Romans 2:28-29 ("He is a Jew who is one inwardly, and real circumcision is a matter of the heart, spiritual and not literal.") and Philippians 3:3 ("For it is we who are the Circumcised, we who worship by the Spirit of God and make our boast in the Messiah Yeshua!") as authority for calling themselves Messianic Jews. I think this is a mistake and a misuse of Scripture.[19] A Gentile believer in Yeshua, called a "Christian" in Acts 11:26, or perhaps a "Gentile Christian" in modern terminology to distinguish him from a "Jewish Christian" (neither term is found in Scripture), is not a Messianic Jew. He may promote Messianic Judaism. He may love Messianic Jews. He may feel an affinity toward Jewish forms of worship which honor Yeshua the Messiah. He may speak of himself metaphorically as having a Jewish heart. But he is not a Jew, Messianic or otherwise. I suggest that in order to distinguish him from Gentiles who have not come to faith in the God of Abraham, Isaac and Jacob through Yeshua the Messiah, while at the same time associating him with the Messianic Jewish movement, one might call him a Messianic Gentile.

---

18. Franz Rosenzweig (1886-1929), an assimilated German Jewish intellectual, considered converting to Christianity until he was won back to Judaism by the beauty of an Orthodox *Yom Kippur* service; he became one of this century's important philosophers. Since he had not grown up observing Jewish practices, he was once asked, after his return to Judaism, "Do you lay *tefillin?*' His answer: "Not yet." (Speculation: Had Messianic Judaism existed then, would Rosenzweig have become a Messianic Jew?)

19. Refer to my notes on these verses in the *Jewish New Testament Commentary* (see below, footnote 20). I occasionally encounter a Gentile Christian who says, "God told me I was Jewish," and proceeds thenceforth to call himself a Jew. Revelation 2:9 has hard words for "those who say they are Jews and are not"; see my note to this verse in the *Jewish New Testament Commentary.*

4. *Sub-Messianic Jews*

With the above definition we can analyze a number of sub-Messianic Jewish positions. These close competitors of Messianic Judaism often have admirable features, yet I would reject them for various reasons.

The following positions are "too Jewish" or "not Messianic enough:"

- "Open" Jews, Jews who are willing to hear about Yeshua and the Gospel but don't get saved. They may have good things to say about Yeshua, the New Testament and believers, but they are not willing to take the step of faith needed to be born again.
- "Secret believers" who remain in the Jewish community without confessing publicly their faith in Yeshua. I must state clearly that these people are not Messianic and have not been born again; for Yeshua said, "Whoever acknowledges me in the presence of others I will also acknowledge in the presence of my Father in heaven; but whoever disowns me before others I will I disown before my Father in heaven."[20]
- Some Jewish believers find themselves uncomfortable in Gentile Christian churches, but are not located near a Messianic Jewish congregation. They don't go to any church but have casual fellowship with likeminded people. Communal aspects of our faith achievable only

---

20. Mattityahu [Matthew] 10:32-33. *Jewish New Testament* (Jewish New Testament Publications, P. O. Box 615, Clarksville, Maryland 21029, USA, 1989; 3rd printing, 1990), my translation of the New Testament which expresses its Jewishness. A companion volume, the *Jewish New Testament Commentary,* deals with Jewish issues raised by the New Testament. See Chapter VII, Section D-l.

in a congregational setting get neglected. The person's faith is Messianic, not "sub-Messianic," but his spiritual growth is stunted by his stand-offishness.

The following positions can be characterized as "too Gentile:"

- Jews who Gentilize themselves in Christian churches, doing all they can to conceal their Jewishness and "pass" as Gentiles. This phenomenon was more prevalent in the eighteenth and nineteenth centuries, when many Jews considered baptism "the passport to Western Civilization." Often Jews who do this lack genuine faith, since their motive is to stop being Jewish, not to come to God.
- Veneer of Jewishness. Often Christian missions to the Jews put a thin veneer of Jewishness, to the best of their ability, over what is clearly a Gentile Christian approach to faith. The complaint of some in the Jewish community that Christians "misuse Jewish sancta" in order to hide the fact that they are trying to win Jews to Christ is most easily demonstrated in connection with such missions and churches. The problem arises from the missionary's unawareness of how Jewish the Gospel really is and of how to express biblical Messianic faith in genuinely Jewish ways.[21]

These involve disturbances in how Jewishness gets expressed:

- Some forms of Hebrew Christianity, as opposed to Messianic Judaism (in the narrow sense), are fossilized. Although Hebrew Christianity from the early 1800's until the 1930's was frequently as radical as Messianic Judaism is considered to be today, some of the people who flock to that banner now do not keep up with what present reality calls for. Instead they canonize earlier

21. See Chapter V, Section C-5; and Appendix, Sections B and C.

approaches that were more relevant when society in general and the church in particular were less open to expressing Jewishness and Messianic faith together. There are some people who are very open to exploring every possibility for expressing Messianic faith in Jewish ways but happen to prefer the term "Hebrew Christianity" to "Messianic Judaism;" they're not the fossils!

- On the other side, there is a genuine danger, noted earlier, of becoming so enamored with Jewishness that the basic truths of the Gospel become neglected. One might expect this of those whose lives were thoroughly immersed in Jewish practice before they came to faith; but actually it seems to work out differently. Often it is Jews who had little education in Judaism before believing in Yeshua who become unduly attached to a few Jewish customs and make these the center of their lives instead of Yeshua.

5. *100% Messianic and 100% Jewish*

The premise of this book is that there is no conflict whatever between being Messianic and being Jewish. Believing in Yeshua, the Jewish Messiah, is one of the most Jewish things a Jew can do. A Jewish believer in Yeshua is not faced with having to give up some Jewishness in order to be more Messianic, or having to give up some of his Messianic faith to be more Jewish.[22] Non-Messianic Jews might try to convince him of this, as might some Gentile Christians, but they would be wrong. The New Testament picture throughout is that Jews who believed in Yeshua remained as fully Jewish as they ever were.[23] The only change required by their faith was not in the direction of less Jewishness but greater godliness. Thus a Messianic Jew does not choose between being, say, 80% Christian and 20% Jewish as over against the reverse; rather, he can and should say that he

22. Except as indicated in Chapter VII, Section F.
23. See footnote 4, above; Chapter III, Section D-3, paragraphs 2 and 3; and Appendix, Section C-l.

is 100% Jewish and 100% Messianic, and then he should seek to express these truths in his life.

But when I call myself both Jewish and Messianic, I am thereby identifying with both the Jewish community and the Church. Although in the New Testament the word "Church" means "God's Messianic Community" of genuine believers, it can also refer to an institution that characteristically includes name-only believers. This makes problems for me; here's a typical one: how do I as a Messianic Jew deal with the Church's persecution of the Jews? If I am fully part of the Church and fully Jewish, then I am one with both the persecutors and their victims. What can that mean? Here is a possible analysis:

- As a victim I feel very negatively toward the persecutor—as a Jew I feel bitter about what the Church has done over the centuries to my people.
- As a Messianic I have gratitude toward the Church, despite its being a persecutor, because the Church, either directly or indirectly, has made the Messiah known to me.
- As a Messianic Jew I can forgive the persecutor (if he wants to be forgiven). That is, the bitterness I might have cherished against the Church as an unsaved person is gone, because of what God has done for me and to me through Yeshua.
- But I am also the persecutor, for identity with the Church as persecutor is inevitably part of the baggage that comes with joining the Messianic Community. To whatever extent I may represent the Church I can be repentant on its behalf and seek the forgiveness of the Jews. But I cannot expect them, as unsaved people, to be willing to forgive me.[24]

---

24. There are Jewish believers in Yeshua who go to Gentile Christian groups—in Germany and elsewhere—proffering forgiveness on behalf of "the Jews" for Christian mistreatment of them. This seems unwise. I can offer my own forgiveness, but "the Jews" have not made me their proxy.

I have two hats, I am part of two communities at odds with each other. Moreover, unless the spiritual transaction which enables people to forgive from their hearts takes place among the Jews, I do not expect "us the Jews" to forgive "us the Church." Appreciate the delicacy and tension in the situation—which, even though it is history's creation, not mine, I cannot escape, because I am part of history. I am not schizophrenic about it; rather, I pray for the promised day when all Israel will be saved, for only in that way will the tension between "me the persecuted" and "me the persecutor" be dissolved.

6. The Challenge of Being A Messianic Jew

From this example we can learn that it is not easy to be a Messianic Jew. It is therefore not surprising if most of us Messianic Jews are ill prepared for our role, which is not merely a matter of private faith but has public implications for two great communities of people set in discord by history. A purpose of this book is to help us Messianic Jews understand who we are and what is expected of us. We need to understand both our Jewish and our Messianic identity better. It is not enough for us merely to proclaim loudly our Jewishness if, like the great majority of Messianic Jews, we are Jewishly unlearned and uninvolved. If we call ourselves Messianic Jews we must intend to back up our words with actions demonstrating that our Jewishness has substance. Likewise, we may know that we have been united with the Messiah by faith, but if we fail to do what our Lord commands and continue in our worldly ways instead of shedding them, we put God to public shame.

We seek to have our Messianic Jewish identity accepted by non-Messianic Jews and Gentile Christians but meet rejection. If we try to forget who we are and seek the world's pleasures, our conscience, with both Jewish and Messianic sensitivities—will not permit us. So we turn to our brother Messianic Jews but too often we find shallowness, self-ghetto-ization, or false bravado. There are communities which have advanced beyond this stage, but others have not. In any case, our numbers are few and we struggle to meet even our own needs (e.g., caring for the Messianic Jewish poor, supporting Messianic Jewish pastors, giving scholarships to those who require them), let alone reach out to others. Our leadership, though dedicated, would be the first to acknowledge its own shortcomings. We are far from being what we would like to be—by the standard of either the Jewish community or the Church.

We say the Messiah has given meaning to our lives. But the words ring hollow \when compared with the smallness of our vision most of the time. We have a full-blown identity crisis.

We Messianic Jews need an ideology and a program to express the inner truth of who we are. For we are 100% Jewish, no matter who denies it. And we are 100% Messianic, no matter who denies it. So it was for the first-century Jewish believers, and so it must be today. This is God-determined truth, in the face of all lies, slanders and disinformation of those who would deny us our true identity. Yet it is up to us to make good our claims. We must, in the Messiah, in obedience to God, through the power of his Holy Spirit, create the visible reality that will validate our rhetoric.

"Let him who would boast, boast in the Lord," we read in both the *Tanakh* and the New Testament.[25] So we will not boast in our Jewish identity, but in the God of the universe who chose to act through a people of whom we are a part. Nor will we boast in our Messianic identity, but in the Messiah who chose from among Jews and Gentiles those who are his, and we are his. And thirdly, we will not boast in our Messianic Jewish identity, but in the Lord who has made us the bridge between the two separated communities of which we are part and given us the work of helping to bring them together. Let us dedicate ourselves to carry out our responsibility by the power of the Holy Spirit in us, so that Yeshua the Messiah and God the Father may be glorified in a united people of God.

---

25. 1 Corinthians 1:31, Jeremiah 9:23-24.

C. TERMINOLOGY

1. *Alternatives to the Term "Messianic Jew"*

A variety of terms have been and are being used to describe Jews who believe in Yeshua. Here are those which have come to my attention, along with my reactions:

- *Jewish believer.* Vague, since it is unclear in what or whom he believes. Orthodox Jews and religious Jews from other streams are also called Jewish believers. But if the context is clear, the term lends variety, and I use it throughout this book.
- *Messianic believer.* Also vague, because although it is clear that the person believes in the Messiah, it is not clear whether he is Jewish or Gentile.[26]
- *Hebrew Christian.* An older term, dating from the nineteenth century—today it sounds a bit quaint to call a Jew a "Hebrew." Nevertheless, the term is important, since it is used by Jews believing in Yeshua who wish to stress the priority of their Christianity over their Jewishness. Some may be using the term out of inertia, or because it is better known in the circles they move in, or to honor the many Jewish believers for whom it was the banner, or to avoid offending Gentile Christians who might be put off by a term that does not include the word "Christian." The terms "Hebrew Christian" and "Messianic Jew" (in the narrower sense) describe different streams or ways of being a Jewish believer in Yeshua.
- *Jewish Christian.* Though easily understood by the public, scholars use this term (and *Judeo- Christian)* narrowly to refer to Jews who accepted Yeshua as Messiah during the first four centuries of the Common Era. In some ways it is a neutral term; yet when one's object is to emphasize the Jewishness of believing in the Jewish Messiah, it is wiser not to employ a word

26. See Section C-3 below.

("Christian") which the New Testament seems to use only for Gentile believers.[27]

- *Christian Jew.* Same idea, although the term is not used by scholars.
- *Completed Jew, Fulfilled Jew.* By accepting New Testament truth a Jew completes and fulfills his Old Testament faith. Traditional Jews may object to the implication that their own faith is incomplete and unfulfilled; but the terms speak for themselves, and the implication is correct: Judaism without Yeshua is less complete and full than it some day will become. Nevertheless, because of inherent tendentiousness, as well as certain vagueness, the term does not commend itself.
- *Biblical Jew,* that is, one who follows what is taught in the entire Bible, both Old and New Testaments. Sometimes it also implies rejection of the Oral *Torah* and "rabbinism" as unbiblical. Again, this seems a needlessly tendentious term, since Jews from other streams consider their own versions of Judaism to be based on the Hebrew Bible. Moreover, many Messianic Jews would on principle not want to imply that they separate themselves from all rabbinic traditions.
- *Jew for Jesus.* The organization "Jews for Jesus", founded in the early 1970's and having as its main purpose the evangelization of Jewish people, was given this name by its detractors. The name was so striking that it stuck. Not only that, but the term came to be applied to the tens of thousands of Jews who believe in Yeshua but who are not members of that organization, as well as to the several dozen who are. Since an organization is called by that name, it is confusing to use the same name for the movement as a whole. Moreover, the organization "Jews for Jesus" has a distinctive style and approach which is not necessarily shared by all Jewish believers in Yeshua.

27. See Section C-4 below and Chapter III, Section H.

2. *"Messianic Jew," Objections and Answers*

The term "Messianic Judaism" has a documented history going back to 1895,[28] it was used again by Theodore Lucky in a controversy with David Baron around 1911, and it appeared in articles in the journal of the International Hebrew Christian Alliance in the early 1920's. But it did not come into common use until the 1960's and 1970's, a period when many Americans were looking for their ethnic roots. In the late 1960's Manny Brotman called his organization "Messianic Jewish Movement International." In 1975 the Hebrew Christian Alliance of America changed its name to "Messianic Jewish Alliance of America" (MJAA); this marks a watershed. From that time the use of the term by those who stress the Jewishness of believing in Yeshua has continued to grow. The formation of the Union of Messianic Jewish Congregations (UMJC) in 1979 brought the term into still wider circulation.

Some object to the term; nevertheless, I am strongly in favor of Messianic Jews' taking the initiative in defining their own identity and using their own terminology. Concerning the main objection to the term "Messianic Jew" raised by traditional Jews (though occasionally by liberal Christians) I can do no better than quote Daniel Juster, first president of the UMJC:

> "The term Messianic Judaism is decried as being unfair; for although *Messiah* is a term which linguistically precedes the word *Christos* in Greek—and is thus properly used to refer to Jews who believe the Messiah, Jesus, has come—it can be argued that all orthodox or Old-Testament-believing Jews are Messianic, since they believe in the coming of the Messiah, or at least in a Messianic Age. No form of Judaism or Christianity, however, has used the term "Messianic

28. David Rausch, *Messianic Judaism: Its History, Theology, and Policy* (New York and Toronto: The Edwin Mellin Press, 1982), pp. 55 ff. According to Robert I. Winer, M.D., the Hebrew form of "Messianic Jews," *Yehudiim Meshichiim*, was carved on stone in New York in 1878 (lecture presented at the 1987 convention of the Messianic Jewish Alliance of America).

> Judaism" as its appropriate designation. For better or worse the meaning of words is given by those who use them. Hence the evolution of language.
>
> "Messianic Judaism" has earned its meaning as a term by those in the grass roots who employ it. The day will come when most Jews and Christians will understand the term as . . . referring to Jews who follow Jesus and maintain a loyalty to their Jewish heritage."[29]

3. *"Messianic" Versus "Messianic Jewish"*

"Did you go to the Messianic conference? We heard some great Messianic music." The speaker is referring to a Messianic *Jewish* conference but doesn't bother to say "Jewish." Since "Messianic" and "Christian" are often taken as synonyms, he could in theory be describing a conference with nothing Jewish about it, a Christian conference of, by and for Gentile Christians. Likewise, the "Messianic" music could have been a concert of 19th-century Protestant hymns. Or Bach cantatas and Haydn masses.

I am enough of a purist to prefer sticking the word "Jewish" in there. I want it heard. There are still people unacquainted with our movement who don't get the point unless both "Messianic" and "Jewish" are said. However, it's probably a losing battle. "For better or worse the meaning of words is given by those who use them. Hence the evolution of language."

4. *Are Messianic Jews "Christians"? Part 1: "Christian" in the New Testament.*

This terminological question generates an amazing amount of heat, as people with various hidden agendas furiously insist that we are or that we are not.

---

29. Juster (*op. cit.* in Chapter I, footnote 8), p. viii.

The answer has two parts. First, since the word "Christian" originates in the New Testament, we need to see how it is used there, in a first-century context. But to answer the question in the twentieth century we need the historical analysis of the next chapter. So, delaying our final discussion till the end of Chapter III, we will here examine the meaning of "Christian" in the New Testament.

According to Scripture the word "Christian" does not denote Jewish believers in Yeshua at all. The New Testament calls them followers of "this way" (Acts 9:2, 22:4) and "Nazarenes" (Acts 24:5). They are natural branches of the tree into which Gentile believers have been grafted (Romans 11:16-26), they are original members of the commonwealth to which Gentile believers have been joined (Ephesians 2:11-16). But the New Testament does not call Jewish believers "Christians." According to New Testament usage the term "Christian" is reserved for Gentile believers in the Jewish Messiah Yeshua.

Acts 11:19-26 tells how in Antioch some Jewish believers from Cyprus and Cyrene did not limit their proclamation of Yeshua as the Messiah to Jews, as had been the norm previously, but broke new ground by proclaiming the Gospel to Greeks as well. Many of these Gentiles came to believe in the *"christos"* (the Greek word translates the Hebrew word *mashiach;* both words mean "anointed," with the one having been brought over into English as "Christ" and the other as "Messiah"). Apparently the other Gentiles in Antioch heard their friends always talking about this *"christos" and* acknowledging him as their leader; so they coined the word *christianoi* ("Christians"), much as the followers of Reverend Sun Myung Moon have been dubbed "Moonies." Thus the term "Christian" was invented by Gentiles to describe Gentiles in a Gentile environment. The New Testament tells us explicitly that "the disciples were first called Christians in Antioch."[30]

The word appears only twice more in the New Testament. In Acts 26:24-29, Sha'ul [Paul], detained in Caesarea until he

30. Acts 11:26.

could be tried before the Emperor in Rome, addressed King Herod Agrippa and his court. Intent at presenting a closely reasoned defense of Yeshua's Messiahship in a Jewish thought-framework, he was suddenly interrupted by the Roman governor, Festus, shouting "at the top of his voice, 'Sha'ul, you're out of your mind! So much learning is driving you crazy!'"

Sha'ul's reply was:

> "No, I am not 'crazy,' Festus, Your Excellency; on the contrary, I am speaking words of truth and sanity. For the king understands these matters, so to him I express myself freely, because I am sure that none of these things have been hidden from him. After all, they didn't happen in some back alley. King Agrippa, do you believe the prophets? I know you believe!"

The sophisticated King Agrippa rebounded off Sha'ul's earnestness (which had been necessary here to counter Festus' outburst), gently twitting him:

> "In this short time, you're trying to convince me to become a 'Christian[5]?"

Rather than "Nazarene," he used the term his Gentile courtiers might be familiar with, even though few would have any more understood the content of the faith than the average person today would understand Reverend Moon's religion.

Neither affirming nor disputing the king's use of the word, "Christian," Sha'ul answered with a light touch, dispelling the derision without demeaning the seriousness of his own message:

> "Whether it takes a short time or a long time, I wish to God that not only you, but also everyone hearing me today, might become just like me—except for these chains!"

"Christian" appears the third time at 1 Kefa [1 Peter] 4:14-16:

> "If you are being insulted in the name of the Messiah *[christos],* how blessed you are! For the Spirit of glory, that is, the Spirit of God, is resting on you! Let none of you suffer as a murderer or a thief or an evil-doer or for being a meddler in other people's affairs. But if anyone suffers as a 'Christian' *[christianos],* let him not be ashamed; but let him bring glory to God in this name."

The letter is addressed "to the elect exiles of the Diaspora of Pontus, Galatia," etc. (1 Kef a 1:1), that is, very explicitly to Jewish believers located in the Diaspora. Kefa tells them not to be ashamed when people—in context, detractors—apply to them the term, "Christian." They should neither get into a dispute about the name nor retreat in depression; rather they should bring glory to God, perhaps by turning the insult into an occasion for pointing the namecaller toward God's mercy in Yeshua. We do not learn that Jewish believers are to call themselves Christians, nor do we learn that Gentile believers are to call Jewish believers Christians; but if the name is applied to them either as an epithet or out of ignorance, Jewish believers should bear it graciously.

I am aware that not all will have been convinced by the above reasoning. Nevertheless my conclusion is that the New Testament gives little or no ground for believers' calling Messianic Jews "Christians." Rather it was the Gentile believers who were called "Christians," and this came about as a result of the early disciples' successful efforts at cross-cultural evangelism. They translated Hebrew words and ideas into Greek; and had they not done so, the word "Christian" would not exist, only "Messianic." The first-century Jewish believers' culture-bridging should not obligate twentieth-century Messianic Jews to use Greek-based terminology in describing themselves. However, two thousand years of history has affected usage. We will conclude the discussion after considering this history in the next chapter.[31]

31. See Chapter III, Section H.

CHAPTER III
HISTORY

A. HISTORY—THE KEY TO EVERYTHING

1. *Focus Elsewhere*

People today are not history-oriented. They may know historical facts and theories, but for most people history is dry and dusty, unconnected to the joys and sorrows of life. Yet history is at the center of existence. History is the key to meaning, purpose and happiness.

Such a statement, if understood at all these days, is a shocker. It runs counter to the conventional attitude so compactly expressed by Henry Ford, "History is bunk." What the inventor meant, of course, is that, loosing ourselves from outworn ways, we should let our thinking soar free beyond the hidebound and traditional. But because the present generation understands freedom not as "freedom to," but "freedom from," history is seen only as a shackle, not as a framework for action. People do not want freedom to change history, they want freedom from history. However, those who are wise will listen to George Santayana: "Whoever will not heed history is condemned to repeat it."

Why have people such an aversion to history? No, that is the wrong question; the right one is: why are people so unconscious of history? Here are some reasons. This generation feels rootless. As a child during World War II I was taught patriotism, which was grounded in American history; but even then, few took seriously what they were taught. Mobility, mass media, and materialism contributed to alienation. Rebellion against authority in the '60's, followed by the "me" generation's turn inward in the 70's focussed attention away from past and future to the present.

False religions too have been a major contributor, for most of them have no sense of history at all. The Eastern ones embed their doctrine of reincarnation in what I call the "yo-yo theory of history: "the individual soul, free on a heavenly plane except for its tie to God, comes down into a body here in this world of illusion, lives a life, then sheds its body and goes back up to heaven, only to descend again in another body, live, die, go back up, down, up, down, . . . until it escapes this recurring wheel of life. In this schema social existence is illusory, without significance; and history means nothing. At one point, before I realized how important history is, I was attracted for awhile to a false religion. At the time I could not have explained why, but now I know it was because this religion had a theory of history. The theory was completely wrong, but at least it said that universal existence has a thread of purpose joining a beginning through a middle to an end. Communism attracts because it roots itself in history (actually it is a false messianism, a biblical heresy). But only the Bible and true religion give the right meaning to history.

Americans are less history-oriented now than ever. We once had slogans that could mobilize the nation—"Manifest destiny!" "Make the world safe for democracy!" No more. Today one rarely finds Americans who think our country has a world mission based on a past to be proud of and a future to be improved. Instead many are ashamed of our past and hopeless about the future, but few understand that such feelings stem from purposelessness. Perhaps the end of the Cold War, the reconfiguring of world alliances, and the growing dangers in the Middle East will reverse Americans' sense of alienation from history.

For several reasons Israelis are more aware of history.

Judaism, a history-based religion which sanctifies time in its holidays, affects everyone. Secular Zionism, another variant of messianism, is also history-centered. Israel's people have a stronger collective spirit and less individualism (in the bad sense) than America's—although that, unfortunately, is changing. Last, Israel's very existence testifies to the working of supernatural power in history—even some atheists agree—and this sense of the miraculous is constantly projected into public life.

2. *The Three Basic Questions*

Why do I say that history is the key to everything? Because I believe that there are but three basic questions to life which everyone asks in his own way, some consciously, others acting them out in total unawareness. The questions are:

- How can one be happy?
- What should one do?
- What does it all mean?

The first is the central question of psychology. The second—once one passes beyond vocational counselling—is the central question of ethics. And the third? The third, you might think, falls in the province of philosophy, but it doesn't. It is the central question of history. As a philosophical question the discussion goes on and on, endlessly and inconclusively, because the question remains abstract, not grounded in events. But history is nothing if not grounded in events—indeed, a two-word definition of history might be "events interpreted." Thus it is in events, in history, that the meaning of life works itself out.

3. *The Meaning of Life*

The question of meaning is the critical one; it subsumes the others. If you know what life means, you will then be able to discern what to do and how to be happy. The pursuit of happiness will fail as an ultimate goal, because it will not lead to discovering the meaning of life—thus the mistake of the 60's and 70's, and perhaps the cardinal mistake of America.

Focusing on what to do will fail, because it analyzes means without considering ends. Sooner or later one will spot this lacuna, and the whole structure of doings will collapse.

In a way, Sartre and the other atheistic existentialists who denied that there was purpose built into the universe and insisted that each of us is responsible to create his own meaning for life, did us a service. By following the logic of their assumption that the God of the Bible does not exist, they exposed the hopelessness and pointlessness of life in such a universe. As Camus put it so clearly in the first sentences of his book *The Myth of Sisyphus,*

> "There is but one truly serious philosophical problem, and that is suicide. Judging whether life is or is not worth living amounts to answering the fundamental question of philosophy."[1]

Or, as I would put it, the fundamental question of history. In other words, whether history is headed toward something worth heading toward is the one crucial question; everything else is bunk.

The meaning of life! Whether the question burns or smolders, how do people answer it? Of those who reject God, some bite Sartre's bullet, attempting to shoulder the full burden of creating meaning in a meaningless universe. But I simply do not see how they can endure such a pointless, thankless, aimless, yet overwhelming task. If Sartre were right, wouldn't one be tempted to answer Camus's question in the irreversible negative? Others evade answering with ambition, with zeal, with good deeds, with supporting good

---

1. Albert Camus, *The Myth of Sisyphus* (New York: Vintage Books, 1959), p. 3. Or Shakespeare's *Hamlet:* "To be, or not to be—that is the question."

causes, with self-gratification, with becoming cultured—as long as the Hound of Heaven[2] will let them.

For only the Bible gives the true meaning of life and of history. "In the beginning God created" man for a purpose, namely, to glorify God. He allowed moral evil; chose through one man, Abraham, to redeem a people, Israel; and through that people, Israel, to bring a Messiah, Yeshua, who would redeem all mankind, so that once again mankind might glorify God. God has as the goal of history the coming in fullness the Kingdom of God, which has already begun to be impressed upon humanity by Yeshua the Messiah and his Body. This present pilgrim people gives an imperfect sense of what the future holds. But the time will come when all Israel will be saved, and the Messiah Yeshua will rule in glory. Thus "In the beginning" is tied through the middle we now live in to the true and glorious end.[3]

4. *Working with God to do His Will*

Once we see that God has implanted history with purpose, we know what to do. We know to work toward the goal God has given, to be nothing less than co-workers with God—not in some crazy, pretentious sense, but with humility. Once we accept that God has given us an inspired Book in which his goals are revealed, our goal becomes simply to forward his goals, to do his will. The issue then devolves to something else: how to know God's will. Suffice for now to note that God has stated

---

2. "The Hound of Heaven," a poem by Francis Thompson, presents Yeshua as pursuing us in supplicating love through our various false refuges until we accept him. Its first lines:

   I fled Him, down the nights and down the days;
   I fled Him, down the arches of the years;
   I fled Him, down the labyrinthine ways Of my own mind . . .

3. See Romans 11:11-32, Yochanan [John] 17:5, 10, 20-22, 24. This philosophy of history has been expressed against the background of modern thought in the works of Francis A. Schaeffer and John Warwick Montgomery.

much of his will in his Word, so that if another means of discerning God's will—such as an inner leading, a dream, a word from a friend, or a heartfelt desire—conflicts with the Bible, then the other means has been proved wrong. "I am *Adonai,* I do not change."[4]

5. *The "A" and the "Z"—Apathy and Zeal*

And here a word about apathy, enthusiasm, zeal and motivation. Apart from knowing God's purpose for history, apathy is the normal human condition, since apathy is the natural response when one finds oneself answering "No" to the questions, "Is there meaning to life? Does anything matter?"

But when one sees that God has answered with his "Yes," the natural response becomes enthusiasm. The word comes from Greek *en* ("in") and *theos* ("God"): being "in God" and having "God in" you. If God's answer is that something does matter, and if you are in God and God in you, as his Word promises will happen, then you will find yourself— literally—enthused.

Moreover, God in you will fill you with zeal to do his will. Scripture warns that zeal, like dynamite, is dangerous. Sha'ul [Paul] testified that while Israel had a "zeal for God," it was "not based on correct understanding."[5] He also wrote, "To be zealous is good, provided always that the cause is good."[6]

Finally, I believe that the strongest motivations to act arise from conflict situations; and the more important, the more fate-fraught the conflict, the greater the motivation an individual can find to help resolve it (and the greater the joy when it is finally resolved). In an electric battery the greater the difference in charge between the terminals, the stronger the current. Likewise the conflict between the Jewish people and the Church is strongly charged with love and hate, positive and negative. Enor-

4. Malachi 3:6.
5. Romans 10:2.
6. Galatians4:17-18.

mous energy has been expended in this conflict, and its importance in history is unequaled. Therefore any individual who is part of it should experience enormous motivation to help resolve it, and its resolution—"when the fullness of Israel comes in, and thus all Israel will be saved"[7]—can be expected to bring joy unequaled in history. Romans 11:15 calls it "life from the dead."

6. *Messianic Judaism at the Center of History*

By virtue of being in both the Jewish community and the Church, Messianic Jews are doubly involved, occupying the position of greatest tension and greatest energy potential, and thus have the greatest motivation to help resolve history's greatest conflict. I have said that it is the destiny of the Messianic Jewish community to do exactly that, thereby cooperating with God in achieving His already stated goal. Messianic Judaism is surely at the focal point of history.

7. *Messianic Jews! Your History Determines Your Calling*

I have written the preceding because I want my Messianic Jewish readers to feel personally involved in the historical analysis to follow. I don't want you merely to think abstractly about "social forces at work in history," as you might in a classroom test. The Passover *Haggadah* enjoins you to experience the Exodus as your own personal history—you personally left slavery under Pharaoh in Egypt and passed through the sea on dry land with Moses to freedom. Similarly, I want you to experience what happened between Israel and the Church as your own story—your tragedy, your hope, and your field for action. Your history, Jewish, Messianic, and Messianic Jewish, determines your calling and it should thrill you! As I said, being Messianic is the most exciting way to be Jewish.

---

7. Romans 11:25-26.

B. ISRAEL, CHURCH AND MESSIANIC JEWS

1. *The Conventional Wisdom*

The conventional wisdom considers Israel and the Church to be separate entities. A "typical Jew" might put it this way: "Yes, Yeshua and his first disciples were Jews, but before long the movement he founded moved away from Judaism. Many Gentiles came in, added their own pagan ideas, and brought Christianity to where it is today—OK for Gentiles but far removed from Judaism. Moreover, what was done to the Jewish people in Yeshua's name removes any vestige of personal interest I might have in finding out more about Christianity. Let Christians worship God as they choose, I'll stay Jewish"—and this whether the person is Orthodox, Conservative, Reform, atheist, or just plain don't-care.

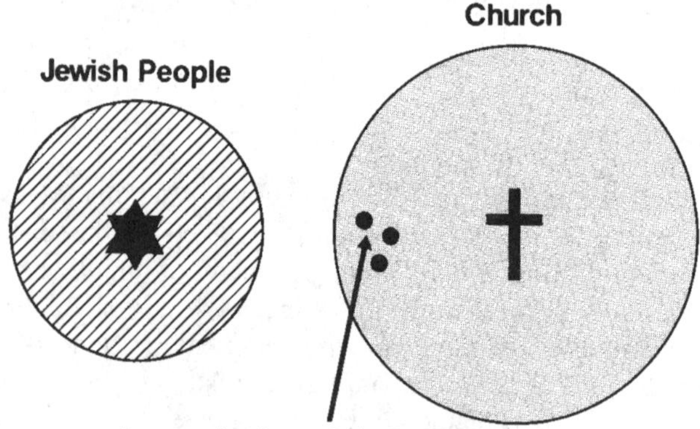
Church
Jewish People
Jews who have left their people,
crossed no-man's land and become
"Christians of Jewish origin"
in order to be saved

FIGURE 1

"The Coventional Wisdom"
About the Jewish People and the Church:
Messianic Judaism is an Empty Set

Likewise, a "typical Christian" might say: "Yes, Yeshua was Jewish, but the Jews rejected him. They have their religion, and I have mine. Let them worship God as they choose, I'll stay Christian,"—and this whether the person is Protestant, Catholic, or Eastern Orthodox, a genuine believer or a Christian in name only.

What both sides see is a picture like Figure 1, in which the small circle represents the Jewish community (smaller because the Jewish community is smaller), while the larger one represents the Church. The circles do not overlap. In order for a Jew to "convert to Christianity"[8] he leaves his people and joins the Church. Simple, easy to understand. But it isn't necessarily true.

2. *Exercise in Logic: All Humanity is Divided Into . . .*

All humanity is divided into two parts—those who say you can divide humanity into two parts, and those who say you can't. I belong to the first group, so—here goes.

We need the following two ways of dividing humanity into two parts in order to explain better than the conventional wisdom the relationship between Jews and Christians.

All humanity is divided into Jews and Gentiles (non-Jews). We discussed earlier the problems of defining a Jew—according to the mother, the father, either, etc. But no matter how the term is defined, logic demands that everybody on earth is either a Jew or a non-Jew—he can't be both, and he can't be neither.

Likewise, all humanity is divided into Messianics and non-Messianics (we avoid the common terms "Christian" and "non-Christian" for reasons discussed elsewhere). Again, there are problems of how one is to define a Messianic—according to faith, community, culture, or whatever. But once

---

8. See Appendix, footnote 5.

more, logic demands that everybody is either Messianic or non-Messianic—he must be one or the other, and he can't be both or neither.[9]

The confusion in thinking about Jews and Christians results from failing to realize that Jew/Gentile and Messianic/non-Messianic are two distinct and logically unrelated ways of describing the human race, two separate dimensions. There are

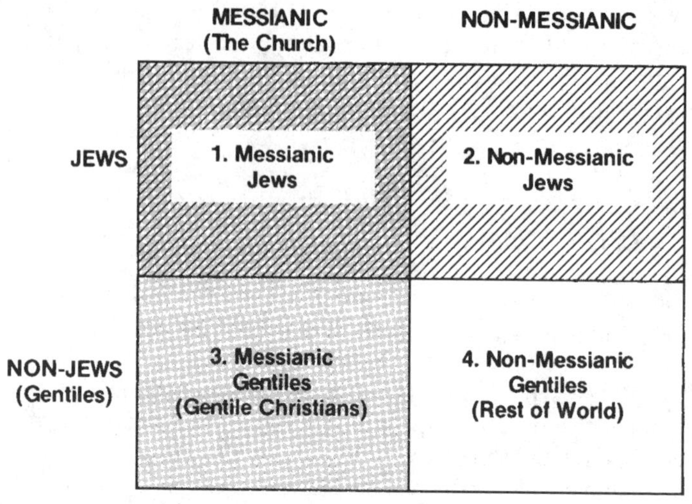

FIGURE 2

Logic of the Relationship
Between the Jewish People and the Church

9. I know someone who says he "neither believes nor disbelieves the Gospel" but calls himself "a friend of the believers." Scripture gives no room for fence-sitting. Yeshua said, "Those who are not with me are against me, and those who do not gather with me are scattering." (Mattityahu [Matthew] 12:30; Zechariah 1:15 and Mattityahu 25:31-46 too exclude a *tertium quid.)*

four possible categories resulting from this two-dimensional classification system (Figure 2), to wit: Messianic Jews (Box 1), non-Messianic Jews (Box 2), Messianic Gentiles (or Gentile Christians, Box 3), and non-Messianic Gentiles (Box 4). Every human being fits in one and only one of these categories.

The confusion is resolved when it is realized that Jews include boxes 1 and 2 (Messianic Jews and non-Messianic Jews), while the Church includes boxes 1 and 3 (Messianic Jews and Messianic Gentiles). Thus—and this is the very simple and obvious point—it is possible, logically, to be both Jewish and Messianic.

Therefore, Figure 2 can be re-drawn (along the lines of Figure 1) as Figure 3. The largest circle represents all humanity.

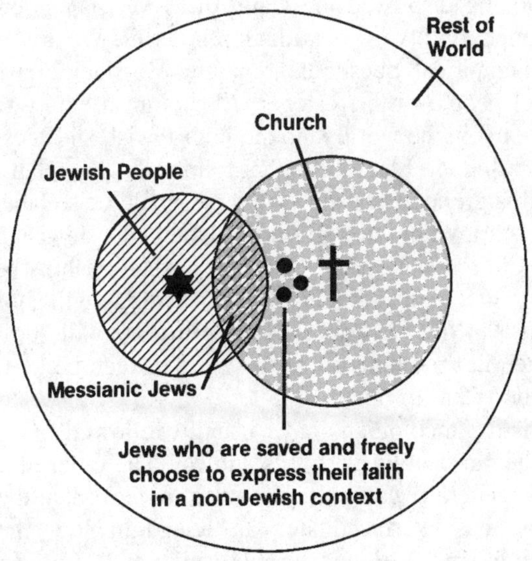

FIGURE 3

The Facts Conform to Logic,
Not to the Conventional Wisdom:
Messianic Judaism is a Non-Empty Set

Again the small circle represents the Jews and the large circle the Church, but now they overlap. The intersection of the two circles represents Messianic Jews. The rest of the Jewish circle represents non-Messianic Jews, while the remainder of the Church circle represents Gentile Christians. The fourth category, the non-Messianic Gentiles, the rest of humanity, who are neither Jewish nor Christian, is represented by the portion of the larger circle outside the two smaller ones.

3. *An Empirical Question: Are There Messianic Jews?*

So far, we have thought about abstract logical categories, and our reasoning disproved the claim that "Messianic Jew" is a logical impossibility, a contradiction in terms. We are left only with an empirical question: are there Messianic Jews? Are there real people in this category? Or is it an empty set? Do persons exist in the world who are both Jewish and Messianic? I say: yes. In fact, I am one. What follows in an explanation of why such a group exists and why they should be so labelled.

We start with three entities—Israel, the Jewish people and the Church—and ask what are the relationships between them both theological and historical. Theology will show eternal truths "in the heavenlies," while history will show what took place in time here on earth. We will then be better able to consider what to do.

Christian theologians have usually followed one of two approaches in dealing with this subject. The older and better known is generally called Replacement or Covenant theology, although it has resurfaced lately as "Kingdom Now" theology, "Dominion-ism," "Reconstructionism" and (in England) "Restorationism." Under any name it says that the Church is the "New" or "Spiritual" Israel, having replaced the "Old" Israel (the Jews) as God's people. In the nineteenth century there arose in Protestant quarters Dispensationalism, which, in its more extreme form, says that the Jewish people have promises only on earth, while the Church has promises in heaven. We will not consider these approaches in detail, but the bottom line is that both oversimplify and in the process arrive at manifestly antisemitic[10] conclusions.[11]

4. *Olive Tree Theology*

The following analysis will show that the separation between the Church and the Jewish people, as it has developed over the last 2000 years, is completely out of God's will, a terrible mistake, what I called earlier the worst schism in history. We will then see that it is our task to rectify that mistake, to throw ourselves fully into what Judaism calls *tikkun-ha'olam,* literally, "fixing up the world," repairing it. According to Jewish tradition such activity hastens the coming of the Messiah; and this corresponds to what Kefa [Peter] encourages believers in Yeshua to do, namely, to hasten the coming of the Day of God.[12] I call this approach "Olive Tree theology," after Sha'ul's [Paul's] allegory in Romans 11:16-26, addressed to Gentile Christians (my translation, from the *Jewish New Testament):*[13]

10. In this book the word "antisemitic" is synonymous with "anti-Jewish." This usage is open to criticism on two counts. First, some Arabs may take offense because they too are Semites; but English-speakers do not mean "anti-Arab" when they say "antisemitic." Second, I have heard a Christian object that the word "antisemitism" too readily connotes the horrors of Hitler's Germany. While I am not trying to dredge up those memories every time the term appears, it must be recognized that antisemitism represents a spectrum not of good but of evil, from relatively minor sins to the worst imaginable.
11. For a brief Messianic Jewish analysis of both theologies see Dan Juster {*op. cit* in Chapter I, footnote 8), pp. 43-45. A popular book refuting Replacement theology and revealing its antisemitism is Hal Lindsey, *The Road to Holocaust* (New York/Toronto/ London/ Sydney/Auckland: Bantam Books, 1989); a useful study is H. Wayne House and Thomas Ice, *Dominion Theology: Blessing or Curse?* (Portland, Oregon: Multnomah Press, 1988).
12. 2 Kefa [2 Peter] 3:12.
13. *Op. cit.* in Chapter II, footnote 20.

"Now if the *challah*[14] offered as firstfruits is holy, so is the whole loaf. And if the root is holy, so are the branches. But if some of the branches were broken off, and you—a wild olive—were grafted in among them and have become equal sharers in the rich root of the olive tree, then don't boast as if you were better than the branches! However, if you do boast, remember that you are not supporting the root, the root is supporting you. So you will say, 'Branches were broken off so that I might be grafted in.' True, but so what? They were broken off because of their lack of trust. However, you keep your place only because of your trust. So don't be arrogant; on the contrary, be terrified! For if God did not spare the natural branches, he certainly won't spare you!

"So take a good look at God's kindness and his severity: on the one hand, severity toward those who fell off; but, on the other hand, God's kindness toward you—provided you maintain yourself in that kindness! Otherwise, you too will be cut off! Moreover, the others, if they do not persist in their lack of trust, will be grafted in; because God is able to graft them back in. For if you were cut out of what is by nature a wild olive tree and grafted, contrary to nature, into a cultivated olive tree, how much more will these natural branches be grafted back into their own olive tree!

"For, brothers, I want you to understand this truth which God formerly concealed but has now revealed, so that you won't imagine you know more than you actually do. It is that stoniness, to a degree, has come upon Israel, until the Gentile world enters in its fullness; and that it is in this way that all Israel will be saved."

14. See entry on *challah* in Glossary.

On pages 50-51 Figure 4 depicts the "cultivated olive tree" as it develops throughout history; the time-line at the left embraces four thousand years. Figure 5 illustrates cross-sections of that olive tree, showing the relationship between the Jewish people and the Church at various points in time.

The olive tree which God cultivated is Israel. Its root is the Patriarchs—Abraham, Isaac and Jacob.[15] From this root grew the Jewish people. Meanwhile, the Gentiles were a wild olive tree to whom God the farmer had not devoted the same kind of special attention. Sha'ul writes that they "were at that time separated from Christ, alienated from the commonwealth of Israel, and strangers to the covenants of promise, having no hope and without God in the world."[16] Figure 5A illustrates this situation, which prevailed until the time of Yeshua's ministry (25 C.E.).

When Yeshua came, he was at the center of the tree, at the center of the Jewish people, the quintessential Jew as well as the quintessential man. He gathered Jewish disciples around him. He died, rose from the grave, and ascended to heaven. The Messianic Jewish community grew—a hundred and twenty (Acts 1:15), three thousand (Acts 2:41), five thousand (Acts 4:4), "and their numbers kept multiplying" (Acts 9:31). See Figure 5B (35 C.E.)

The non-Messianic Jews reacted against the Messianic Jews, pushing them away from the center (Acts 4-9, 12). Meanwhile, the message spread to Gentiles—Cornelius (Acts 10), Antioch (Acts 11); see Figure 5C (50 C.E.).

---

15. "While some take *e riza* [Greek: "the root"], to refer to Christ, and some take it to refer to the Jewish Christians, there is a very widespread agreement among commentators that it must refer to the patriarchs. ..." (C. E. B. Cranfield, *Romans (International Critical Commentary)*; Edinburgh: T. & T. Clark, Ltd., 1981; volume 2, p. 565). That the root is the Patriarchs is confirmed by Romans 4:16 ("Abraham the father of us all") and Galatians 3:7, 29. Also compare with Sha'ul's olive tree and root a first-century B.C. E. Jewish source, the Book of Enoch 93:5: "And his *[sc.* Abraham's] posterity shall become the plant of righteousness for evermore."
16. Ephesians 2:12, Revised Standard Version.

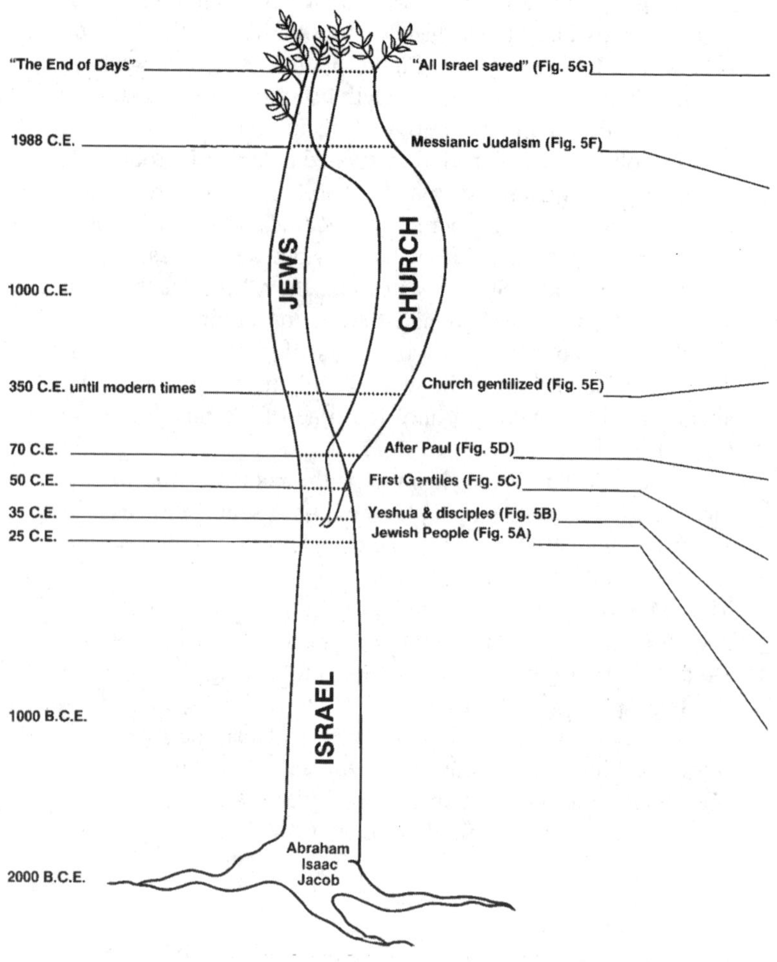

FIGURE 4

The Cultivated Olive Tree:
The Church and the Jewish People
Through History

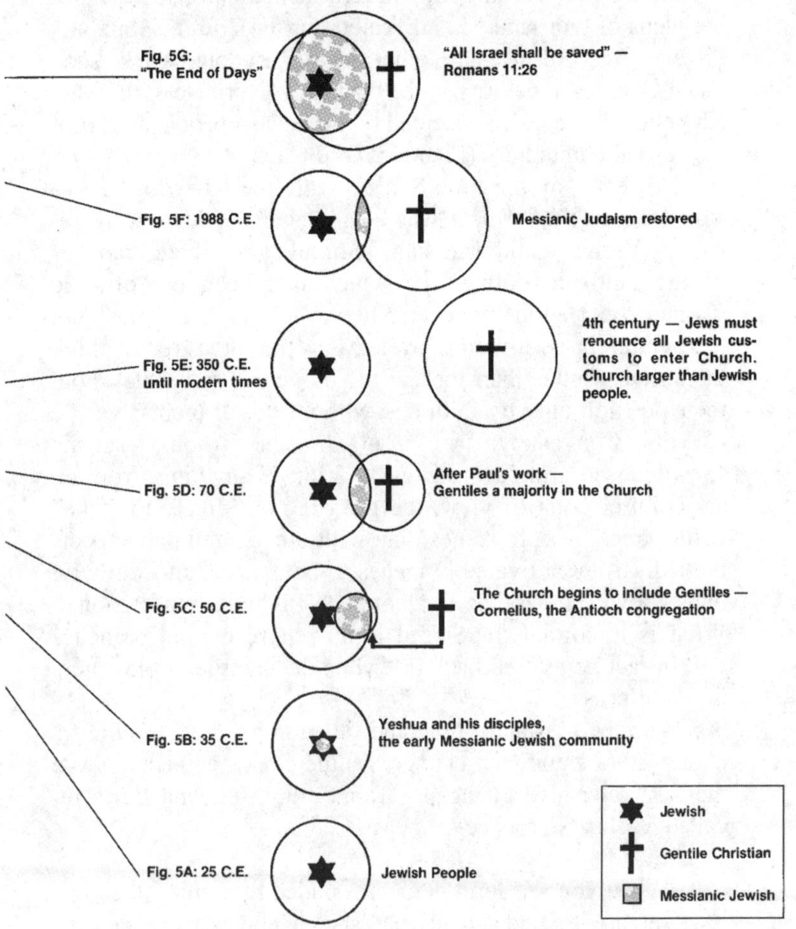

FIGURE 5

Cross-Sections of the Olive Tree:
The Church and the Jewish People
At Specific Points in History

Although Messianic Jews in Jerusalem alone came to number "tens of thousands, ... all zealots for the *Torah*,"[11] Sha'ul's travels (Acts 13-28) and other missionary outreaches soon made Gentiles a majority in the Church. Nevertheless, the Jewish believers were still accepted by the Jewish people as part of the Jewish community (Figure 5D, 70 C.E.).

However, by the time Sha'ul wrote the letter to the Romans (about 57 C.E.), it was clear that most Jews were rejecting Yeshua as the Messiah.[18] Sha'ul called them branches of the cultivated olive tree which had been cut off. He warned the Gentile believers, however, that they must not take undue pride in being grafted into the olive tree or think themselves better than the cut-off branches, since they hold their position only by faith and without it will themselves be cut off. Conversely, the cut-off branches (non-Messianic Jews) can be grafted in again by faith; if anything, from an agricultural point of view, the graft is more likely to "take" with a tree's own branches than with others, and one expects the fruit from cultivated branches to be better than from wild ones (however, God is not bound by human expectations). What is important for Sha'ul is that these natural branches will in fact be grafted back in "when the Gentile world enters in its fullness."

With the passing of time, the situation for Jewish believers underwent a significant change. As the clouds gathered before the first Jewish revolt against Rome, the Messianic Jews recalled Yeshua's prophecy,

> "When you see Jerusalem surrounded by armies, then you are to understand that she is about to be destroyed. Those in Judea must escape to the hills, those inside the city must get out, and those in the country must not enter it."[19]

---

17. Acts 21:20, *Jewish New Testament (op. cit.* in Chapter II, footnote 20).
18. For anon-Messianic Jewish view of this critical period, 50-135 C.E., see Schiffman *(op. cit.* in Chapter II, footnote 17).
19. Luke 21:20-21, *Jewish New Testament.*

They fled to the city of Pella, thus escaping the destruction of the Temple (70 C.E.) and the Roman slaughter of nearly a million Jews (according to Josephus; fewer by other estimates). For this prudence the Zealots who led the rebellion regarded the Messianic Jews as traitors.

During the second revolt (132-135 C.E.), the Jewish believers initially acquiesced; but when Rabbi Akiva renamed the Jewish military leader Shim'on Bar-Kosiba "Bar-Kochva", declaring him to be the long-promised "star [Aramaic *kochva]* out of Jacob" of Numbers 24:17, that is, the Messiah, they could no longer cooperate, since they would not switch allegiance from the true Messiah, Yeshua. This also was branded treason, and the rest of the Jewish community became sealed in bitterness against them.

Besides political tension, witness the addition to the synagogue liturgy of the *Sirhat-HaMinim* (the Benediction against the "sectarians," generally understood to be the Jewish believers) around 90 C.E. Clearly the Messianic Jews were being excluded from the unbelieving Jewish community.

Moreover, from the Gentile Christian side, the orthodoxy of the Jewish believers' faith increasingly came under scrutiny if they held to Jewish customs and loyalties. In the *Dialogue With Trypho, A Jew,* by Justin Martyr, a Gentile Christian (about 160 C.E.), one sees a limited tolerance of Messianic Jews who retain Jewish distinctives.[20]

---

20. Justin Martyr, "Dialogue With Trypho, A Jew" in Alexander Roberts and James Donaldson, editors, *The Ante-Nicene Fathers* (Grand Rapids, Michigan: Wm. B. Eerdmans Publishing Company, 1975), Volume I, pp. 194-270. The following selection from section xlvii (page 218) illustrates this "limited tolerance":

> "If some, through weak-mindedness, wish to observe such institutions as were given by Moses, from which they expect some virtue, but which we believe were appointed by reason of the hardness of the people's hearts, along with their hope in this Christ, and [wish to perform] the eternal and natural acts

But after Christianity became the state religion of Rome in the early fourth century, many unsaved Gentiles entered the institutional Church. It grew to be far larger than the entire Jewish population of the world, became fully Gentilized, regarded the Jews as a vanquished competitor, and had little understanding of Jewish believers who wanted to retain their Jewishness. It became impossible for a person to express publicly both Jewish and Messianic identity. A Jew who wanted to accept the Jewish Messiah had to leave his people and cross over into the Church (Figure 5E, 350 C.E.). Jews who came to faith in Yeshua were required to separate themselves utterly from Judaism, the Jewish people and their Jewish customs. Here is a confession typical of those which Messianic Jews had to affirm:

> "I renounce ail customs, rites, legalisms, unleavened breads and sacrifices of lambs of the Hebrews, and all the other feasts of the Hebrews, sacrifices, prayers, aspersions, purifications, sanctifications and propitiations, and fasts, and new moons, and Sabbaths, and superstitions, and hymns and chants and observances and synagogues, and the food and drink of the Hebrews; in one word, I renounce absolutely everything Jewish, every law, rite and custom . . . and if afterwards I shall wish to deny and return to Jewish superstition, or shall be found eating with Jews, or feasting with them,

---

> of righteousness and piety, yet choose to live with the Christians and the faithful, as I said before, not inducing them either to be circumcised like themselves, or to keep the Sabbath, or to observe any other such ceremonies, then I hold that we ought to join ourselves to such, and associate with them in all things as kinsmen and brethren."

He adds that he disapproves of Judaizers but believes that Judaized Gentile believers will be saved. However, those "who have gone back from some cause to the legal dispensation, and have denied that this man is Christ, and have repented not before death, shall by no means be saved."

> or secretly conversing and condemning the Christian religion instead of openly confuting them and condemning their vain faith, then let the trembling of Cain and the leprosy of Gehazi cleave to me, as well as the legal punishments to which I acknowledge myself liable. And may I be anathema in the world to come, and may my soul be set down with Satan and the devils."[21]

Crude as this confession may seem to the modern reader, it is representative—admittedly in the extreme form suited to the fanaticism of the fourth and fifth centuries—of attitudes that have persisted in the Church for hundreds of years. The Spanish Inquisition scrutinized Catholics of Jewish origin to see whether they retained Jewish customs. Out of Gentile distaste for Jewishness emerged Christian persecution of Jews—Crusades, Inquisition, pogroms, Nazi Germany (yes, there was Christian involvement, both for evil and for good)—with all the pain and ugliness that Jews cannot forget, and the Church will not be permitted to forget until all Christians (not just some) learn the lesson.

So until very recently the Jewish people and the Church have remained separate, with no place for Messianic Judaism, since both the majority of Jews (unsaved people whose experience with the Church had been mostly negative) and the majority of Christians (Gentiles who misunderstood their own faith as it relates to the Jewish people) wanted it that way.

* * * * *

Leaving for a moment the historical development of this tragic division of the cultivated olive tree into two seemingly separate

---

21. "Profession of Faith, from the Church of Constantinople: From Assemani, Cod. Lit., I, p. 105," as cited in James Parkes, *The Conflict of the Church and the Synagogue* (New York: Atheneum, 1974), pp. 397-398.

peoples of God, let us examine the extended metaphor of the olive tree with a view to understanding its implications for theology. There is only one cultivated tree, and that means that there is only one Israel, not two. The wild branches (Gentiles) have been grafted in through faith in the Messiah, "brought near in the blood of Christ,"[22] so that they are now included in the commonwealth of Israel. But they are not, as Replacement theology would have it, a New Israel. Nor do Jewish and Gentile believers together constitute a New Israel, since the cut-off branches too are still identifiable as Israel even though they do not have the living sap of the tree flowing through them. For God is miraculously preserving them, so that instead of drying out, as detached branches normally do, they are able to be grafted back in by faith. Thus unsaved Jews (cut-off natural branches), saved Jews (natural branches attached to the tree), and Gentile believers (grafted-in wild branches) each have their own kind of ongoing participation in the one Israel; and this fact needs to be taken into account in any correct theology of Israel and the Church. Not a word is said in the "olive tree" passage or anywhere else in Scripture about splitting the promises into earthly ones for the Jews and heavenly ones for the Church. However, God has made two kinds of promises. In regard to the promises which relate to individual salvation, there is neither Jew nor Gentile (Galatians 3:28), no distinction between them (Romans 10:12), no dividing wall of hostility (Ephesians 2:14-19). On the other hand, there remain promises to national Israel, the Jewish people, in which Gentile nations corporately and Gentile believers individually have no direct share—although it is worth noting that there are also promises to certain Gentile nations (as an example, Isaiah 19:24-25 gives assurance that God will bless Egypt and Assyria along with Israel; so that Gentile believers who are part of those nations will experience those blessings).

22. Ephesians 2:13, Revised Standard Version.

The present situation with commonwealth Israel is that Gentiles from many nations recognize the Jewish Messiah, yet the majority of national Israel do not. Suppose citizens of Canada, India, Nigeria, Australia, and other members of the British Commonwealth of Nations recognized Elizabeth II as their Queen, but most individual Englishmen, as well as the British government, did not. In this circumstance it would be wrong to say that Great Britain was no longer a member of the Commonwealth—when in fact it would still be the central member among equals. It would also be incorrect to agree with the British that Elizabeth was not the Queen. Rather, one could only try to convince them—both individual Englishmen and their governmental establishment—to honor Elizabeth II, who is in fact the Queen.[23]

In the future, "all Israel will be saved." In the *Tanakh* ["Old Testament"], that is to say, in Hebrew thinking, the word *kol* ("all") in reference to a collective does not mean every single individual of which it is composed, but rather the main part, the essential part, or the considerable majority. Therefore I believe that when "all Israel" is saved, it will not be that every Jew believes in Yeshua, but that the Jewish nation will have a believing majority and/or a believing establishment. To use Moses' metaphor, the Messianic Jews will be "the head and not the tail."[24] (See Figure 5G.)

I believe that the reappearance of a Messianic Jewish community in our day is a significant phase in God's process of saving all Israel. If Figure 5G is the ultimate goal, and Figure 5E (which is virtually the same as Figure 1, the conventional wisdom) shows the situation as it actually existed until recently, then Figure 5D not only depicts an ancient historical stage, but also resembles the present and the immediate future, represented by Figure 5F, showing that we are beginning to

23. I am indebted to Daniel Juster, *Growing To Maturity,* ([Gaithers-burg, Maryland: Union of Messianic Jewish Congregations], 1982), pp. 253-254, for this analogy.

24. Deuteronomy 28:13.

recover our past. Moreover, it teaches us that events are beginning to conform more to logic (Figures 2, 3 and 5F) than to the conventional wisdom (Figures 1 and 5E). It has once again become possible for a Jewish believer in Yeshua to identify himself as both Jewish and Messianic, and to express this identification in a socially recognizable way.

This has come about historically because of the great growth of freedom in Western political, economic and social life during the last three hundred years, a phenomenon which surely demonstrates God's love for humanity. Previously a tiny minority could not have hoped to effect fundamental change in two much larger opposed social entities by claiming to be part of both. Today our freedom to attempt this outrageously improbable task (improbable by the world's standards but not by God's) is protected in pluralistic democratic countries. As political freedom grew, already by 1718 John Toland in his book *Nazarenus*[25] could suggest that "Christians from among the Jews" should observe the *Torah*. As economic freedom grew, the Hebrew Christian movement could advance with few impediments in nineteenth-century England. And as social freedom has grown, along with the advance in communications, it is possible for us, today, to dare expect that Messianic Judaism will succeed in reaching its goal of healing the split between the Church and the Jewish people.

It is the task of Messianic Jews and of sympathetic Gentile Christians to undertake the *tikkun-ha'olam* of which we spoke earlier. These are the ones who, because of their common trust in the Jewish Messiah Yeshua, can work together to undo the damage caused by the division of the Jewish people and the Church into two apparently separate peoples of God. The Jewish people must be brought to understand—freely, willingly, not by coercion or deception—that the age-

25. John Toland, *Nazarenus,* 1718; quoted in both Rausch *(op. cit.* in Chapter II, footnote 28) and Schonfield *(op. cit.* in footnote 45 below).

old goals of Jewish endeavor will be achieved only when the Jewish people come to understand and trust in Yeshua, the Jewish Messiah. The Church must be brought to understand—freely, willingly, not by coercion or deception—that its goals will be achieved only when any form of overt or covert antisemitism or stand-offishness has disappeared, and intimate unity with the Jewish people has been acknowledged.

Can there be a grander goal? We live in an exciting age, as we see the momentum of history sweeping toward the fulfillment of Sha'ul's prophecy that all Israel will be saved. And as we work toward accomplishing that end, it is essential that we be armed with a right understanding of the relationship between Israel and the Church.

C. MESSIANIC JUDAISM AND HISTORY

Each of humanity's four categories has a history. Jewish history is 4,000 years old; Church history distinct from the Jewish history on which it builds is 2,000 years old, as is distinct Messianic Jewish history (even though during many centuries Messianic Jewish history becomes difficult to see). The history of the rest of the world is of course the longest; the others are embedded in it. Now precisely because Messianic Jews are both Jewish and Messianic, we must relate to .., of these histories as our own.

But a word of caution is in order. It is interesting to have four histories, but we cannot pick and choose. We must accept the bad along with the good, the unfaithful and despicable characters and incidents along with the faithful remnant and the events worth celebrating. Honesty is the best policy for historians. Moreover, there is a wonderful precedent for it—the Bible, which does not shrink from reporting the unpleasant side of the truth.

As we proceed, I will be using a term which I like very much: "salvation history." It means the record of God's acts and interventions in human affairs in order to redeem mankind from sin and its consequences. It pictures the whole sweep of human history from the point of view of God saving us. The term has built into it God's main purpose for humanity, his primary reason for letting history continue at all. Unfortunately the German liberal scholars who invented and used this term (in German, *Heilsgeschichte)* did not believe in God as the Bible portrays him. As a result, some Bible-believers are put off by these scholars and by the terms they use. But I think good and truth are where you find them, so I am going to use the term "salvation history" anyway.

D. MESSIANIC JUDAISM AND JEWISH HISTORY

1. *Do Gentile Christians Share in Jewish History?*

Gentile Christians necessarily and legitimately regard the story of God's people Israel in the Hebrew Bible as their own, because it records the salvation history in which they, through New Testament faith, have come to share. The record continues through intertestamental times (400 B.C.E. until the time of Yeshua), and particular attention is paid to Judaism and the Jewish environment of the first century, with its various trends, parties and sects, because Yeshua arose then, in consequence of which Gentiles began to be systematically joined into God's people through faith in the Jewish Messiah but without their converting to Judaism.

But at that point Gentile Christians bid farewell to Jewish history. A few—too few—may have an intellectual interest and even a genuine, heartfelt concern and sympathy for the fortunes and misfortunes of the Jewish people during the last two thousand years; but I am not talking about that. Rather, I mean that Gentile Christians are not personally involved with post-New Testament Jewish history. This is true for one right reason and one wrong one: the right reason is that post-New Testament Jewish history is not their own. The wrong one is that they think Jewish history after Yeshua is no longer part of salvation history, which it most certainly is.

2. *Why Jewish History is My History.*

The reason why Jewish history is my history is that I am not a Messianic Gentile but a Messianic Jew. A non-Messianic Jewish objector might ask, "Why is Jewish history important for you? Be Christian and find your place in your own stream of history." No, that is unsatisfactory for several reasons.

First, Jewish history is mine because I am Jewish. I reject the claim that I am not. Jewish history leads to me and explains who I am.

Second, Jewish history is important for me because Judaism has preserved some elements of truth better than Christianity has. For example, the system which generates *halakhah* in Judaism has produced better application of biblical truth to many specific ethical decisionmaking situations than the usual Christian arrangements, which tend to be more *ad hoc* and therefore less well designed for preserving wisdom. Moreover, phenomena such as the sanctification of time in festivals and *Shabbat,* and the introduction of holiness into daily life through repeated activities such as laying *tefillin,* reciting prayers in a synagogue, and even seeing the *mezuzah* on the door express in practical ways the immanence of God. Thus modern Jewish history and the Judaism it has produced help us Messianic Jews to understand our faith. But actually this would be a good reason for Gentile Christians as well to involve themselves with Judaism—and indeed this may well have been what Ya'akov [James] had in mind when, after the Jerusalem Council decided that Gentile Christians had to obey only four *mitzvot* to be accepted as brother believers, he said, "For from the earliest times, Moses has had in every city those who proclaim him, with his words being read in the synagogues every *Shabbat.*"[26]

And third, Jewish history is mine because if we Messianic Jews are to undertake our task to help heal the split between

26. Acts 15:21.

the Church and the Jews, as insiders to both, we must be fully identified with Jewish as well as Christian history.

So the Rambam is my Rambam, and David Ben-Gurion is my Ben-Gurion, and so are Moses Mendelssohn and Moshe Feinstein and Solomon Schechter and Stephen Wise and Judah HaNasi and Raba and Abaye and Meyer Lansky and Albert Einstein and the Marxes—Karl and Groucho—and Peres and Shamir and Rav Kahane and Charlie Biton. All mine! And I, a Jew who honors the Jewish Messiah Yeshua, am theirs.

3. *Why Messianic Jews Are Jewish*

Yes, I am theirs. So it is strange that some non-Messianic Jews try to exclude Messianic Jews from the Jewish community. It certainly was not that way at the beginning. The facts are simply not up for debate. For years all Yeshua's disciples were Jewish. The New Testament was entirely written by Jews (Luke being, in all likelihood, a proselyte to Judaism). The very concept of a Messiah is nothing but Jewish. And Yeshua himself was Jewish—was and is, since nowhere does Scripture say or suggest that he has stopped being a Jew. Could Revelation 5:5 call the glorified Messiah "the Lion of the tribe of Judah" if he were not still Jewish? Could the eternal King of the Jews become a Gentile? It was Jews who brought the Gospel to non-Jews. Sha'ul, the chief emissary to the Gentiles, was a lifelong observant Jew. Indeed the main issue in the early Church was whether without undergoing complete conversion to Judaism a Gentile could be a Christian at all. The Messiah's vicarious atonement is rooted in the Jewish sacrificial system; the Lord's Supper is rooted in the Jewish Passover traditions; baptism is a Jewish practice; and indeed the entire New Testament is built on the Hebrew Bible, with its prophecies and its promise of a New Covenant, so that the New Testament without the Old is as impossible as the second floor of a house without the first.

Moreover, much of what is written in the New Testament is incomprehensible apart from Judaism. Here is an example.

Yeshua tells us in the Sermon on the Mount, "If thine eye be evil, thy whole body shall be full of darkness."[27] What is an evil eye? Someone not knowing the Jewish background might suppose Yeshua was talking about casting spells. But in Hebrew, having an *'ayin ra 'ah,* an "evil eye," means being stingy; while having an *'ayin tov,* a "good eye," means being generous. Yeshua is warning against lack of generosity and nothing else. Moreover, this fits the context perfectly: "Where your treasure is, there will your heart be also. . . . You cannot serve both God and money."[28]

Some non-Messianic Jews acknowledge that there was a Jewish Christian community in ancient times but deny the possibility of a Messianic Jewish Community today. Consider the remarks of Justice Shamgar in the Dorflinger decision:

> "For this purpose [to convince the court she was a Jew entitled to make *ally ah* under Israel's Law of Return] she made exaggerations with long and tortuous arguments concerning the possibilities of her being a Jew who believes in Jesus' being the Messiah, as if we are still living in the beginning of the first century of the Christian Era, as if since then nothing had occurred in all that relates to the crystallization of the religious frameworks and the separation from Judaism of all those who chose another path."[29]

Can the clock be turned back or not? Zionists did exactly that, recreating a Jewish state after a 2,000-year hiatus. It is

---

27. Mattityahu [Matthew] 6:23, King James Version.
28. Mattityahu [Matthew] 6:21, 24. For other examples of New Testament textswhich, when perceived against their first-century Jewish background, yield meanings different from those commonly taught, see Chapter V, Sections B-5 (on Mattityahu 18:18-20) and C-2.
29. Israel High Court of Justice Case No. 563 / 77. See above, Chapter II, Section B-l, and below, Chapter VII, Section E-3.

time to "decrystallize the religious frameworks" and reverse the "separation from Judaism" of Messianic Jews.[30]

4. *Jewish Attitudes Toward Yeshua and the New Testament*

But perhaps all of this can be understood best if we take note of five basic attitudes a Jew can have toward Yeshua, the New Testament and Christianity. These may not be the only possible positions, but I cannot recall hearing a viewpoint that did not express in greater or lesser degree one of these attitudes. I have appended brief responses of my own.

- Yeshua was bad, Sha'ul [Paul] was bad, the New Testament is bad, Christianity is bad, the Church is bad, the whole thing is bad. One expects this attitude to be held most virulently by active anti-missionaries, but it can be found among every category of non-Messianic Jew—Orthodox, Reform, secular. The Orthodox who hold to this position regard Yeshua as an impostor who led the Jewish people astray, from which point things got only worse.

  Generally people with this view live in their own world. They will not deal with the ancient documents seriously, are not interested in understanding them in their Jewish context, and cannot even entertain the possibility that what they say might be true. Time spent arguing with them is time wasted. One can only appreciate the depth of their pain and pray that the Holy Spirit will open their hearts to consider the truth-claims rationally.

- Yeshua is good, but Sha'ul was bad. This is the view of those who wish to reclaim Yeshua for the Jewish people. Yeshua was a good Jew, not the Messiah and

30. My appreciation to Menahem Benhayim and Ari Sorko-Ram for pointing out that the Zionists accomplished what Justice Shamgar thought impossible.

of course not the Son of God, but one of the greatest teachers, from whom we can all learn, one of the finest men who ever lived, whom we can all emulate. The villain of the piece is Sha'ul. He tried to make Judaism easier for the pagans around him and introduced idolatrous ideas garnered from their religions. Yeshua did not teach that the *Torah* had been abolished, but Sha'ul did. Yeshua did not claim to be a god, but Sha'ul made him into one. Yeshua demanded righteous behavior, but Sha'ul taught that faith is all you need, so that what you do doesn't matter.

Yeshua himself taught that he was the Messiah, divine, the atonement for the sins of the world. If he was such a wonderful teacher, one should believe what he taught! Or, as C. S. Lewis put it, given what Yeshua said about himself one cannot conclude that he was simply a good teacher. "He would either be a lunatic—on a level with a man who says he's a poached egg—or else He would be the devil of hell. You must make your choice. Either this man was, and is, the son of God: or else a madman or something worse."[31] Also this view misunderstands Sha'ul, who introduced no pagan ideas, made nothing easy, and did not teach the *Torah* is abolished (as we will see in Chapter V).

- Yeshua was good, Sha'ul was OK, and I have nothing against the New Testament either—great literature. The problem came when Gentiles came to outnumber Jews in the Church and gained power in the fourth century under Emperor Constantine. Paganism, antisemitism and politics came to dominate the Church, and the damage done to the Jews by Christians since then has made it impossible for us to consider the New Testament's claims today.

One very simple answer: Truth does not depend on how people respond to it. If the Church misused

31. C. S. Lewis, *Mere Christianity* (New York: MacMillan, 1958), p. 41.

and misapplied the New Testament, this cannot affect the truth of what the New Testament says.

- Yeshua was good, Sha'ul was good, the New Testament is good, the Church is good—but it's not for us. This is the two-covenant theory, that Gentiles come to God through Yeshua, but Jews don't need him because they are already close to God.

  Yeshua presented himself to the "House of Israel" as the Jewish Messiah, and the Gospel is "for the Jew first." The two-covenant theory attempts to reduce the pressure to believe, but it does so by picking and choosing texts from the New Testament which agree with its predetermined conclusions and finessing those which do not.[32]

- Yeshua is good, so was Sha'ul, so is the New Testament—and I believe it.

  This is my position, that of a Messianic Jew.

E. MESSIANIC JUDAISM AND THE CHURCH

Messianic Jews tend to be neurotic in relating to the rest of the Church, going to one of two extremes. They either submerge themselves in the Church environment altogether, rejecting all or portions of their Jewishness; or they hold Church history and Christendom generally at arm's length, disassociating themselves from the Church and what it has done. Neither does justice to the reality of being a Messianic Jew, fully Jewish and fully Messianic.

1. *Neurosis No. 1: Anti-Jewishness*

For example, there was a Jewish believer named Moses Margoliouth (1820-1881) who in 1843 published a book called

32. For a more extensive description and refutation of the two-covenant theory, see Appendix, Section C-3-c.

The Fundamental Principles of Modern Judaism Investigated. One can learn from this book, but one has constantly to battle its style, which can only be called anti-Jewish; and from the pen of a Messianic Jew that is a shame. This can be seen from the following quotation of less than one sentence:

> "The Rabbies [sic], who require our Jewish brethren to believe them 'even when they tell them that right is left and left is right,' (as stated in Rabbi Jarchi's commentary on Deut. 17.11), attempt to persuade them that the Divine Being wears Phylacteries, and try to prove it in a most absurd and extravagant manner; which is another instance of their wilful perversion of the word of God; as we shall see from the following extract found in ...," etc.[33]

He also wrote, "I make a wide difference between *Jews* and *Modern Judaism.* The former I esteem, respect and love ... ; whilst the latter, ... I found to be wanting."[34] Margoliouth, who became an Anglican vicar shortly after the above was published, undoubtedly loved the Lord and the Church, but with such a negative attitude toward Judaism it is hard to imagine him effectively expressing the "esteem, respect and love" which he said he had for his fellow Jews. There are truths in traditional Judaism, so that even if some Jewish environments can be oppressive (as can Christian ones), it would be better to be less scattershot and more moderate in pointing out abuses. Moreover, the remarks about God laying *tefillin* are misdirected, since the Jewish source is *aggadic,* presenting a *drash* (homily), not a literal description. In conclusion, it seems to me that he felt at peace with the Church, but not with his Jewishness.

Some Jews who accepted the Messiah during the Middle Ages became tools of the institutionalized Church

---

33. Moses Margoliouth, *The Fundamental Principles of Modern Judaism Investigated (London:* B. Wertheim, 1843), p. 28.
34. *Ibid.*, p. 192.

against their fellow Jews. These include Pablo Christiani (d. 1274), whose debate with Rabbi Moshe ben Nachman (Nachmanides) is recorded; Avner of Burgos (Paulus de Santa Maria, 1351-1435), Nicholas Donin (13th century) and Johann Josef Pfefferkorn (1469-1522) too are among the villains—they encouraged pogroms, burned *Talmuds* and made false charges of various kinds against the Jews. Jews have antennae sensitive to antisemitism. Messianic Jews should not let their own antennae grow calloused, especially in regard to their own actions.

2. *Neurosis No. 2: Anti-Christianity*

On the other hand, I have encountered a number of Jewish believers who ignore or deny certain aspects of what the Church is about.

Some take issue with doctrines that simply cannot be compromised, for example, the inner nature of God and the divinity of Yeshua. The word "trinity" is not found in Scripture, so there is no need to extract from any believer a confession of the word "trinity." But that to which the word refers—what John Fischer calls God's "unique unity"—is nonnegotiable: God is in fact Father, Son, Holy Spirit. For this there is more than adequate scriptural proof, consisting of not only many verses in the New Testament, but some hints in the *Tanakh* as well. Some wish to regard Yeshua as "less than" the Father. This can be done within the framework of orthodox Christian theology, because any orthodox theology of God's inner nature must deal with both equality and hierarchy. On the one hand Father, Son and Holy Spirit are equal; on the other, the Father is greater than the Son, and both are greater than the Holy Spirit. Again, there is no shortage of scriptural proofs for both aspects. I have no trouble with Jewish believers who choose to talk more about hierarchy than equality—it may even be precisely what the Gentile Christians around them need to hear. But if I cannot get a

Jewish person who claims to be a believer in Yeshua to admit that Yeshua is God (which is not the same as saying that God is Yeshua; that statement is at best off-target and at worst heretical), and that Father, Son and Holy Spirit are, in at least some sense or senses, equal, then I must conclude either that the person is not saved or—more generously and more usually—that he doesn't know what he's talking about. The point of saying all this is that sometimes Jewish believers, out of a desire to present their Messianic faith in a Jewish way, produce sub-Messianic expressions that need to be corrected.

Another form of anti-Christianity is refusal to come to terms with the fact that Christians have persecuted Jews. We take as given that antisemitism is incompatible with biblical faith.[35] At Zechariah 2:8 God says, "He who touches you"—the Jewish people—"touches the apple of my eye," that is, the pupil, the most sensitive and useful part. At Genesis 12:3 God assures Abraham, the father of the Jewish people, "I will bless those who bless you and curse him who curses you."

Nevertheless both individuals and the Church as an institution have taught antisemitic doctrines and committed antisemitic acts in the name of Christ. Moreover, although some of these individuals were Christians in name only, displaying no evidence of genuine faith, others were people who according to any criterion except that of the antisemitism itself really were Christians—such as Augustine and Martin Luther. In fact, even though he inaugurated the Protestant Reformation one can seriously wonder, in the light of the standard set by Genesis 12:3, if the man who filled his tract, "On the Jews and their Lies,"[36] with imprecations against Abraham's descendants was saved.

---

35. See Appendix, Section C-2; also a study by the Messianic Jew, Menahem Benhayim, *Jews, Gentiles and the New Testament Scriptures: Alleged Antisemitism in the New Testament* (Jerusalem: Yanetz, 1985).

36. Martin Luther, "On the Jews and Their Lies" (1543), translated by Martin H. Bertram, edited by Franklin Sherman: Volume 47, pp. 121-306 of Jaroslav Pelikan and Helmut T. Lehmann, *Luther's*

I think it is appropriate for Gentile Christians and Messianic Jews to take responsibility for these things, to be humble about them, to acknowledge personally the Church's guilt before Jews without necessarily expecting to be forgiven by them. In other words, we must agree that antisemitism is bad without glossing over the Church's antisemitism; to do less is anti-Christian.

This is the appropriate place to mention another phenomenon found among Messianic Jews: anti-Gentilism. Generally this sinful attitude is left over from the person's life as a Jew before he was saved, although occasionally it develops afterwards. If Gentile Christians must give up anti-Jewish prejudice, Messianic Jews must give up anti-Gentile prejudice and

---

Works (Philadelphia: Fortress Press and St. Louis: Concordia Publishing House, 1962-1974). The following is selected from pp. 268-278:

> "What shall we Christians do with this rejected and condemned people, the Jews? . . . I shall give you my sincere advice: First, to set fire to their synagogues . . .in honor of our Lord and of Christendom, so that God might see that we are Christians. . . . I advise that their houses also be razed and destroyed. . . . I advise that their prayerbooks and Talmudic writings . . . be taken from them. . . . I advise that their rabbis be forbidden to teach henceforth on pain of loss of life and limb. . . . [W]e will believe that our Lord Jesus Christ is truthful when he declares of the Jews who did not accept but crucified him, 'You are a brood of vipers and children of the devil. . . .' I have read and heard many stories about the Jews which agree with this judgment of Christ, namely, how they have poisoned wells, made assassinations, kidnapped children . . . I have heard that one Jew sent another Jew, and this by means of a Christian, a pot of blood, together with a barrel of wine, in which when drunk empty, a dead Jew was found."

It does not make edifying reading. The only mitigating factor, if it may be called one, is that Luther was equally excessive in spewing vitriol on all his perceived enemies, Christian and non-Christian alike. Further analysis is contained in my unpublished paper, "Luther's View of the Jews: A Lesson For Our Time," 1974.

seek God's healing. If the feelings won't leave, one should conform one's actions to scriptural standards and trust God to change the feelings. No Jewish believer should tolerate anti-Gentilism in himself or in other believers.

3. *No Neurosis*

The Messianic Jew has two non-neurotic roles to play in the Church. First, he must do his best to correct the Church in its relationship with Jews, Judaism and Jewishness. For example, the issues raised in this book need to be brought to the attention of all in the Church, Gentile Christians as well as Messianic Jews. Many Messianic Jews will feel that God is calling them to precisely that task.

The second role he has to play is being instrumental in fostering Jewish evangelism, helping the Church to bring the Gospel "to the Jew first,"[37] as Scripture requires.

4. *Gentile Christian Attitudes Toward Messianic Jews*

Gentiles in the Church take one of four positions toward Messianic Jews: for us, against us, ignoring us, or using us.

The most common stance is to ignore us. Not that we are ignored as people, we are ignored as Jews. It is assumed that the middle wall of partition's being broken down means that we Jews are supposed to act like Gentiles. Our Jewish concerns concern no one else, so that the Jewish aspect of our being simply has to be put on ice. This is, of course, precisely the opposite of what the New Testament teaches. Sha'ul insisted that Gentiles did not have to act like Jews to become Christians.[38] The opposite possibility, that Jews in the Church would one day be expected to act like Gentiles, did not occur

37. Romans 1:16; for a discussion of this phrase see Appendix, Section C-4.
38. Galatians 2:11 -20, Acts 15:1-2.

to him; but it is unthinkable that he would have countenanced it. Indeed, proving that he was *not* teaching Jews to abandon the *Torah* of Moses cost him his freedom—and ultimately perhaps his life.[39]

Other Gentile Christians use us. We spoke of it earlier;[40] here I will add only that although putting a Jewish believer on display is nearly always a matter not of malice but enthusiasm, it would be better to meet him as a person and learn what his needs and abilities are, so that he can serve the Body as he should.

There are two ways of being against us. Churches still exist where a Jewish believer is unwelcome simply because he is Jewish. I praise God that I have not encountered them, but I hear stories. Clearly the phenomenon was more widespread in times past, when cultural conformity was more easily mistaken for theological orthodoxy. In those days, the Gentile Christians, not knowing how to deal with this oddity in their midst, the believing Jew, tended to distance themselves from him or look down on him as a second-class Christian.

However, there is a phenomenon I do encounter, which I call unconscious or latent antisemitism. The people who have it may consciously intend the opposite, but their antisemitic habit patterns and attitudes are so deeply built in that they cannot control them and are in fact unaware of them. My wife and I were talking with the pastor of a nationally known church with more than 5,000 members about a mutual acquaintance, a Jewish believer who is serving the Lord well. "I really appreciate his ministry," he began, "but I must ask: Why does he have to act so Jewish?" Martha and I were both nonplussed at his question, but she was the first to recover sufficiently to answer—in a typically Jewish way, with a question—"Why do *you* have to act so Gentile? " The point is that the Gospel does not require a person to "act" at all. There are required behaviors; and there is the promise that

39. Acts 21:20 ff., 2 Timothy 4:6-8, 16.
40. Chapter II, Section A-3.

God, working in believers, will give them power to behave as they should. But the Gospel is not tied to a particular culture, so there isn't any reason in the world why a Messianic Jew shouldn't "act Jewish." Through this Gospel Gentiles come to know the God of the Jewish people *without* having to change cultures. Therefore it is a double error to expect Messianic Jews not to act Jewish: first, because the Gospel was Jewish to start with, and second, because the very essence of the Gospel is not to require de-culturization of believers.

Another example we encountered was when we were served a *table d'hote* meal in a restaurant. Gentile Christians seated with us watched us picking at the food in an effort to keep a semblance *of kosher.* When we explained what we were doing, their response was to remind us to "Eat what is set before you."[41] Had they been our hosts, we would have done exactly that, without demur, even though the verse quoted has nothing to do with Jews' observing the dietary laws. But in a restaurant no one's feelings are hurt by what we eat or don't eat. When we explained to them about Messianic Judaism they became interested and could empathize with us. But their unconscious initial reaction was anti-Jewish.

The second form of opposition I encounter from Gentile Christians is not to me either as a person or as a Jew, but to my desire to foster a movement, to develop Messianic Judaism as a viable communal expression of New Testament faith. The reasons for such opposition are generally not personal but theological; nevertheless, I believe they are wrong. This book is my answer to such mistaken theology.

Finally, there is the attitude I like to see—favor. There are Gentile Christians who understand that there is a Jewish component to my nature, that I have ambitions for Messianic Judaism as a communal movement, that the Church needs to appreciate its own Jewish background more and understand the Jewish people better, and that they as Christians are

41. 1 Corinthians 10:27.

grafted into a Jewish root. When we Messianic Jews find ourselves surrounded by such Gentile Christians encouraging, nurturing and supporting us, I am sure that our Church neuroses will drop away.

F. MESSIANIC JEWISH HISTORY

1. *Review of Messianic Jewish History*

As we saw earlier, Messianic faith began within Judaism; indeed it could not have happened otherwise. We saw that the Messianic Jews would have remained within the Jewish community, but insufferable pressures caused them to be excluded by the second century (perhaps in some areas the third or fourth), and they ceased to exist as an identifiable movement by the fifth century, with possible minor exceptions. The history of the early Jewish Christians has been studied, although less is known about them than one might wish.

From the 5th to the 18th century there was no room, either in the Church or in the Jewish community, for Messianic Jews who wished to retain their dual identity. A Jew who wanted to honor Yeshua had to leave his people and join the Gentile-dominated Church. During that period the Church and the Jewish community developed their own histories, but Messianic Jewish history ceases to be communal and becomes the stories of individual Jewish believers in relationship to the Jewish, Christian and secular communities.

The modern revival of Messianic Judaism begins in idea form, as we said, with the suggestions of John Toland, Christian outreaches to Jews in Holland and Germany in the seventeenth and eighteenth centuries, and the Hebrew Christian movement in early 19th-century England. Occasional efforts were made to retain a Jewish approach, e.g., Rabbi Isaac Lichtenstein, who preached Yeshua from the pulpit of his synagogue in Tapio-Szele, Hungary (late 1800's); Josef Rabinovich, who founded a Messianic synagogue in Kishinev in the 1880's; Yechiel Lichtenstein's commentaries on the New Testament (1891-1904); Mark John Levy and Theodore Lucky (early 1900's). But because the movement was still pervasively Gentilized, it won mostly marginal Jews, as B. Z. Sobel's book, *Hebrew Christianity: The Thirteenth Tribe* devastatingly documents in a sociological case study of a small missionary organization active in the early 1960's.[42]

Recently the Messianic Jewish congregations movement has implemented principles of evangelism that do not demand conformity to the dominant culture but allow people to retain their own customs except where prohibited by Scripture. Jewish cultural emphasis is thus encouraged not merely for the individual or within a fellowship group of subsidiary importance, but in the congregation itself, which expresses its Jewishness as much as it wishes. The development of Messianic Judaism in the last twenty years, including the emergence of Messianic Jewish congregations by the dozens, suggests that the time for this book has come.

We will discuss today's Messianic Jewish movement further in Chapter VII, Section A.

2. *Books On Messianic Jewish History*

There are several books on the Jewish Christianity of the first through fifth centuries.[43] The late Jacob Jocz, a Jewish believer, wrote both history and theology in *The Jewish People and Jesus Christ*[44]. But it is to be regretted that more than half a

42. B. Z. Sobel, *Hebrew Christianity: The Thirteenth Tribe* (New York: John Wiley & Sons, 1974).
43. B. Bagatti, *The Church From the Circumcision* (Rome: Pontifical Biblical Institute, 1971); Jean Danielou, *The Theology of Jewish Christianity* (London: Dalton, Longman & Todd, 1964); Schoeps *(pp. cit.* in Chpter II, footnote 6): Ray A. Pritz, *Nazarene Jewish Christianity* (Jerusalem: The Magnes Press, and Leiden: E. J. Brill, 1988).
44. *Op. Cit.* in Chapter I, footnote 11.

century after the late Hugh Schonfield wrote *The History of Jewish Christianity,* it still remains the only comprehensive study tracing the fortunes of the Messianic Jews through all of the last two thousand years. Although his later books, such as *The Passover Plot,* are dominated by wild speculation, he took relatively few liberties in this early work. Unfortunately it has long been out of print and is hard to find.

Another book which is out of print and hard to find is Bernstein's *Some Jewish Witnesses For Christ.*[46] It contains biographies of several hundred Jewish believers from the first century until the date of publication (1909).

Unfortunately no similar work has been produced describing as broad a cross-section of twentieth-century Messianic Jews, although several smaller books have appeared. It would be an inspiration to Jewish believers to learn about others who share our faith. If the Jewish community can point to its Freud, Marx and Einstein, why should we not reclaim the Messianic Jewish composer Felix Mendelssohn (1809-1847), whose oratorios *Elijah* and *Paul* testify to his faith? Likewise, Benjamin Disraeli (1804-1881) was the first and only Jewish prime minister of England; less well known is the fact that he was also its only Messianic Jewish prime minister.

We can be proud of some of our history—and ashamed of other parts; but all in all, it is ours, and we deserve to know it; in order to know it we have to research it and write it!

G. JEWISH-CHRISTIAN RELATIONS

An area of particular interest to Messianic Jews is Jewish-Christian relations.[47] In the following list of forms which Jew-

---

45. Hugh Schonfield, *The History of Jewish Christianity* (London: Duckworth, 1936).

46. A. Bernstein, *Some Jewish Witnesses For Christ (London:* Operative Jewish Converts' Institution, 1909).

47. Of the immense literature of Jewish-Christian relations the following three items may be of particular interest to many readers of this book: Marc H. Tanenbaum, Marvin R. Wilson and A. James Rudin, eds., *Evangelicals and Jews in*

ish-Christian relations can take, keep in mind that Messianic Jews are almost never included as a distinct third party entitled to its own voice.

1. *Opposition*

The Church coerced, the Jewish people resisted. It hardly needs to be said that this was the paradigm for centuries.

2. *Separatism*

In other words, live and let live. This is perhaps the first choice of many Jewish people and not a few Christians; however, it is isolationist, ignoring the flow of history bringing people ever more closely together in the global village.

3. *Tolerance*

Being against tolerance is like being against motherhood, and I am not against it. But I view tolerance as separatism concealed by a veneer of courtesy. It's better than discourteous separatism and better than intolerance and bigotry, but it's not the ultimate goal. In order for tolerance to work, the participants implicitly agree to avoid raising the elements they regard as nonnegotiable in their respective worldviews. Nevertheless, it can be a useful early step in improving relations.

To the extent that tolerance of Judaism by Christianity and vice versa is desirable, to that same extent tolerance of Messianic Judaism by non-Messianic Jews and Gentile Christians and vice versa is desirable. Therefore representatives of Messianic Judaism ought to be included in activities intended to promote tolerance.

Conversation on Scripture, Theology and History (Grand Michigan: Baker Book House, 1978); same editors, *Evangelicals and Jews in an Age of Pluralism* (Baker, 1984); and Merrill Simon, *Jerry Falwell and the Jews* (Middle Village, New York: Jonathan David Publishers, 1984.

A number of interesting birds make their home in the tree of tolerance. One is interfaith dialogue, valuable because any communication is better than none. The National Conference of Christians and Jews and the Anti-Defamation League of B'nai Brith are two well-known organizations working in this area. But Messianic Jews are rarely asked to participate; I hope this will soon change.

Another expression of tolerance is cooperation or alliance between Christians and Jews for limited purposes, for example, to help Jews leave Russia, or to support the State of Israel. This is another kind of arm's length relating, which, again, is better than none. It become, testy when one side questions the other's motives.

Tolerance sometimes leads to mutual assistance. As an expression of human kindness, who can object? Yet it is problematical to help a community or organization whose purposes are perceived as directly opposing one's own. Ultimately this must limit the degree of assistance.

"Ecumenism" is a term worth bringing up here. If it is another way of saying "interfaith dialogue," nothing more needs to be added. If it means inter-denominational cooperation and possibly merger, it is unthinkable that there would be a merger between a Christian and a Jewish denomination.

4. *Syncretism*

Syncretism is the uniting of two religious beliefs, without their being fully integrated with each other, and often involving compromise, illogical eclecticism, uncritical acceptance of mutually inconsistent principles, or incorporation of undigested lumps of doctrine or practice. The so-called Judeo-Christian tradition has elements of sycretism about it, as does American "civil religion." "All paths lead to God" is a false proposition which, if developed beyond slogan form, necessarily involves syncretism. "Taking the best of all religions" really means founding one's own personal religion and usually proves to be another name for syncretism. No thoughtful Jew or Christian would ever be satisfied with a syncretistic approach to Jewish-Christian relations.

5. Assimilation

In the New Testament the Judaizers wanted to require Gentiles to assimilate to Judaism before they could be accepted as Christians. Today assimilation means Jews becoming less Jewish and more like the so-called "Christian culture" around them. From a Jewish communal point of view assimilation is an enemy feared more than death. For as Jews leave Judaism and the Jewish community, the community diminishes; and if assimilation were total, the Jewish community would cease to exist, so that—as the Post World War II Jewish writers have put it—Hitler would have a posthumous victory.[48]

It should be pointed out that the culture around us is by no means Christian in any scriptural sense; and being baptized is no longer the entry card to Western civilization. Assimilation is more often to the Gentile culture with its many pagan and non-Christian elements.

The Messianic Jewish response to the problem of assimilation is that a Jew does not need to stop being Jewish when he believes in the Jewish Messiah, Yeshua. In fact, many Jews become more Jewishly conscious when they come to New Testament faith, rather than less.

---

48. See Emil Fackenheim, "Jewish Faith and the Holocaust," *Commentary*, 1967; quoted in his *God's Presence in History* New York: Harper & Row, 1970), p. 84. But contrast this remark of Vera Schlamm, a Jew who survived the concentration camps, in her testimony of how she came to faith in Yeshua: "If we allow the memory of the Nazis to keep us from Messiah, we give Hitler the power to reach beyond the grave and destroy us in an awful way that even his evil mind could not imagine." (Ruth Rosen, ed., *Jesus for Jews* (San Francisco: A Messianic Jewish Perspective, 1987), pp. 106-107).

In terms of Jewish-Christian relations, assimilation is no answer at all. True, Arnold Toynbee declared that Judaism was a "fossil" with no current function, which implies that he thought it should assimilate and be done with itself. But, God be praised, that is simply not about to happen.

6. *Compromise*

Compromise is different from assimilation, since it involves both sides and is voluntary. But it is premised on the idea of giving up something good to get something good. With denominational differences and ecumenism compromise has some auspicious history. But between Judaism and Christianity it is not a promising approach, since each regards some issues as uncompromisable. Reconciliation, on the other hand, as we will see, is premised on the idea of conforming to God's will, which can only be good. In other words, compromise is a "zero-sum game," in which what one side wins the other loses; whereas reconciliation, like economic production, is a "positive-sum game," in which both sides can gain.

7. Evangelism, Conversion and Competition

These are interrelated and will be dealt with together. Evangelism is spreading the Gospel. Conversion, scripturally, means coming to genuine faith in Yeshua the Messiah. However, in the popular sense, it means moving from one religious community to another. According to this popular definition, conversion is no solution to Jewish-Christian relations, since it too is a zero-sum game: every Jew won to Christianity is a Jew lost to Judaism. Conversion of this kind solves no problems, so long as one side holds out.

But the popular definition of conversion is premised on the idea that the circles representing Judaism and Christianity do not overlap (Figures 1, 5E). If, as I claim, they do overlap (Figures 3, 5F), then a Jew who comes to faith in Yeshua need not leave Judaism, so the popular definition of conversion cannot be applied.

Evangelism takes place when believers in New Testament truth reach out to nonbelievers with that truth. There was a time when Judaism was a missionary religion,[49] but for the most part it no longer is—although Reform Judaism has proposed missionizing "unchurched" Gentiles, and the Lubavitcher Hasidim energetically attempt to bring non-Orthodox Jews into their sect (this is not missionizing, since the people targeted are already Jewish; however, their methods resemble those of some missionaries).

Conversion (in the popular sense), evangelism and missionizing all imply a competitive relationship between religious communities. This is not a bad thing; indeed, in the case of evangelism it follows from the objective fact that the truth is what it is.

Evangelism and interfaith dialogue are sometimes considered incompatible. Supposedly a dialogician must not have the attitude, "I'm right and you're wrong." But why not? After all, dialogue is only two people talking. People can talk without setting preconditions on each other's attitudes. All it takes is being willing to listen to what the other has to say, and being willing to speak honestly. Put another way, the conflict between evangelism and dialogue disappears if the goal is reconciliation without preconditions.

8. *Reconciliation*

Reconciliation is the ideal. To be real, it must be based on truth, not on surface tolerance; that is, it must be without preconditions, except the precondition that both sides are willing to conform to what is true. In my opinion, reconciliation will involve change in both Judaism and Christianity in a direction that Messianic Judaism can help make visible, even though Messianic Judaism makes no claim to have itself already

49. Mattityahu [Matthew] 23:15.

arrived at the ultimate goal. Moreover, reconciliation is consistent with any form of evangelism that uses honest methods and is willing to respect the free choice of those being evangelized. Messianic Judaism clearly has a role to play in reconciliation.

H. ARE MESSIANIC JEWS "CHRISTIANS"? PART 2: AN OPEN DEBATE.

We are ready at last to tackle the rest of the question raised at the end of the previous chapter. There we looked at how the term "Christian" is used in the New Testament. To examine whether "Christian" should be applied to Messianic Jews in the twentieth century, I will construct an imaginary conversation between several people who have followed the analysis to this point.

Someone begins by saying: What's the problem? The word used to describe a person who believes in Yeshua as Messiah and accepts the New Testament is "Christian," so it's simply a matter of using language in the normal way.

Messianic Jew: We have seen already that the New Testament does not show believers calling Messianic Jews "Christians."[50] We should use the Bible's technical terms the way the Bible uses them.

But even if we put that argument aside, words have connotations as well as denotations. The connotations of the word "Christian" to non-Messianic Jews vary, but few of them are good. It can signal "persecutor," and I am not a persecutor. It can signal "Gentile" and I have not become a Gentile. It can call up a vision of statues and candles and idols, and I have nothing to do with these. It can signal hating or rejecting my Jewish people, and I haven't done it.

Anti-Missionary: You have! You have! Liar! Traitor! Any-

50. See Chapter II, Section C-4.

one who turns to "that man" has left his people! Call yourself a Christian, but don't call yourself any kind of Jew!

Messianic Jew: Apparently the analysis we have just been through has passed you by.

Gentile Christian: Excuse me, but it seems to me that if you won't call yourself a Christian, then you aren't one. Why should I regard you as my brother in the Lord if you won't identify yourself by the name nearest and dearest to my heart?

Another Gentile Christian: I will consider you my brother in Christ, but it does seem your faith is deficient and you are a very weak brother indeed if you balk at using the label "Christian" for yourself.

First Gentile Christian: In any case, it's a fact of history that the word "Christian" has been used for centuries to describe any believer in Jesus—Gentile or Jewish. Do you think you can change history?

Messianic Jew: I can try! Listen, both of you, try to understand! Why should I create wrong impressions in the minds of other Jewish people by using a word that connotes things about myself that just aren't so? I am fighting the misimpression of Jewish believers which my fellow Jews have had in the past and often still have. They're on a train, going down the track ninety miles an hour in the wrong direction, and I am trying to stop the train! Once the train is stopped and reversed, we can talk about whether I should call myself a Christian or not. If you want to call me one, it's okay, since you and I both understand that I have not left either the Jewish people or the Jewish religion by believing in Yeshua. But they don't understand it. They think I have changed religion . . .

Jewish person: Well, haven't you? I'm not religious myself, but I know one thing: Jews don't believe in Jesus. If you can't admit . . .

Messianic Jew: You too! Try to understand! You are secular, but I am religious. Not Orthodox, not Conservative, not Reform, not Reconstructionist but Messianic.

Jewish person: I would say that if you don't call yourself a Christian you are being deceptive. You're trying to convince us that you're not something which in fact you are. You use a term like "Messianic Jew" to worm your way back among our people and try to convert us. If you would simply call yourself a Christian, we would all know where you stand. Then I could respect you for what you are.

Messianic Jew: You wouldn't at all know where I stand!—Because you're putting me in a box, you're stretching me to fit your Procrustean bed. Your problem is that you don't want to think about whether Yeshua really is the Messiah of the Jewish people, and whether a Jew can honor him in a Jewish way. Here is what I will admit: if he isn't *our* Messiah, then he isn't *anybody's* Messiah.

Look, I have already said I am 100% Jewish and 100% Messianic. "Messianic" means I believe in Yeshua. I've followed the *Torah* to where it leads, and it leads to the Messiah, so now I'm a Jew who knows who the Messiah is. What do you want from me?

* * * * *

There it is, and we'll leave it at that.

CHAPTER IV
THEOLOGY

A. THE NEED FOR MESSIANIC JEWISH SYSTEMATIC THEOLOGY

Christian theology tends to underplay or misrepresent Jewish phenomena. Jewish theology ignores the New Testament. Since any genuine reconciliation of the Church and the Jewish people must conform to biblical truth, what is needed before any program of action can be designed is a thought framework that can do justice to both the Messianic and the Jewish elements of any theological topic. The name for such a thought framework is Messianic Jewish systematic theology. (However, in this book I do not offer finished theology—if there is such a thing. Rather, I am pointing out topics which need theological treatment and hinting at ways to go about it.)

1. *Consumer-Oriented Theology And The Four Audiences*

I define systematic theology as the presentation of biblical truth in an organized fashion, by subject matter, in a manner that will be understood by its intended audience. My emphasis on the audience is purposeful; I do not believe that theology should be merely whatever its author wishes to say, placed in the marketplace for whoever will buy. A producer-oriented theology is selfish; theologians ought to consider the consumer.

Although this is a general principle applicable to any theology, it is an absolute must for Messianic Jewish theology, because we have not one audience but four. They are the four mutually exclusive categories of humanity mentioned in the preceding chapter: Messianic Jews, non-Messianic Jews, Gentile Christians and the rest of mankind. Confusion is created and damage done when theologians write about Messianic Jewish subjects without considering who will read what they have written.

This problem could be dealt with by using the procedure of Thomas Aquinas in his *Summa Theologica.* He states a theological principle, follows with possible objections, then answers them. A Messianic Jewish theologian too might state a principle, divide the objections into those he would expect from each of the four audiences, and conclude with his replies.

A theologian targeting one of the four audiences must remember that the other three exist. Messianic or non-Messianic Jews may be reading over the shoulder of the Gentile Christian for whom he is writing. Non-Messianic Jews and Gentile Christians may be eavesdropping when he speaks to Messianic Jews.

When addressing any one of the audiences, a theologian should deal with what bothers them, rather than irritate them by discussing issues in which they have neither interest nor a need to have interest awakened. In other words, scratch where it itches, not where it doesn't!

But when we are in the role of eavesdropper on a message not meant for us, we should put ourselves in the place of those being spoken to, rather than criticize the speaker for failing to consider our concerns or ride our hobby-horses.

If a theologian changes intended audiences, he should be clear about it. Sha'ul [Paul] knew how. In Romans 11 he begins by addressing both Jewish and Gentile believers. But in verse 13, he turns specifically to Gentile Christians. Then at 12:1 he once again speaks to all believers as "brothers."

2. *Differences within the Four Audiences*

None of the four groups is monolithic. Non-Messianic Jews, for example, not only fall into the familiar categories of Orthodox, Conservative, Reform, Reconstructionist, Humanist and secular, but each of these has subgroups. The modern Orthodox Jew, such as might be graduated from Yeshiva University, may take a less rigid stand on certain points than those affiliated with the *yeshiva* world;[1] the approach of both would be different in some respects from that of the *Hasidim;* and within the *Hasidim* are strenuously conflicting camps. Some Orthodox are willing to recognize the Conservative and Reform denominations, others are not. Some Orthodox Jews acknowledge Messianic Jews as Jews; others do not. Likewise, the revisionist branches of Judaism—Conservative, Reform, Reconstructionist, Humanist—each has its right and left wings and its internal differences. Among secular Jews, labels such as "agnostic" and "atheist" may be misleading, since some secular Jews may have considered spiritual issues with care before arriving at their present conclusions, while others may be unaware, uneducated or uninterested. And since being Jewish is not only a matter of religion but of peoplehood, another way to categorize is according to involvement with Jewish people generally or with the organized Jewish community in particular. Still another way is by attitude toward Israel: Zionist, non-Zionist, anti-Zionist, or unaware/don't care.

The denomination of a Gentile Christian will cast light on his faith, attitudes and concerns. Another factor is his place on the right-to-left scale of fundamentalist-evangelical-liberal. A third dimension is his attitude toward Messianic Judaism—in favor, inclined toward, neutral, opposed, uninformed but curious to learn more, or hopelessly uninterested.

The distinctions made for non-Messianic Jews and for Gentile Christians would both apply to Messianic Jews.

---

1. See William B. Helmreich, *The World Of The Yeshiva: An Intimate Portrait Of Orthodox Jewry* (New York: The Free Press, 1982).

Non-Christian Gentiles have a philosophical or religious viewpoint, whether it be another religion, a sect or a cult; adherence in a religious fashion to principles of psychology, philosophy, economics, or a political ideology; secularism, atheism, hedonism; or just apathy. One of our mentors, Sha'ul from Tarsus, said that he tried to put himself in the position of anyone he spoke with, in the hope that by trying his best to deal with how that person acted and thought and felt about life, the person might be saved.[2]

B. INTRODUCTORY OBSERVATIONS

1. *Our "Enemies" Are Our Best Friends*

Those most critical of us are usually the most articulate about why they oppose us and thus provide our clearest guidelines for improvement. Christians who write against Messianic Judaism or against Jewish evangelism clarify the theological issues we must address to defend Messianic Judaism within the Church. Non-Messianic Jews doing apologetics against the New Testament and against Christian understandings of the Hebrew Bible, such as the sixteenth-century Karaite rabbi, Yitzchak of Troki, show us areas needing clarification, especially areas where the Messianic Jewish position may need to be distinguished from more traditional Christian views that do not adequately take into account the Jewish background of the New Testament.[3] Similarly, by sharpening our perception of

2. 1 Corinthians 9:20-23.
3. Isaac Troki, *Faith Strengthened*(1593) (New York: Ktav Publishing House, 1970). His arguments have been answered point-by-point in A. Lukyn Williams, *A Manual Of Christian Evidences For Jewish People* (London: Society For Promoting Christian Knowledge, 1919, 2 volumes), although some of the rebuttals would be unacceptable from a Messianic Jewish perspective; unfortunately the book is out of print. Most modern anti-missionary literature consists of rather boorish replays of Rabbi Yitzchak's arguments. See, for examples, Samuel Levine, *You Take Jesus, I'll Take God: How To Refute Christian Missionaries (Los* Angeles: Hamoroh Press, 1980); two pamphlets by Shmuel Golding, *A Guide To The Misled*

Jewish attitudes against institutionalizing Jewish belief in Yeshua as the Messiah, someone like Sobel[4] points out directions for bettering our movement.

2. *The Liberal-Orthodox Spectrum*

A confounding factor in communicating with both friends and "foes" is the liberal-orthodox spectrum found within both Judaism and Christianity. This spectrum arises in part from the philosophical and epistemological presuppositions which people bring to their understanding of religion—presuppositions which they usually do not want questioned. Both Orthodox Jews and orthodox Christians regard Scripture as the inspired word of God, they interpret it literally, accept miracles as real, and believe that the only way to reach or please God is by means of the procedures God has authorized. Liberals, on the other hand, take the opposite positions on all of the above: Scripture is merely human, miracles are fraudulent or illusory, and all paths lead to God.

An untested hypothesis which casual observation leads me to believe is true is that Jews and Christians find it easiest to understand each other when they occupy about the same spot on their own orthodox-to-liberal spectrum. In the case of liberals, it means that they can comfortably engage in interfaith dialogue without either for a moment trying to persuade the other to change. More particularly, liberal Christians feel no need to evangelize their Jewish counterparts, which of course alleviates

---

(Beersheva, Israel: 1986) and *A Counselor's Guide: Jewish Answers To The Missionary Problem* (Jerusalem, 1986); the anonymously written book, *The Disputation* (Salford, England: Scholarly Publications, 1972); and Gerald Sigal, *The Jew And The Christian Missionary: A Jewish Response To Missionary Christianity* (New York: Ktav Publishing House, 1981), in answer to which Dr. Louis Goldberg, a Messianic Jew, has written the pamphlet, *A Jewish Christian Response* (San Francisco: Jews for Jesus, 1986). See also footnotes 55 and 56, below.

4. See Chapter III, footnote 42.

the tension many Jews feel when they know they are being targeted for the Gospel.

The right-wing case is interesting: on the one hand, both believe that Scripture is inspired—but they differ as to what is to be defined as authoratively from God. Orthodox Jews accept the *Tanakh* [the "Old Testament"] plus the Oral *Torah,* orthodox Christians the *Tanakh* plus the New Testament. Both accept miracles. Both accept resurrection from the dead as real, although of course Christians believe in Yeshua's resurrection and Orthodox Jews (Pinchas Lapide[5] excepted) do not. Both agree that one comes to God only in God's way, but they differ as to what that way is. Orthodox Jews expect Gentiles to obey the Noachide Laws[6] and Jews to obey the *Torah* of Moses as interpreted by the rabbis, while Orthodox Christians are certain that no one, Jew or Gentile, comes to the Father except through Yeshua the Messiah[7] and the New Covenant inaugurated by his atoning death on the execution-stake.

3. *Same Conclusions, Different Methodology: Using The Jewish Theological Agenda.*

It has been said that Gentile Christian theology moves from the Pauline epistles backward and finds justification in the Old Testament, whereas Messianic Jewish theology should start with *Torah* and move forward to new *Torah* discoveries that would not have been found without the New Testament. In principle, since both use the same texts and the truth is one, the results should be the same; but one expects the methodol-

---

5. Pinchas Lapide, *The Resurrection of Jesus: A Jewish Perspective* (Minneapolis: Augsburg Publishing House, 1983). The author, an Orthodox Jew, accepts the resurrection of Yeshua as a genuine historical event but does not find in it a reason why the Jewish people should accept him as the Messiah. His argument is that while the entire population of Israelites witnessed God on Mount Sinai, only a small coterie (several hundreds) saw the risen Yeshua.
6. See Chapter V, Section B-7.
7. Yochanan [John] 14:6, Acts 4:12.

ogy to be different. Moishe Rosen once put it this way: we need a biblical theology that does not rest on New Testament assumptions but comes to New Testament conclusions.[8]

It would be wise, therefore, to use the Jewish theological agenda when doing Messianic Jewish theology. This may suggest interacting with traditional Jewish materials such as the *Talmud, Midrashim,* codes and response, with anti-Christian polemics and apologetics, and with current Jewish writings, perhaps by writing commentaries on them. It may also imply making use of the thought framework of Jewish theology, for which the main topics are God, Israel and *Torah,* rather than the Christian agenda of theology, anthropology, soteriology and eschatology.

4. *Dealing With Secular Judaism*

Relating theologically to secular Jews differs from addressing "true believers" of some sort. The following issues are among those which arise: Does God exist at all, and does he intervene in human history? This discussion must necessarily distinguish the God of the Bible from the imaginary "God" the secular person has substituted for him.[9] Is God both just and merciful? This leads to the question of how he could allow the Holocaust, and who or what is responsible for it. Epistemological questions arise, such as how we can know there is a God, how we can know the Bible is true, and what constitutes proof. Finally, there is the embarrassment of being "chosen"— Tevye's complaint.[10] These are the same questions non-Messianic religious Judaism has to deal with when appealing to secular Jews.

---

8 Private conversation, February 16, 1977.

9 Two popular treatments of the subject by Christian theologians are Francis A. Schaeffer, *The God Who Is There* (Downers Grove, Illinois: Inter-Varsity Press, 1968), and J. B. Phillips, *Your God Is Too Small (New* York: Macmillan Publishing Co., Inc., 1961).

10 In the musical, "Fiddler on the Roof," based on Sholem Aleichem's stories, the leading character, Tevye, complains to God about it: "Why don't you choose someone else for a change!"

5. *Jewish Theology Of Christianity*

Non-Messianic Judaism has been forced by circumstances to deal with Christianity. Like all religions it has developed apologetics (defense of its own views) and polemics (attacks on other views). But in addition, I believe the pressure has been so great that it has developed two additional elements *vis-a-vis* Christianity. The first is defensive theology, by which I mean that it has taken theological positions in reaction to Christian theological positions. Because Christianity has taken such-and-such a stand, Judaism has taken a stand more oppositional than it would have taken, had Christianity not existed. Second, Judaism has had to develop its own theology concerning important Christian ideas. That is, Judaism has had to think about subjects that would not have arisen at all if Christianity had not been there.

For example, the Christian doctrines of the Incarnation and Trinity are described in Jewish thought as *shittuf,* "participation" or "association." Christianity is perceived as teaching that Yeshua "participates" in the divinity which rightfully belongs to God alone *(i.e.,* in Christian terminology, to God the Father alone)—a human being is wrongfully elevated to the position of God and worshipped as such. In the Middle Ages opinions among Jewish writers were divided over whether this constituted idolatry; today, with some exceptions, Jewish thinkers are satisfied that *shittuf does* not prevent Christianity from being a non-idolatrous, monotheistic religion.

Likewise, Judaism has its own theology of Christian baptism. Christians discuss whether baptism is into the Messiah or into the Church. Judaism doen't care much what Christian baptism is "into;" its concern is with what baptism is "out of." For most Jewish thought Christian baptism signifies that the individual has left the Jewish community and moved to the Christian community. This conceptualization in terms of leaving one community and entering another should not surprise us, since Judaism is more community-centered than Christianity. An implication is that a Jew can entertain whatever "crazy" ideas he wishes privately—and perhaps even publicly if it doesn't upset the community—perhaps even including the belief that his sins have been forgiven through the death of Yeshua the Messiah. But if he undergoes baptism, which is perceived not as heralding a new relationship with the God of Israel through the Jewish Messiah, but as initiation into Christianity, he also "exitiates" himself out of Judaism. However, in terms of the analysis of Chapter III, this understanding of baptism assumes that one cannot be both Jewish and Messianic; if, as we claim, one can be, then this theology is false. Moreover, it is inconsistent with *halakhah,* which says that "a bad Jew is still a Jew" and there is no act by which he can de-Jew himself.

No one source presents a comprehensive Jewish theology of Christianity, but Jewish studies of Christianity and polemic literature against Christianity reveal most of its elements. Messianic Judaism will find it useful to systematize these ideas.

6. *Christian Theology Of Judaism*

Similarly, Messianic Judaism can benefit from studying how Christians have understood Judaism. Much of this book is occupied with correcting Christian mis-impressions of Jewish ideas and practices; this is as important as correcting wrong Jewish attitudes toward the New Testament message."

C. THEOLOGY PROPER

In theology proper, the study of the nature of God, one can begin with the elements common to Jewish and Christian understanding or "Judeo-Christian tradition"—for example, the oneness, eternality, omnipotence and holiness of God. But soon one must deal with the two chief issues which divide, the divinity of the Messiah and the inner nature of God.

---

11. See, for example, Clemens Thoma, *Christian Theology of Judaism* (New York: Paulist Press, 1980; Franz Mussner, *Tractate on the Jews* (Philadelphia: Fortress Press, 1984). Both are Roman Catholics.

History has brought non-Messianic Judaism to the point of utterly denying the possibility of the incarnation and insisting on the absolute unity of God in a way that negates most Christian assertions about the Trinity (this is an example of "defensive theology"). Nevertheless, there are within Judaism hints that the opposition was not always so monolithic.

Misconceptions must be cleared up on both sides. Jews often suppose Christians think that Yeshua became God. They do not understand that the New Testament teaches the opposite; God—or, more precisely, the eternal Word of God—without compromising or diluting his God-ness, took on flesh and became man.[12] Another common Jewish idea is that Christians believe in three gods. But Yeshua quoted the *Sh 'ma* as the most important commandment: "Hear, O Israel, the Lord, our God—the Lord is one. And you shall love the Lord your God with all your heart and with all your soul and with all your strength."[13]

On the Christian side, the tendency among the masses of Christians if not among the theologians is to ignore the Father and turn exclusively to Yeshua, or, in the case of some charismatics, to the Holy Spirit. Yeshua instructed his disciples to pray to the Father; and the "Lord's Prayer," which he taught them, is addressed to the Father. But Christians often use the names of the three persons of the Trinity interchangeably, which suggests a practical tritheism both offensive to Jews and unconscious of the Jewishness of the Gospel.

D. SIN, ATONEMENT, FAITH, WORKS

1. *Man in the Image of God*

Again it is well to begin with the commonalities. For example, Jews and Christians agree that man is made in the image of

12. Yochanan [John] 1:1, 14.
13. Mark 12:28-30, quoting Deuteronomy 6:4-5. For more on theology proper, see above, Chapter HI, Section E-2, paragraph 2.

God. Some Christian theologies suppose that sin has damaged this image, whereas others locate the damage elsewhere. Jewish theology does not speak of a damaged image. In any case, I submit "God created man in his image" as my candidate for the most profound statement in the entire Bible.

2. *Sin*

Jews and Christians acknowledge the rather obvious fact that human beings sin. Beyond this, the theologies of sin move in opposite directions. The Christian notion of "original sin" strikes many Jewish people as grossly unfair—why should we today be punished for the sin of Adam long ago? Likewise "total depravity" suggests that everyone practices the grossest forms of vice; but this is not what theologians mean by the term. Is man a sinner because he sins, or does he sin because he is a sinner? Jews say the former, Christians the latter. But does the answer matter practically? No matter which is right, the fact remains that people do violate God's will—as the *Tanakh* reminds us, "there is no one who does [only] good and doesn't sin."[14]

Although the Jewish theology of sin is "defensive," it strikes me that Christian theories of sin too follow a hidden agenda, which is to impress on people how seriously God takes sin. Possibly that goal can be achieved with descriptions of man's sinful character which pose fewer intellectual problems and are just as true to the scriptural facts as the Augustinian versions that have dominated Christian thinking since he wrote. And in fact these other versions exist; were the theories of Arminius, Cocceius and John Wesley (none of whom are considered heretical like Augustine's opponent Pelagius) better known in Jewish circles, some of the problems in this area of theology might be alleviated.

14. Ecclesiastes 7:20.

3. *Repentance, Atonement, Forgiveness*

On the matter of atonement for sin, Messianic Judaism should be sure to bring out all that the New Testament teaches on the subject, for Christianity tends to gloss over the very elements which Judaism stresses. In order for Yeshua's atonement to be effective, a person who has sinned must not only admit his sin, he must repent—which means being determined not to commit the sin again; he must be sorry—not out of self-pity but out of distress at having offended other people or God; and he must make restitution to the person wronged. From Christianity one seems to hear mostly how willing God is to forgive, from Judaism how crucial it is for us to do all we can to right the wrong. But righting wrongs is scriptural in both the *Tanakh* and the New Testament, as is God's desire to forgive the repentant sinner.

Individual responsibility, taught already by Moses and reaffirmed by Ezekiel, is clearly in view in the New Testament.

There has been Christian misunderstanding of the *Kol Nidre* prayer,[15] which strikes the uninitiated reader as offering "cheap grace;" but this misunderstanding is easily cleared up when the historical context is understood.

The sacrificial system must be discussed. Christians must understand that the *Tanakh's* system of sacrifices, although it looked forward to Yeshua the Messiah's final sacrifice for sin, was efficacious. Jews must come to realize that it takes more

15. The *Kol Nidre* prayer preceding the service for the Day of Atonement asks God to forgive certain false vows knowingly made. "... the context makes it perfectly obvious that no vows or obligations toward others are implied [only vows toward God]. ... *Kol Nidre* acquired intense significance particularly during the period of persecutions in Spain, where some hundred thousand Jews were forced to forswear their faith and adopt a new religion. Many of these attended the synagogue in secret at the risk of their life and used the *Kol Nidre* text as a form of renouncing the vows imposed upon them by the Inquisition." Philip Birnbaum, translator and annotator, *High Holyday Prayer Book* (New York: Hebrew Publishing Company, 1951), pp. 489–492.

than "prayer, repentance and charity" to "avert the evil decree,"[16] because the decreed penalty for sin is death (Genesis 2:17): hence the need for a sacrifice, a death. The practice of *kapparot* (sacrificing a chicken) at *Yom Kippur* in some Orthodox Jewish circles witnesses to a vestigial awareness of the importance of sacrifice, but this custom is probably not even known to the majority of Jews.

Jews question how Yeshua's sacrifice can have been effective, given that God hates human sacrifice. First, no other human being's sacrifice could have been effective, because no one else was sinless, without blemish, as is required of sacrifices. Second, God's hate for human sacrifice shows all the more how much he loved us: he sacrificed his son despite it. Thus God's sacrifice was real.

Has the Levitical system of sacrifices been abolished by the New Covenant? The New Testament book of Messianic Jews [Hebrews] is devoted to the subject, but a careful reading shows that only the sin offering has been canceled, replaced by Yeshua himself. It appears that if and/or when the Temple is rebuilt (the propheteers have varying opinions on this),[17] the other sacrifices (continual offering, thank offering, grain offering, etc.) would continue.

Jews suppose the ideas of vicarious atonement and mediation between God and man are Christian; but they are entirely Jewish, illustrated in the *Tanakh* by the animal sacrifices and the priests, respectively. Once more, the basic New Testament source on these subjects is Messianic Jews [Hebrews], especially Chapters 7–10, which relate the animal sacrifices and Levitical priesthood of the *Torah* to Yeshua's once-for-all, death-conquering self-sacrifice and consequent eternal high-priesthood. Yet his being high priest forever does not necessarily invalidate the Levitical priests, since their service is on earth, while his is in heaven.

---

16. These are the final words of the *Un'tanneh tokef prayer* from the High Holydays *Machzor;* see *ibid.*, p. 359-362.
17. See below, Section F-3.

4. *Man's Moral Duty*

Judaism emphasizes man's moral duty, the requirement that he obey God, that he should be holy because God—in whose image he is created—is holy, and it stresses that he has free will to do these things. Christianity, usually considered in Jewish circles to stress man's inability in these areas, actually says that the believer "can do all things through the Messiah, who strengthens" him[18]—hardly a teaching of despair. The moral demands of the New Testament are not less than those of the Old; in fact, comparison itself is a mistake, since the comparison is between God and God—he does not change.

5. *Faith And Works*

Finally, since Judaism considers itself "works-oriented" and Christianity for different reasons agrees with this self-evaluation, a clear understanding of the relationship between works and faith must be developed. Faith must be understood in the Jewish sense as *emunah,* "trusting faithfulness;" good works must be understood as stemming from this trusting faithfulness;[19] and it must be clear that good works performed out of anything but trusting faithfulness, though useful to others and perhaps helpful in training the individual, nevertheless do not credit his own account with righteousness.[20] In any case, legalism is as fatal to faith and good works in Christianity as in Judaism, and neither religion at its best espouses legalism. It must be stressed that no quantity or quality of good works that we can muster in our own strength will be good enough to earn us God's applause.

Jews who have no inclination to perform a particular *mitzvah* are sometimes told by their rabbis, "Do it anyway, the desire may come later." Christians seeing such a procedure as legalism should remember that they tell people, "Don't go by

18. Philippians 4:13.
19. Ephesians 2:10.
20. Isaiah 64:5-6; Romans 4:3, 14:23.

feelings, go by God's word." As I see it, that amounts to the same thing.

E. THE PEOPLE OF GOD: COVENANTS, CORPORATENESS, PROMISES, AND THE GOSPEL

The people of God are a chosen people, a kingdom of priests, a holy nation, witnesses for God, a people with a mission, a people with a Book, a blessing to the nations. The Jews are God's people, and the Church is God's people—as we saw in Chapter III, Section B. Other biblical concepts which need to be integrated into any Messianic Jewish theology include the "faithful remnant" and the "Israel of God."[21]

Three important subjects which require a correct understanding of the people of God are: covenants, corporate aspects of the Gospel, and the relationship between the Gospel and God's promises to Israel.

1. *Covenants*

One of the most important theological topics is covenants (contracts between God and human beings), because these frame all of salvation history. Our theology must consider the covenants with Noah, Abraham, Moses, David and Yeshua in relation to Jews, Gentiles and Messianic Jews.

a. All Five Covenants Remain In Force Today.

A key point of departure from many Christian theologies is insistence that all five of these covenants remain in force today.

- God's covenant with mankind through Noah (Genesis 9) is, in Jewish tradition, the basis for the "Noahide Laws," under which Gentiles receive salvation. Although the New Testament asserts that salvation for

---

21. Galatians 6:16.

Jews and Gentiles alike is only through Yeshua, the outcome of the Jerusalem Conference (Acts 15), which set forth the minimal conditions for acceptance of Gentiles into the Body of the Messiah, parallels the Noahide Laws. For further discussion see Chapter V, Section B-7.

- God's covenant with Abraham (Genesis 12, 13, 15, 17) created the Jewish people. Except for the requirement of circumcision it is an unconditional covenant promising that the Jews are to be a blessing to all mankind. This has proved true especially through Yeshua the Messiah, the "seed of Abraham," who came forth within the Jewish people and whose just rulership over all nations will extend from Jerusalem the Jewish capital. The covenant now applies to both Jews and Gentiles who follow Yeshua, as explained in Romans 4 and Galatians 3. The Jewish people will one day bless the world in unprecedented ways (Zechariah 8:23; Revelation 7, 14).

- God's covenant with the Jewish people through Moses provided the *Torah* to exhort and guide them into righteous living, to increase their awareness of sin and of their need to repent, and to teach them to accept God's provision—at first the animal sacrifices, and in the fullness of time Yeshua's sacrifice—for healing the separation from God caused by sin.

  In relation to its blessings and curses the Mosaic covenant is conditional from the Jewish side—but not from God's side, for God is faithful even when his people are not (Romans 3:2-3). According to Scripture, the Jewish people, having broken that covenant (Jeremiah 31:31-32), are currently recipients of its curses and not its blessings (Deuteronomy 28). When Jewish individuals become obedient and cease to break the covenant, God blesses them individually. When the Jewish people become obedient and cease to break the covenant, God will fulfill his promise to bless them as a nation.

However, the *Torah* supplied under this covenant was given forever and never abolished, and that *Torah* is still in force. Because this important truth runs against the current of so much Christian theology, its implications will be explored at length in Chapter V; see also below, Section E-l-b.

- God's covenant with David (2 Samuel 7) established the throne of his kingdom forever. For this reason the expected Messiah was and is called the Son of David. Messiah Yeshua, a descendant of David, will ascend the throne in the Father's good time (Acts 1:6-7, Revelation 20:2-6).
- God's New Covenant with the house of Israel and the house of Judah (Jeremiah 31:30-34) through Yeshua the Messiah blesses all mankind by providing the final and permanent atonement for sin and by promising that the Holy Spirit of God will write the *Torah* on the heart of anyone with faith. It thus complements the earlier covenants without annulling them (Galatians 3). It was promised in the *Tanakh,* and the books of the New Testament elaborate on it.

b. Messianic Jews [Hebrews] 7-8—Has The "Old" Covenant Been Abolished By The "New"?

This seems an appropriate place to look more intensively at how the Letter To A Group Of Messianic Jews ["To The Hebrews"] deals with the "old" and "new" covenants.

> "For if the system *oicohanim* is transformed, there must of necessity occur a transformation of *Torah*.... Thus, on the one hand, the earlier rule is set aside because of its weakness and inefficacy (for the *Torah* did not bring anything to the goal); and, on the other hand, a hope of something better is introduced, through which we are drawing near to God."[22]

22. Messianic Jews 7:12, 18-19, *Jewish New Testament (Op. cit.* in Chapter II, footnote 20).

But "a transformation of *Torah*" does not imply its abolition. Specific rules are set aside—for example, the *Torah* has to be adjusted to take account of Yeshua's role as *cohen gadol* [high priest]. Yet the *Torah* itself continues in force and is to be observed, just as the Constitution is not abolished by being amended. Chapter V deals with this controversial issue.[23]

> """See! The days are coming," says *Adonai,* "when I will establish . . . a new covenant . . .'" [Jeremiah 31:30- 34] In saying 'new' he has treated the first covenant as 'old;' and something being made old, something in the process of aging, is near vanishing."[24]

Yeshua's second coming is "near" ("The Lord is near,"[25]), but it has not happened yet![26] Likewise, although the "first" or "old" covenant *(i.e.,* the Mosaic Covenant) is "near vanishing," it has not yet vanished but is in a "process of aging." As I write I am fifty-two years old, and I too am in a process of aging; but I hope that no one will treat me as if I have vanished—at least, not for a while! We do not know when the "old" covenant will vanish; but we do know that Yeshua said, "Until heaven and earth pass away, not so much as *ayudor a* stroke will pass from the *Torah*—not until everything that must happen has happened."[27] Meanwhile, the Mosaic Covenant is here to be observed and not broken from our side (even though our fathers did break it[28]), since it has never been broken from God's side.

2. *Corporate Aspects Of The Gospel*

There are aspects of the Gospel which are corporate, not just related to individuals. Christians who understand that it is right

---

23. Note particularly Chapter V, Section A-2-d, which proves, on the basis of Messianic Jews [Hebrews] 8:6, that the New Covenant "has been given as *Torah.*"
24. Messianic Jews 8:9, 13, my translation.
25. Philippians 4:5. See also Mattityahu [Matthew] 24:42-50, 25:1-13; Luke 12:35-40; Romans 13:11-12; 1 Corinthians 7:29-31; Ya'akov [James] 5:8-9; Revelation 1:1-3, 22:6-10.
26. 2 Thessalonians 2:1-2.
27. Mattityahu [Matthew] 5:18, *Jewish New Testament.*
28. Jeremiah 31:31-32, Messianic Jews [Hebrews] 8:10.

to preach the Gospel to Jews often offer a Gospel which is inadequate because it is oriented only toward the individual and does not deal with the Jewish people as a corporate entity. In my view a gospel only for individuals is inadequate not only for Jews, but for Gentiles as well.

What is the Gospel for the individual? The New Testament's most complete statement of it is in the Letter to the Romans, Chapters 1-8, although every essential part can be found in the *Tanakh* as well. Chapters 1-3 tell us that everyone has sinned and falls short of fully obeying God (1 Kings 8:46, Ecclesiastes 7:20), that this sin builds a wall between him and God (Isaiah 59:1 -2), that the penalty for sin is death (Genesis 2:17), and that no one can restore the relationship with God by his own efforts (Psalm 143:2, Isaiah 64:5-6), but that God, from his side, by his own sovereign act of offering Yeshua the Messiah as an atonement for sin, has bridged the gap and restored fellowship between the individual and his God (Isaiah 52:13-53:12). Chapters 4-6 explain that what a person must do to have his own individual relationship with God restored is to put his trust in God, accepting personally what God has already done for him through Yeshua (Genesis 15:6). Chapters 7-8 add that such trust from the heart (Hebrew *emunah,* Greek *pistis),* which the New Testament makes clear is not merely intellectual affirmation of certain facts (Ya'akov [James] 2:14-26), will lead to his both wanting and being able—by the power of the Holy Spirit in him—to do those deeds which are pleasing to God.

In America, where the individual's right to pursue his own happiness has for more than two centuries been regarded as virtually a law of nature (what the Declaration of Independence called an "inalienable right"), the Gospel for the individual is conveniently presented in little booklets containing four or five "spiritual laws;" and it is possible to suppose that that's all there is to the Gospel. But salvation is corporate, for the community as well as for the individual. Any study of the word *yeshu'ah* ("salvation, deliverance") in the Hebrew Bible will show that deliverance is never thought of as being for the individual alone, although individual salvation definitely is part of the Old Testament message.[29] Nevertheless salvation for the individual Jew apart from concern for the deliverance of the Jewish people as a whole is simply not found in the *Tanakh.* On the contrary, much of its discussion of salvation is focussed on the integrity and holiness of the Jewish people as a whole, witness, for example, the frequent explanation in Deuteronomy for capital punishment or excommunication, "so that the evil may be purged from among you;" and compare the story of Achan in Joshua 7.

Since most Jewish people, after 4,000 years of communal history, have a strong sense of peoplehood,[30] an individual Gospel seems to them both selfish and insufficient, since it does not touch directly on national and universal aspirations. On average, Jews live more corporately than most individualistic Westerners—and I say this to the shame of the Church, which the New Testament proclaims to be "one body." Indeed, the Church can and should learn from the Jewish people what it means to care for one another.

To put this idea another way, my individual tie to God is direct, yet it is not alone—it is intertwined with yours. A Gospel which ignores the intertwining of lives together in "nations

---

29 See Psalm 51:12 (51:14 in some versions).

30 See, for example, Mordechai M. Kaplan, *The Greater Judaism In The Making* (New York: The Reconstructionist Press, 1960), especially the more than 100 page references under "Jewish people-hood" in the index. A sample, from pp. 30-31:

> "The Jewish People seem to have achieved a more intense and permanent ethnic consciousness than any other ancient people. ... The entire education of the Jewish child was confined to writings which dealt with the Jewish people. The main purpose of that education was to cultivate in him a loyalty and devotion to Israel and Israel's God, and to teach him the facts he had to know and the duties he had to perform as a member of the Jewish people.... [Communion with God in worship] was not in terms of an I-Thou but of a We-Thou relationship, the "We" being the Jewish people which God had chosen to make Him known to all the world."

and kindreds and people and tongues" is overly simple, escapist. "No man is an island, entire of itself." Scriptural religion is not practiced in the lotus position. Not only will an overly inward-directed Gospel fail to attract people more attuned to the good of society, which many Jewish people are, but it fails to represent fully the concerns of God.

For Gentiles, who must be saved in spite of their culture and religious background, one could argue that the individual aspect is the key. This is why Sha'ul [Paul], the emissary to the Gentiles[31] emphasized it so much. Likewise, the individual aspects of the Gospel may speak adequately to the hearts of assimilated or troubled Jews whose involvement with the Jewish community is weak. But Jews who feel part and parcel of their people—and not a few socially oriented Gentiles as well—need to hear the corporate aspects of the Gospel too, or they may dismiss it as shallow and not get saved.

Moreover, even people whose interest is their own personal well-being need to hear the corporate aspects of the Gospel. In fact, they need it even more, since a major aspect of salvation for them may involve turning from a selfish, egocentric approach to life and adopting God's approach to life, which is oriented toward others.[32] Thus a Gospel lacking a focus on corporate and societal elements fails to be "the whole counsel of God"[33] for anyone.

3. *Yeshua Is Identified With The People Of Israel*

An interesting way to think about the Gospel as simultaneously individual and corporate is to consider the ways in which the Messiah Yeshua stands for and is intimately identified with his people Israel. Just as the individual who trusts Yeshua becomes

31. Romans 11:14.
32. Leviticus 19:18, Philippians 2:1-11.
33. Acts 20:27.

united with him and is "immersed" (baptized) into all that Yeshua is, including his death and resurrection—so that his sin nature is regarded as dead, and his new nature, empowered by the Holy Spirit, is regarded as alive—just as this intimate identification with the Messiah holds for the individual, so the Messiah similarly identifies with and embodies national Israel.

In the New Testament one encounters this notion first at Mattityahu [Matthew] 2:15, where it is said of Yeshua's being taken to Egypt, "This happened in order to fulfill what *Adonai* had said through the prophet, 'Out of Egypt I called my son.'" The verse quoted is Hosea 11:1. However, in context the prophet Hosea was clearly speaking not about a future Messiah but about the nation of Israel and the Exodus.

Some accuse Mattityahu of misusing Scripture here, recklessly taking a verse out of context and applying it to Yeshua. Is he guilty? To answer, we should take note of the four kinds of Scripture interpretation which the rabbis used:

- *P'shat* ("simple")—The plain, simple sense of the text, what modern interpreters call grammatical-historical exegesis.

- *Remez* ("hint")—Peculiar features of the text are regarded as hinting at a deeper truth than that conveyed by its plain sense.

- *Drash* or *midrash* ("search")—Creativity is used to search the text in relation to the rest of the Bible, other literature or life in order develop an allegorical or homiletical application of the text. This involves eisegesis—reading one's own thoughts into a text—as well as exegesis, which is extracting from a text its actual meaning.

- *Sod* ("secret")—One operates on the numerical values of the Hebrew letters; for example, two words whose letters add up to the same amount would be good candidates for revealing a secret through "bisociation of ideas."[34]

The accusation that Mattityahu is misappropriating Scripture stands only if he is dealing with the *p 'shot.* For as we have said, the *p'shot of* Hosea 11:1 applies to the nation of Israel and not to Yeshua.

But perhaps Mattityahu is making a *midrash,* reading the Messiah into a verse dealing with Israel? Many rabbis used the same approach; his readers would not have found it objectionable.

Nevertheless, I believe Mattityahu is doing neither but giving us a *remez,* a hint of a very deep truth. Israel is called God's son as far back as Exodus 4:22. The Messiah is presented as God's son a few verses earlier in Mattityahu 1:18-25, reflecting *Tanakh* passages such as Isaiah 9:6-7, Psalm 2:7 and Proverbs 30:4. Thus the Son equals the son; the Messiah is equated with the nation of Israel. This is what Mattityahu is hinting at by calling Yeshua's flight to Egypt a "fulfillment" of Hosea 11:1.

The idea that one stands for all can be found throughout the Bible, sometimes for weal and sometimes for woe—in the story of Achan's sin (Joshua 7), in the relationship between Israel and her king (many places in the *Tanakh,* for example, 1 Kings 9:3-9), in Romans 5:12-21, in 1 Corinthians 15:45-49, and in the debate over the "servant passages" of Isaiah (42:1-9, 49:1-13, 50:4-11, and 52:11-53:12). In fact, the controversy over whether Isaiah 53 refers to Israel or to a then unborn Messiah dissolves when it is remembered that Israel's Messiah embodies his people. Likewise, consider these phrases from Isaiah 49:1-6:

Adonai . . . said to me, "You are my servant, Israel, in whom I will be glorified.". . . And now, *Adonai* says, . . .

---

34. The term was coined by Arthur Koestler, the assimilated Jewish cosmopolitan political philosopher and novelist, in his book, *The Act Of Creation* (1964). It means a creative putting together of two ideas in a way previously not thought of or exploited.

> "It is too light a thing that you should be my servant, to raise up the tribes of Jacob and to restore the preserved of Israel; I will give you as a light to the nations, that my salvation may reach to the end of the earth."

Does Israel restore the preserved of Israel? Who is the "light to the nations"? Judaism understands this as a goal to be fulfilled by the Jewish people. Christians think at once of Yochanan [John] 8:12, where Yeshua said of himself, "I am the light of the world." I suggested at the beginning of Chapter I that the Jewish people will be the light to the nations that we ought to be when we have in us him who is the light of the world.

This concept, that the Messiah embodies the Jewish people, should not seem strange to believers, who learn precisely that about Yeshua and the Church. What else does it mean to talk of the Church as a body of which the Messiah is the head? Or a temple of which he is the chief cornerstone? The concept of one standing for all is familiar. But the Church has not clearly grasped that the Holy One of Israel, Yeshua, is in union not only with the Church, but also with the Jewish people. When Christians have fully digested this and can communicate to Jews that through Yeshua the Messiah, by virtue of his identification with Israel, the Jewish people will achieve their destiny, then the Jewish people will have been presented a less alien and more attractive Gospel. And the Church will have become more faithful to it.

"The truth, the whole truth, and nothing but the truth"? Yeshua said, "I am . . . the truth." But he identifies with Israel. A believer in the Gospel acquires truth by identifying with Yeshua. But if so, he too, whether Jewish or Gentile, must identify with the Jewish people, with whom Yeshua identifies. Otherwise he has not identified with Yeshua. That's the truth! "Ye shall know the truth"—Yeshua, who identifies with the Jewish people—"and the truth shall make you free."[35]

35. Yochanan [John] 8:32.

4. *God will Fulfill His Promises to the Jewish People*

A major corporate element in the Good News is the guarantee that God will fulfill his promises to the Jewish people as a people. These promises appear in the *Tanakh* over and over; two of the most important are that the Jewish people will return from Exile to possess and inhabit *Eretz- Yisrael* [the Land of Israel], and that the Kingdom will be re-established with the Son of David on the throne.

a. The New Testament Proves It

Many Christians are unaware that the New Testament affirms the future fulfillment of God's promises to national Israel. We shall examine two texts by way of demonstration.

The first is Mattityahu [Matthew] 23:37-39. After excoriating a particular group of Torah-teachers ["scribes"] and *P'rushim* ["Pharisees'[1]] whose hardened hearts had turned against spiritual truth, Yeshua exclaimed,

> "Jerusalem! Jerusalem! You kill the prophets! You stone those who are sent to you! How often I wanted to gather your children, just as a hen gathers her chickens under her wings, but you refused! Look! 'God is abandoning your house to you, leaving it desolate.' [Jeremiah 22:5] For I tell you, from now on, you will not see me again until you say, 'Blessed is he who comes in the name of *Adonai.*™ [Psalm 118:26]

Regardless of whether the Messiah calling "Jerusalem! Jerusalem!" is addressing all Jewish people or only the Jewish establishment centered in the Holy City, it is obvious that he is speaking not just to individuals but to the nation as a whole, promising that national salvation will come to Israel when she says, as a nation, "Blessed is he who comes in the name of the Lord."

Another key passage affirming that God will fulfill his promises to national Israel is Romans 9-11. This section of the Book of Romans is not, as some extreme Dispensationalists claim, a "parenthesis" unrelated to what Sha'ul writes before and after. Rather, it answers a key question raised by the last verses of Chapter 8, where Sha'ul promises that believers in Yeshua, having been chosen, will be glorified (v. 30), and that nothing can prevent it (vv. 31-39). The natural response of the first-century reader to this assurance that God will keep his promises to anyone who has faith must have been, "What about Israel? I don't see God keeping his promises to them. The Messiah came and went, and the Jewish people are not following him. What about Israel?" The answer of Romans 9-11 is that God will indeed keep his promises to Israel—in his own way and in his own time—so that in the end, "all Israel," that is, Israel as a national entity, "will be saved."

Thus we see that the future of national Israel is indeed mentioned in the New Testament; moreover, these two passages are by no means the only places.

b. The Tanakh Proves It

Even if the New Testament had made no mention of promises to the Jewish nation, we would still have them as stated in the *Tanakh,* which is, after all, still the Word of God. What Christians call the Old Testament was Yeshua's only Bible, and he believed it with all his heart. In fact, referring to the *Tanakh* and its promises, he said, "Scripture cannot be broken." Likewise Sha'ul wrote that "All Scripture," *i.e.,* the entire *Tanakh,* "is inspired by God and is profitable for doctrine. .. ."[36] The New Testament does not cancel or replace the *Tanakh;* rather, it is built upon it—or, more accurately, assumes it. That is, everything written in the *Tanakh* is assumed by the New Testament to be faithful and true, including all the promises to national Israel.

36. Yochanan [John] 10:35, 2 Timothy 3:16.

Moreover, the *Tanakh's* promises of a New Covenant and a new heart and spirit for the Jewish people are coupled with the promise that they will remain a nation and will live safely in the Land of Israel (Jeremiah 31:30-37 and Ezekiel 36:22-36). If we believe that the prophecies of a New Covenant found in these passages are fulfilled by Yeshua, we should also believe that the associated prophecies of Israel's return from Exile to the Land will also be fulfilled. The Bible does not allow itself to be cut in pieces according to the reader's preconceived notions.

c. Refutation Of Arguments That God Is Finished With The Jews (2 Corinthians 1:20, Mattityahu [Matthew] 5:17)

Yet there are those whose theology does not admit that there remain promises to the Jewish nation as such. In fact, most forms of Replacement theology say that when the Jewish people failed to accept Yeshua as the Messiah, they forfeited all the blessings of the Old Covenant, and what remains to them as a people is only the curses. We have already indicated that Replacement theology is based on a wrong understanding of the relationship between Israel and the Church;[37] but because its influence is great, we will analyze two New Testament verses which it uses to deny God's promises to the Jewish people, demonstrating instead that these verses actually confirm them.

> "For all the promises of God find their Yes in him," that is, in Yeshua (2 Corinthians 1:20).

Replacement theology understands this to mean that all the Old Testament promises have in some mystical sense been fulfilled in the Messiah already, so that none remain for the Jews. But the verse does not say or mean that all the promises have been fulfilled already, but that whenever God's promises are

37. On Replacement theology, see Chapter III, Section B-3 with footnote 11.

fulfilled, they are fulfilled in, through or by Yeshua. He is the instrument through whom God the Father has fulfilled, is fulfilling and will fulfill every promise he has ever made to the Jewish people—including the promise that they will return from Exile to possess and live in the Land of Israel and the promise that the Kingdom will be restored, with the Son of David on the throne. A text which assures that God will fulfill every one of his promises to the Jews must not be turned into a pretext for cancelling them!

> "Do not think that I came to abolish the Law or the Prophets; I did not come to abolish, but to fulfill" (Mattityahu [Matthew] 5:17).

Replacement theology likewise understands that Yeshua at his first coming fulfilled the *Torah,* so that we don't have to (the logic leading to this conclusion is unclear); and that he fulfilled all the Old Testament prophecies, so that, once again, none remain for the Jews.

But the word usually translated "fulfill", *Greekpleroo,* does not necessarily convey this specific sense. Rather, it is a very common word which simply means "fill," "fill up," "make full," as in filling a cup or a hole. It should be evident that the actual meaning is as rendered in the *Jewish New Testament:* "Don't think that I have come to abolish the *Torah* or the Prophets. I have come not to abolish but to complete"—that is, to "make full" the meaning of what the *Torah* and the ethical demands of the Prophets require. In fact, this verse, so understood, states the theme of the entire Sermon on the Mount—in which six times the Messiah says, "You have heard of old time" the incomplete meaning or a distortion, "but I say to you" the complete, full spiritual sense that you should understand and obey.

As with 2 Corinthians 1:20, Yeshua does fulfill the predictions of the Prophets; likewise, he kept the *Torah* perfectly. But that is not what Yeshua is talking about here in the Sermon on the Mount. He will indeed fulfill every unfulfilled prophecy concerning himself, and he will also be the means by which God the Father will cause to be fulfilled every as yet unfulfilled prophecy concerning the Jews.

To sum up, the Hebrew Bible's promises to the Jews are not cancelled in the name of being "fulfilled in Yeshua." Rather, fulfillment in Yeshua is an added assurance that what God has promised the Jews will yet come to pass. "For the gifts and the call of God are irrevocable."[38]

5. *The Promise Of The Land*

Certainly one of the most important aspects of the Jewish Gospel is the promise that Israel will return from the Exile to *Eretz-Yisrael.* True, not every Jew thinks of his Diaspora existence as Exile. Many Jews regard America (or whatever country they happen to live in) as flowing with more milk and honey than the Promised Land. But God presents in his Word a contrary opinion, and it is his opinion which will in the end prevail. In the manner and time of his choosing, God will gather Jewish people from the nations of the earth back to the Land which he gave us "as an inheritance forever."[39]

Of course, this promise is rooted in the *Tanakh;* but an interesting New Testament reference to the Land is in the Olivet Discourse, where most translations distort the meaning. According to Mattityahu [Matthew] 24:30, when the sign of the Son of Man appears in the sky, "all the tribes of the Land will mourn"—*not* "all the tribes o" the earth," as in most versions, because Yeshua is alluding to Zechariah 12:10, 14. Mattityahu comes to tell us that when the Messiah returns "on the clouds of heaven, with tremendous power and glory," the twelve tribes of Israel will be living in the Land of Israel, and they will see him.

Replacement theology sometimes bases its view that there is no longer any valid Jewish claim to the Land of Israel on the notion that with the coming of Yeshua the Mosaic Covenant,

---

38. Romans 11:29. Sha'ul writes this strong word of assurance when discussing the promise that "all Israel shall be saved" (Romans 11:26). But this great overarching promise subsumes the entire panoply of promises God made to the Jewish people in the Hebrew Bible.
39. See references to Genesis and Exodus in text, two paragraphs below.

with its promise of the Land, was abolished. Although I do not agree that this covenant has been abolished any more than the Abrahamic one has, it is useful to point out that the promise of the Land predates Moses. This promise was made to Abraham (Genesis 12:7, 13:14-17, 15:7-21, 17:7-8, 24:7), Isaac (Genesis 26:2-4, 28:3-4, 13-15) and Jacob (Genesis 35:11-12), long before Moses came on the scene, although the promise was repeated to him as well (Exodus 32:13). By the logic of Galatians 3:15-17, which says that a later covenant does not alter an earlier one, the promise of the Land made to the Patriarch would be altered neither by the coming of the New Covenant nor by the supposed abrogation of the Mosaic one.[40]

Today, when the issue of who has which rights to the Land of Israel is constantly in the newspapers,[41] Christians need to know what the Bible says. Let them not be taken in by Colin Chapman's book, *Whose Promised Land?*[42] which uses Replacement theology as its basis for denying that the Land of Israel is any longer promised by God to the Jews.

On the contrary, I like a formula suggested to me by Joseph Shulam, leader of the "Netivyah" Congregation in Jerusalem: "Although the Arabs do not have the right *to* the Land, they do have rights *in* the Land." God has promised governance over *Eretz-Yisrael* to the Jewish people, but "dwellers in the Land" who wish to live at peace have the right to peaceful and undisturbed use of property to which they have title, and the right to be paid a fair price for land purchased from them, the right not to be exploited or shamed or mistreated. We Israeli Jews who are currently ruling the Arabs in the Territories by a military administration have no better guide to behavior than the *Torah* and the Prophets:

> "*For Adonai* your God is God of gods and Lord of lords, the great, the mighty, the awesome God. He is not partial and he takes no bribe; he executes justice

40. See Section E-l above.
41. I am not adjusting this section to match the rapid pace of Middle East political events but leaving it as modified in 1990, before the Oslo Peace Process began.
42. Colin Chapman, *Whose Promised Land?* (Tring, Herts, England: Lion Publishing, 1983).

> for the fatherless and the widow; he loves the sojourner, giving him food and clothing. So thus you are to love the sojourner, for you were sojourners in the land of Egypt."
>
> "He has shown you, O man, what is good—and what does the Lord require of you except to do justice, love kindness, and walk humbly with your God?"[43]

While on the subject, let me say a few words about peace between Jews and Arabs. Some Jews despair of achieving any sort of peaceful coexistence with Arabs, while others attempt contact and understanding. I think the one great hope for genuine peace with justice lies in loving fellowship between Aarab Christians and Messianic Jews based on our common faith in Yeshua (in Arabic, *Yesua).* Only the Messiah in the hearts of Arabs and Jews can make peace between us. Efforts are being made in this direction right now. The path is long, the dangers and opportunities for mistakes are many; yet I can see no other hope, because the enmity between Jews and Arabs has theological overtones which only our common trust in the Messiah has any possibility of bridging. For the Jews are God's measuring stick—"I will bless those who bless you and curse him who curses you," said God to Abraham (Genesis 12:3), and this applies to Arabs too when they bless or curse the Jewish people. On the other hand, God reserved blessings for Ishmael; he would make him a "great nation" (Genesis 21:13).

The efforts at fellowship between Arabs and Jews to date are promising, hopeful, moving—in this age *of intifada* (uprising) some Arab Christians meeting with Messianic Jews risk their lives. Still, we have far to go. We sing each other's songs, and rejoice in each other's testimonies of coming to faith. But we must yet pour out our hearts to each other, acknowledge and repent of our sins, forgive and seek forgiveness, reveal our inmost desires. We must also submit our own

43. Deuteronomy 10:17-19, Micah 6:8

ideas on the Land to each other and to the discipline of Scripture, with the object of reaching theological agreement. Pray for us.

And as for politics? Hawks? Doves? War? Peace? I believe with perfect faith that if enough Jews and enough Arabs are won to putting their trust in Yeshua, the King of Israel, and submitting to him, there will be peace.

Messianic Jewish theology of the Land, after dealing with biblical, Christian, Jewish and Arab views of whose it is, must discuss how believers ought to regard the present State of Israel. While the secular State of Israel is obviously not the Messianic state, it does appear to be a phase of *tikkun-ha'olam.* Joseph Shulam, using the *Tanakh's* principle of the "faithful remnant," has taught that God protects the State of Israel for the sake of its Messianic Jews, who constitute the present-day remnant of Israel. Yeshua called believers "the salt of the Land,"[44] salt being a preservative, so that one might say the Messianic Jews preserve the State of Israel in the Land of Israel.

Messianic Judaism will eventually be centered in Israel; "for out of Zion shall come forth *Torah* and the word of *Adonai* from Jerusalem."[45] When all Israel is saved, Israel's establishment *(i.e.,* a majority thereof) will be Messianic Jewish.

After what has been said, the next question may seem strange: should a Messianic Jew be a Zionist, a non-Zionist or an anti-Zionist? There are Jewish anti-Zionists, both ultra-Orthodox and liberal. The ultra-Orthodox reject the current State because it has not been set up by the Messiah. The liberals reject it because they believe Jewish particularity is an anachronism; however, their numbers have dwindled greatly in the forty years since the State was founded. In Jewish circles anti-Zionism is increasingly equated with antisemitism. But Palestinian Arabs "use the word 'Zionists' when they want to scare

44. Mattityahu [Matthew] 5:31; in most translations, "the salt of the earth."
45. Isaiah 2:3.

their children" (I am quoting an Arab Christian friend).[46] There are non-Zionist Jews, or, perhaps one should call them indifferent Jews, who have no strong feelings or thoughts concerning the Jewish State, except, possibly, that it's fine for those who need it—refugees, the poor, the persecuted. And finally, there are those who favor the State. They may not favor everything its leaders do, but they are very much delighted that the State exists. The logical next step for them would be to make *aliyah,* but very few American Jews do.

With Messianic Jews it ought to be different. Because of one verse, Isaiah 35:10, every Messianic Jew not living in Israel ought to be thinking seriously about moving there. The verse says that "the redeemed of the Lord shall return and come with singing unto Zion, and everlasting joy shall be upon their head. They shall obtain gladness and joy, and sorrow and sighing shall flee away." If "the redeemed of the Lord," in context, are not the faithful remnant—the Messianic Jews—then who are they? Every year the Passover *Seder* concludes with the words, *HaShanah HaBa'ah BiYerushalayim!* ("Next year in Jerusalem!"). So—why not?[47]

6. *The Promise Of The Kingdom*

God promised that there would always be a descendant of David to rule the Jewish people.[48] As is well known, the popu-

46. As given here, this is an inflammatory statement, so I want to provide some context. Knowing the person who said it as I do, I am convinced that he is speaking of Zionism in its political and not its theological sense. If Zionism were only a political movement, like the world's other "liberation fronts," it could be evaluated entirely on practical, political and social grounds. One would expect some to favor it and others to oppose it. Perhaps the Zionism of people who do not believe the Bible ought to be judged this way. But to the degree that Zionism is theological, reflecting the Bible's statements about the relationships between God, the Jewish people and the Land of Israel, it must be evaluated by the Word of God. And to this same degree no one should be scaring his children with it.
47. For my pitch encouraging Messianic Jews to make *aliyah,* see Chapter VII, Section E-3.
48. 2 Samuel 7:14.

lar expectation at the time of Yeshua was that the Messiah would restore the national fortunes of Israel, freeing her from the Roman yoke and re-establishing the kingship. So anxious were some of Yeshua's hearers to have this dream fulfilled that they tried to achieve it by force.[49]

During his three-year ministry Yeshua kept his disciples from pestering him about it by teaching them that he had to die for the sins of mankind and rise from the dead. But when he had accomplished these things it was not unreasonable for them to ask him,

> "Lord, are you at this time going to restore self-rule to Israel?" He answered, "You don't need to know the dates or the times; the Father has kept these under his own authority."[50]

His answer may not have been what they wanted to hear, but we do learn from this New Testament text that *whether* God will "restore self-rule to Israel" is not in question. The only uncertainty is *when.*

7. *Conclusion*

In conclusion, the promises of God to the Jewish nation are a key element in biblical religion. Who knows whether without them the Jewish people would have survived? They remain central to Jewish community life. A Gospel which has nothing to say about them is a Gospel few committed Jews can consider. Fortunately, as we have seen, the real Gospel, the Jewish Gospel of Yeshua the Messiah, confirms those promises; indeed, it is through him that they are all Yes.

49. Yochanan [John] 6:15.
50. Acts 1:6-7, *Jewish New Testament.*

F. ESCHATOLOGY

1. *The Messiah*

Obviously a major topic for any Messianic Jewish theology is the subject of the Messiah and the different meaning assigned to this concept in Judaism and Christianity. Proper interpretation of the relevant *Tanakh* passages is both the start and the goal. Although one does not expect much new evidence to emerge, the differences between Jewish and Christian understandings of the texts must be compared, explained in the light of presuppositions and history, and ultimately reconciled to the extent allowed by Scripture.

Subtopics include the Messiah's first and second coming; views of the Messiah in Jewish writings; Messianic speculation among the Jews; false Messiahs; what is considered evidence for who the Messiah will be; the person and work of the Messiah; the Messianic Age—with or without a personal Messiah; the relationship between the Messianic Age and the Kingdom of God; and finally, of course, presentation of Yeshua as the Messiah.

2. *Reward And Punishment*

Reward and punishment are downplayed in modern Judaism, which espouses the idea that actions done for the sake of God are superior to actions done for the sake of worldly or heavenly reward. Messianic Jewish theology should be able to bring this attitude into harmony with the elements of Scripture that stress the importance of the reward. Likewise the Jewish stress on living this life properly is sometimes contrasted with a supposed Christian overemphasis on the world to come. This too is a matter of emphasis rather than substantive contradiction, so it too can be harmonized.

3. *End-Time Prophecy*

Since so many of the biblical prophecies about the *acharit-hayamim* ("the end of days") involve the Jewish people, it is not surprising that there is intense excitement among many Messianic Jews awaiting their imminent fulfillment. Likewise, the arguments which can emerge between those who differ on the interpretation of these prophecies can be intense. This book is not the place for me to enter the fray. Movement leaders and theologians seem to be well aware that opinions about the future are best held lightly, since they could prove wrong.

At the same time, prophecy is not to be ignored or discounted either. For some of the most important prophecies came from the mouth of Yeshua the Messiah himself. Also, our faith is in very great measure grounded in the fact that Yeshua fulfilled all the prophecies in the *Tanakh* that pertain to the Messiah's first coming. If we pay attention to fulfilled prophecies, we should also give weight to the unfulfilled ones, as indeed we are instructed to do in Scripture.[51]

G. THE INSPIRATION AND AUTHORITY OF SCRIPTURE

1. *What Constitutes God's Word?*

A major disagreement between Judaism and Christianity is over what constitutes Scripture. Judaism and Christianity agree that God inspired the Hebrew Bible, the *Tanakh,* what Christians call the Old Testament. But to this common core Judaism adds the material of the Oral Law—the *Mishna, Gemara,* codes, and halakhic responsa; while Christianity adds the New Testament.

51. For more on these admittedly fascinating matters, consult Millard J. Erickson, *Contemporary Options in Eschatology;* R. Ludwigson, *A Survey of Bible Prophecy;* William E. Biederwolf, *The Second Coming Bible;* and J. Barton Payne, *Encyclopedia of Biblical Prophecy.* Two books by Hebrew Christians are Charles Lee Feinberg, *Israel In The Spot light (Chicago:* Moody Press, 1975) and Arnold G. Fruchtenbaum, *Footsteps Of The Messiah* (San Antonio, Texas: Ariel Press, 1982); and no serious student of eschatology or God's people should ignore his *Israelology: The Missing Link in Systematic Theology (P.* O. Box 3723, Tustin, CA 92681, USA: Ariel Ministries, 1989).

The difference seems irreconcilable, and frustration at this leads to premature oversimplification of the issues. All Jews properly called Messianic, along with all Gentiles properly called Christian, affirm the divine inspiration and authority of the *Tanakh* and of the New Testament. But a few Messianic Jews are so enamored of the Oral Law that they acknowledge all of it as inspired and commanding obedience; while many more seem ready to discard the Oral Law and everything connected with it as sub-inspired, unauthoritative, and therefore irrelevant. We will look into these questions more deeply in Chapter V, but meanwhile I can say categorically that Messianic Jewish theology will get nowhere with either attitude. Messianic Judaism needs to take all of these materials into account in a considered manner when formulating its theology of Scripture. But, just as non-Messianic Judaism is willing to judge rabbinic writings by the *Tanakh,* so Messianic Judaism should judge these same writings by the New Testament as well. Some portions will not meet the test, some will be altogether satisfactory as they stand, and some will need modification to meet New Testament standards.

A useful tool for dealing with these matters will be the exploration of the differences between Jewish and Christian concepts of inspiration. Christian concepts tend to be colored black or white—either a document is inspired or it isn't. Judaism has the notion of greater or less inspiration: the five books of Moses are the most highly inspired, and other writings are on a scale downward. A concept of Karl Barth could be of value here: the notion of the inspired Word as (1) incarnate, (2) written, and (3) preached. Question: in what way is the preached word inspired? And what about the "word" of "two or three" deciding questions of New Testament *halakhah*.[52]

52. See below, Chapter V, Section B-5.

2. *The Jewishness Of The New Testament*

The New Testament is thought by many Jews to be a Gentile book. As I said earlier, it is Jewish from every direction. The ongoing work of Messianic Jewish biblical theology must be to recover the first-century Jewish background of the New Testament wherever possible. Messianic Jewish systematic and practical theology must show the relevance of the New Testament for Jewish communal and individual life today. I am attempting to contribute to these goals in the *Jewish New Testament* and the *Jewish New Testament Commentary.*[53]

3. *Antisemitism In The New Testament?*

The New Testament is accused of being antisemitic. Even some Christians have bought that line. A superficial examination can lead to that conclusion on the basis of passages such as Mattityahu [Matthew] 27:25; references to the *Ioudaioi* in Yochanan [John], translated "Jews" in most versions but usually "Judeans" in the *JNT*; and 1 Thessalonians 2:15, where also *Ioudaioi* means "Judeans." But a more open-minded reading will reveal that antisemitism is absent from the New Testament just as it is from the *Tanakh.*[54] However, the unconscious antisemitism pervading Christendom has caused translators of the New Testament and commentators on it to come up with antisemitic interpretations, so that it can appear antisemitic where it isn't. Messianic Judaism must root out the antisemitic presuppositions and replace them with the real meaning of the text, based on the Jewish background to it.

H. APOLOGETICS

Precisely because we Messianic Jews are speaking both to non-Messianic Jews and to Gentile Christians we have a double apologetic task. That Jews have objections to Yeshua, to the

53. *Op. cit.* in Chapter II, footnote 20; also see Chapter VII, Section D-l.
54. See Chapter III, footnote 35.

New Testament, to Christianity, to Messianic Judaism, and to dozens of specific points is well known.[55] The history of defense literature is long; we must be prepared to take the torch from those who have carried it before us.[56]

Likewise, we must be able to defend before Gentile Christians our ideas about evangelism of Jews, Messianic Jewish identity within the Church, antisemitism, and other issues.

Because apologetics has of necessity become one of the more developed areas of Messianic Jewish theology, there is no need to dwell on it at length here.

---

55. See footnote 3 above. Three more Jewish apologetic works are: David Berger and Michael Wyschogrod, Jews and *"Jewish Christianity" (New* York: Ktav Publishing House, 1978); Abba Hillel Silver, *Where Judaism Differed* (New York: The Macmillan Company, 1956); and Trude Weiss-Rosmarin, *Judaism and Christianity: The Differences* (New York: Jonathan David, 1968). See also Chapter VII, footnote 14.
56. Messianic Jewish and Hebrew Christian apologetic works include those cited in Chapter 1, footnotes 8-11; Arnold Fruchtenbaum, *Jesus was a Jew* (Nashville, Tennesssee: Broadman Press, 1974); Authur W. Kac. *The Messianic Hope* (Grand Rapids, Michigan: Baker Book House 1975); Authur W. Kac, compiler: *The Messiahship Of Jews: What Jews And Jewish Christians Say* (Chicago: Moody Press, 1980); Aaron J. K Kligerman, *Messianic Prophesy In The Old Testament* (Grand Rapids. Michigan: Zondervan Publishing House, 1957); Moishe Rosen, Y'shua: *The Jewish Way To Say Jesus* (Chicago; Moody Press, 1982); Barry Rubin, *You Bring the Bagels; I'll Bring the Gospel: Sharing the Messiah with Your Jewish Neighbor* (Clarksville: Lederer Books, 1997); Michael Brown, *Answering Jewish Objections to Jesus 1-4* (Grand Rapids: Baker Books, several pub. dates)

CHAPTER V

TORAH

A. TORAH INCOGNITA

1. *Christian Theology's Greatest Deficiency*

I have given an entire chapter to the question of how Messianic Judaism is to relate to the *Torah* because I am certain that the lack of a correct, clear and relatively complete Messianic Jewish or Gentile Christian theology of the Law is not only a major impediment to Christians' understanding their own faith, but also the greatest barrier to Jewish people's receiving the Gospel. Even though many Jews do not observe *Torah,* often neither knowing nor caring about it, I stand by this statement; because attachment to the *Torah* is rooted deep in the Jewish people's memory, where it affects attitudes unconsciously.

While ultimately the issue becomes who Yeshua is—Messiah, Son of the Living God, final Atonement, Lord of our lives—the Church's problem here is mainly one of communication, of expressing the truth in ways that relate to Jewish world-views. But the Church hardly knows what to make of the *Torah* or how to fit it together with the New Testament. And if the Church doesn't know, don't expect the Jews to figure it out for them! I believe that Christianity has gone far astray in its dealings with the subject and that the most urgent task of theology today is get right its view of the Law.

Christianity organizes systematic theology by subjects it considers important. Thus topics like the Holy Spirit and the person and work of the Messiah take a healthy amount of space in any Christian systematic theology. Judaism too organizes its theological thinking into categories reflecting its concerns, and as we noted earlier, its three main topics are God, Israel (that is, the Jewish people) and *Torah.*

Comparing Jewish and Christian theology, one finds that both devote much attention to God and to the people of God (in the one case the Jews, in the other the Church). It is all the more striking, therefore, to notice how much Jewish thought and how little Christian theology addresses the topic of *Torah*—generally rendered in English as "Law," although the meaning of the Hebrew word is "teaching." As a rough measure, I checked the subject index of Augustus Strong's *Systematic Theology* and found under "Law" 28 pages out of a total of 1,056 (less than 3%). In L. Berkhof s *Systematic Theology* there are 3 pages out of 745 (less than 1/2%). And in Lewis Sperry Chafer's 7-volume work with the same title, there are only 7 out of 2,607 (about 1/4%). On the other hand, Isidor Epstein's *The Faith of Judaism* has 57 pages on *Torah* out of 386 (15%), Solomon Schechter's *Aspects of Rabbinic Theology* has 69 out of 343 (20%), and Louis Jacobs' *A Jewish Theology* 73 out of 331 (22%) (these three authors are Orthodox, Conservative and Liberal (Reform), respectively). One is forced to the conclusion that the topic interests Jews and not Christians.

And that is unfortunate for the Christians. It means, first, that most Christians have an overly simplistic understanding of what the Law is all about; and, second, that Christianity has almost nothing relevant to say to Jews about one of the three most important issues of their faith. In short, *Torah* is the great unexplored territory, the *terra incognita* of Christian theology.

The main reason for this is that Christian theology, with the anti-Jewish bias it incorporated in its early centuries, misunderstood Sha'ul [Paul] and concluded that the *Torah* is no longer in force. This is not the Jewish Gospel, nor is it the true Gospel. It is time for Christians to understand the truth about the Law. Christian theologians in the last thirty years have made a beginning.[1] Messianic Jews should now move to the front lines and spearhead this process.

2. *Nomos In The New Testament*

A good starting place would be a thorough study of the Greek word *nomos* ("law," *"Torah ")* and its derivatives as used in the New Testament. Unfortunately there is not space in this book to undertake it, since the word and its cognates appear some 200 times. The sampling which follows is intended to whet the appetite and encourage further investigation.

a. Romans 10:4—Did The Messiah End The Law?

Consider Romans 10:4, which states—in a typical but wrong translation—"For Christ ends the law and brings righteousness for everyone who has faith." Like this translator, most theologians understand the verse to say that Yeshua terminated the *Torah.* But the Greek word translated "ends" is *telos,* from which English gets the word "teleology," defined in Webster's Third International Dictionary as "The philosophical study of the evidences of design in nature; . . . the fact or the character of being directed toward an end or shaped by a purpose—used of... nature . . . conceived as determined . . . by the design of a divine Providence. . . ."The normal meaning *of telos* in Greek —which is also its meaning here—is "goal, purpose, consummation," not "termination."

---

1. See W. D. Davies, *Paul and Rabbinic Judaism,* 4th ed. (Philadelphia: Fortress Press, 1980); Daniel P. Fuller, *Gospel and Law: Contrast or Continuum?* (Grand Rapids, Michigan: Eerdmans, 1980); Hans Huebner, *Law in Paul's Thought* (Edinburgh: T. & T. Clark, 1984); Jacob Jervell, *The Unknown Paul* (Minneapolis: Augsburg Press, 1984); E. P. Sanders, *Paul, the Law, and the Jewish People* (Philadelphia: Fortress Press, 1983); E. P. Sanders, *Paul and Palestinian Judaism* (London: SCM Press, Ltd., 1977); Gerard S. Sloyan, *Is Christ the End of the Law?* (Philadelphia: Westminster Press, 1978); Clark M. Williamson, *Has God Rejected His People?* (Nashville, Tennessee: Abingdon, 1982).

The Messiah did not and does not bring the *Torah* to an end. Rather, attention to and faith in the Messiah is the goal and purpose toward which the *Torah* aims, the logical consequence, result and consummation of observing the *Torah* out of genuine faith, as opposed to trying to observe it out of legalism. This, not the termination of *Torah,* is Sha'ul's point, as can be seen from the context, Romans 9:30-10:II.[2]

2. The next six verses of Romans introduce another issue clouded by the translators. The familiar King James Version serves as well as any to demonstrate the problem. Romans 10:5 mentions "the righteousness which is of the law;" and verse 6 begins, "But the righteousness which is of faith. ..." Every translation I know of, by rendering the first word of verse 6 (Greek *de)* as "but," seems to imply that there are two different, contrasting ways to attain righteousness. Theologians take this "but" as a strong adversative meaning "on the contrary," and are thus led down the primrose path of regarding "the righteousness which is of the law" as bad and "the righteousness which is of faith" as good. From here it is only a short step to considering the *Torah* bad and the Gospel good.

But Greek has a different word, *alia,* for "on the contrary." The word *de* here is weaker; it can be rendered "and,""also,""moreover," implying that what follows continues the previous thought and does not contrast with it. Or it can mean "but" in the sense of limiting the previous statement rather than contrasting with it. In any case, there is only one way to attain righteousness, not two. Sha'ul's point is that righteousness, which truly comes if one observes the *Torah* (v. 5), is achieved only if one hasfaith(vv. 6-8). (He said the same thing a few verses earlier, in Romans 9:30-32.)

It is highly significant that he brings his evidence for this from the *Torah*—Leviticus 18:5 in verse 5 and Deuteronomy 30:11-14 in verses 6-8—showing that the *Torah* itself mandates faith in order to attain righteousness. If there were two ways to attain righteousness, one in the *Torah* and another in the Gospel, he would be guilty of citing the *Torah* against itself. But never in any of his writings does Sha'ul demonstrate one part of the Bible inconsistent with another.

Here is what Romans 10:5-10 teaches. The righteousness which is of the law says that he who "does these things," he who does what God commands to be done, *will* attain life through doing them (v. 5). *But* that very righteousness which is "of the law" must *also, necessarily,* be "of faith" if it is to be efficacious (vv. 6-8). "Doing these things" legalistically will never bring eternal life. Only if obeying God's *Torah* commands is grounded in the kind of faithful trusting that does not demand going up to heaven or across the sea to bring the Messiah (these being legalistic self-efforts at attaining righteousness), but simply waits on God to provide him and acknowledges him now that he has come (vv. 9-10), will salvation be assured.

b. "Under The Law" and "Works Of The Law"

Much of Christian theology about the *Torah* is based on a misunderstanding of two Greek expressions which Sha'ul invented. The first is *upo nomon;* it appears 10 times in Romans, 1 Corinthians and Galatians, and it is usually rendered "under the law." The other is *erga nomou,* found with minor variations 10 times in Romans and Galatians, translated "works of the law."

Whatever Sha'ul is trying to communicate by these expressions, one thing is clear: Sha'ul regards them negatively: being "under the law" is bad, and "works of the law" are bad. Christian theology usually takes the first to mean "within the framework of observing the *Torah*" and the second, "acts of obedience to the *Torah.*" This understanding is wrong. Sha'ul does not consider it bad to live within the framework of *Torah,* nor is it bad to obey it; on the contrary, he writes that the *Torah* is "holy, just and good" (Romans 7:12).

C. E. B. Cranfield has shed light on these two phrases; his first essay on the subject appeared in 1964,[3] and he summarized it in his masterly commentary on Romans.[4] There he writes,

> ". . . the Greek language of Paul's day possessed no word-group corresponding to our 'legalism,' 'legalist' and 'legalistic.' This means that he lacked a convenient terminology for expressing a vital distinction, and

I am indebted to a former professor of mine, Daniel P. Fuller (op. *cit.* in footnote 1 above, especially Chapter 4, "Paul's View of the Law") for these insights, but I do not claim he would agree with my formulation.

3. C. E. B. Cranfield, "St. Paul and the Law," in *Scottish Journal of Theology* (1964), pp. 43-68.

4. C. E. B. Cranfield, *Romans (International Critical Commentary)* (Edinburgh: T. & T. Clark, Ltd., 1981), volume 2, pp. 845-862.

> so was surely seriously hampered in the work of clarifying the Christian position with regard to the law. In view of this, we should always, we think, be ready to reckon with the possibility that Pauline statements, which at first sight seem to disparage the law, were really directed not against the law itself but against that misunderstanding and misuse of it for which we now have a convenient terminology. In this very difficult terrain Paul was pioneering."[5]

If Cranfield is right, as I believe he is, we should approach Sha'ul with the same pioneering spirit. We should understand *erga nomou* not as "works of law, "but as "legalistic observance of particular *Tor ah* commands." Likewise, we should take *upo nomon* to mean not "under the law" but "in subjection to the system that results from perverting *Tor ah* into legalism." This is how these phrases are rendered in the *Jewish New Testament.*

The expression "in subjection" is important because the context of *upo nomon* always conveys an element of oppressiveness. Sha'ul is very clear about this, as can be seen from 1 Corinthians 9:20, where, after saying that for those without *Torah* he became as one without *Torah,* he stressed that he was himself not without *Torah* but *ennomos Christou,* "en-lawed" or "en- bra'zed of Messiah." He used a different term, *ennomos* in place of *upo nomon,* to distinguish his oppression-free relationship with the *Torah,* now that he is united with the Messiah, from the sense of being burdened which he noticed in people (probably Gentiles![6]) who instead of happily "en-lawing" themselves to God's holy, just and good *Torah,* subjected themselves to a legalistic perversion of it.

If the above renderings of *upo nomon* and *erga nomou* were used in the 20 passages where these phrases occur, I

5. *Ibid.,* p. 853.

6. Sha'ul has already spoken of Jews in 1 Corinthians 9:20; "those under law" are another category, namely, Judaized Gentiles. See my notes to this verse in the *Jewish New Testament Commentary (op. cit.* in Chapter II, footnote 20).

believe it would change Christian theology of *Torah* for the better.

c. Galatians 3:10-13—Redeemed From The Curse Of The Law?

Galatians 3:10-13 presents a number of stumblingblocks in most translations. As an example, here is the New American Standard Bible's rendering, which strikes me as neither better nor worse than most:

> "[10] For as many as are of the works of the Law are under a curse; for it is written, 'Cursed is every one who does not abide by all things written in the book of the Law, to perform them. [11] Now that no one is justified by the Law before God is evident; for, 'The righteous man shall live by faith. '[12] However, the Law is not of faith; on the contrary, 'He who practices them shall live by them.' [13] Christ redeemed us from the curse of the Law, having become a curse for us—for it is written, 'Cursed is every one who hangs on a tree.'"

These verses appear as follows in the *Jewish New Testament:*

> "[10] For everyone who depends on legalistic observance of *Torah* commands *[erga nomou]* lives under a curse, since it is written, 'Cursed is everyone who does not keep on doing everything written in the Scroll of the *Torah.'* [Deuteronomy 27:26] [11] Now it is evident that no one comes to be declared righteous by God through legalism [*nomos*], since 'The person who is righteous will attain life by trusting and being faithful.' [Habakkuk 2:4] [12] Furthermore, legalism *[nomos]* is not based on trusting and being faithful, but on a misuse of the text that says, 'Anyone who does these things will attain life through them.' [Leviticus 18:5] [13] The Messiah redeemed us from the curse pronounced in the

> *Torah* [*nomos*] by becoming cursed on our behalf; for the *Tanakh* says, 'Everyone who hangs from a stake comes under a curse.' [Deuteronomy 21:22-23]"

"The curse of the law" is not the curse of having to live within the framework of *Torah,* for the *Torah* itself is good. Nor is it the curse of being required to obey the *Torah* but lacking the power to do so—this would be a kind of "Catch 22" unworthy of God, although there are theologies which teach that this is exactly the case. Rather, it is "the curse pronounced in the *Torah*" (v. 13; see v. 10) for disobeying it. Sha'ul's point is that that curse falls on people who are actually trying to *obey* the *Torah* if their efforts are grounded in legalism (vv. 11a, 12). For Sha'ul, such a legalistic approach is already disobedience; for the *Tanakh* itself requires genuine obedience to emerge from faith (v. 1 Ib). There is not space here to prove that this is the case or to deal with other controversies raised by the above rendering of these four verses; my *Jewish New Testament Commentary* addresses these matters.

d. Messianic Jews [Hebrews] 8:6—The New Covenant Has Been Given As Torah

One of the most surprising discoveries I made in the course of preparing the *Jewish New Testament* is that the New Covenant itself has actually been given as *Torah*—as much as, and in exactly the sense that, what Moses received on Mount Sinai was given as *Torah.* The verse which hides this extremely well kept secret is Messianic Jews [Hebrews] 8:6, which reads, in a typical translation,

> "But as it is, Christ has obtained a ministry which is as much more excellent than the old as the covenant he mediates is better, since it is enacted on better promises."

The passage would seem poor ore for my mining efforts. But upon examining the Greek text I noticed that the phrase "is enacted on" renders the word *nenomothetetai,* a compound of our friend *nomos* ("law, *Torah")* with the common verb *tithemi* ("to put, place"). If the subject matter of the Letter to a Group of Messianic Jews were, say, Greek law, or the Roman Senate, it would be appropriate to translate this word as "enacted, established, legislated," that is, "put" or "placed as law."

But in the letter to these Messianic Jews, the word *nomos,* which appears 14 times, always means *Torah* specifically, never legislation in general. Moreover, the only other appearance of *nenomothetetai* in the New Testament is a few verses back, at Messianic Jews 7:11, where it can only refer to the giving of the *Torah* at Sinai (the related word *nomothesia,* "giving of the *Torah"* at Romans 9:4 is equally unambiguous). Therefore the *Jewish New Testament* renders Messianic Jews 8:6:

> "But now the work Yeshua has been given to do is far superior to theirs, just as the covenant he mediates is better. For this covenant has been given as *Torah* on the basis of better promises."

So the New Covenant has been "given as *Torah"* which implies that *Torah* still exists and is to be observed in the present age—by all Jews and by all Gentiles, as we shall see. However, precisely what is demanded of "all Jews" and of "all Gentiles" is not quite so obvious. We will address this question in a limited way, but comprehensive treatment is beyond the scope of this book.

3. *The Gospel With An Ended Law Is No Gospel At All*

The statement has been made (I'm not saying I agree) that of the three items mentioned earlier as most important on the Jewish theological agenda, Reform Jews focus mainly on "God," the Conservatives on "Israel," and the Orthodox on

"Torah." Reform and secular Jews disagree with the Orthodox and Conservative over whether the *Torah* is binding forever, while Conservative Jews deny the exclusive claim of Orthodoxy to determine specific applications of what they agree is the eternal *Torah.* Nevertheless, although Orthodox Jews constitute only 15-20% of the Jewish population in Israel and less in the United States, their view of *Torah* as eternal has found a very deep place in the heart of the Jewish people; so that the non-Orthodox find themselves somewhat in the role of upstarts trying to dislodge a clever, experienced and self-confident ruler.

Now if Christianity comes into such an environment with the message that the *Torah* is no longer in force, the line of communication with Orthodox Judaism is simply cut. There is no longer anything to discuss. Moreover, if I am correct about the role of the Orthodox Jewish view of *Torah* in the Jewish mentality, then even the secular Jew "knows" at some level, whether correctly or not, that Orthodoxy is right. In fact there are secular Jews who, though not religious themselves, regard the Orthodox as the preservers of the Jewish nation.

Thus, if Christianity cannot address the issue of *Torah* properly and seriously, it has nothing to say to the Jewish people. Individual Jews may be won away to Christianity, across the wide gap between the Jewish people and the Church (look back at Figure 5E); but the central concern of Orthodox Judaism itself is dismissed, perhaps with a casual and cavalier citation of Romans 6:14, "We're not under the law but under grace." In my opinion this shallow, sterile way of thinking has gone on too long in the Church, and it serves no purpose but the Adversary's!

Moreover, this way of thinking is not only shallow, but perverse! Yeshua said very plainly in the theme sentence of the Sermon on the Mount, "Do not think that I came to abolish the Law . . .; I did not come to abolish, *butplerosai,* "to fill." We learned earlier[7] that Yeshua's "filling" here means making clear

7. Chapter IV, Section E-4-c.

the full and proper sense of the *Torah;* and we pointed out that even if *pier* meant "fulfillment," it could not be twisted to mean "abolition," in contradiction to what he had said three words earlier. This seems so clear that it is hard for me to understand how Christian theology has even dared to propose the idea that the *Torah* is no more. I myself believe it came about because of anti-Jewish bias infused into the Gentile Church in its early centuries;[8] this bias is now so pervasive and difficult to root out that even Christians without any personal antisemitism whatever are unavoidably affected by it.

The remedy is to reassess the theology of *Torah.* I am convinced it will be found that the *Torah* continues in force. When I say this, I am not making a "concession to Judaism," as some Christian critics might suppose. Nor am I somehow expressing *anti-Torah* theology in hypocritical, deceptive and confusing *pro-Torah* language, an accusation I could expect from a few non-Messianic Jews. Rather, I am stating as clearly as I can what I believe the New Testament teaches. It will prove to be neither a concession nor a confusion, but a challenge—to both Jews and Christians.

For a key element of the New Covenant, both as promised by Jeremiah and as cited in the Letter To A Group of Messianic Jews ["To The Hebrews"] is that the *Torah* is written on people's hearts (Jeremiah 31:30-34, Messianic Jews 8:9-12). It takes unacceptable theological legerdemain to conclude that when God writes the *Torah* on hearts he changes it into something other than the *Torah.*

But if Messianic Jews and Messianic Gentiles acknowledge the ongoingness of the *Torah,* then the question arises,

8. It was the Adversary (Satan) who infused this anti-Jewish bias into the Church. He hates the Jews with unending fury because God chose to act in history through them. But Satan can enter only where there is no defense against him (Mattityahu [Matthew] 12:43-45). See also Appendix, Section C-2, and the paragraph on "unconscious or latent anti-semitism" in Chapter II!, Section E-4.

"Just what does the *Torah* require, now that Yeshua the Messiah has inaugurated the New Covenant? What is the New Covenant *halakhah?*[9] And this is already a Jewish question, and, as we will see, an essential element of the Gospel.

For there is a tradition within Judaism which says that when the Messiah comes he will explain the difficult questions of *Torah.* Another tradition says he will change the *Torah.* Yeshua the Messiah has already come; some things he has explained—for example, in the Sermon on the Mount—and other things have been changed, as we learn later in the chapter. (When he comes the second time he may give more explanations and make more changes!) A Jew can cope with this kind of approach to *Torah.* And the Christian will just have to get used to it.

B. THE TORAH OF THE MESSIAH, A TREE OF LIFE

> I give you good instruction; do not forsake my *Torah.* It is a tree of life to those who take hold of it, and those who hold fast to it are happy. Its ways are ways of pleasantness, and all its paths are peace.[10]

9. *Halakhah* means, literally, "way of walking;" but, depending on the context, it can convey either the broad sense, "way of living, according to the *Torah,*" or the narrow sense, "the rule to be followed" in a particular situation. In Jewish discourse when one speaks of "the *halakhah,*" one is bringing to mind the whole framework of Jewish life as seen from a particular viewpoint. Sometimes the intent is to know what is permitted and what is forbidden by Jewish law; however, just as often the concern is not "legal" but simply related to finding out what the customs are, and perhaps why they are that way. The phrase "the *halakhah*" connotes Jewish peoplehood spanning centuries and expressing itself through ordinary Jews consulting with their rabbis in order to learn more about how God wants them to live.
10. Proverbs 4:2 and 3:18, as quoted in the *Siddur* [Jewish prayerbook] and recited in the synagogue after the public reading from the *Torah* scroll.

1. *Should Messianic Jews Observe The Torah?*

As we are saying here and there throughout this book, Jewish believers have an identity crisis, and it is not of their own making, it is not a psychological problem. Rather, it is caused by historical developments over the last two thousand years for which they are not responsible." The identity crisis consists in how to put together and express the Jewish and Messianic elements in their own lives.

The question which resonates this conflict the loudest is: "Should Messianic Jews observe the *Torah*?" Most Jewish believers find themselves wrestling with it sooner or later; eventually it penetrates the consciousness even of those who have had no connection with religious Judaism. What happens in the present phase of Messianic Jewish history is that individual Messianic Jews or individual Messianic Jewish congregations work out their own ways of relating to the *Torah,* each doing what is right in his own eyes. But this approach reflects communal failure; and the way to deal with this failure is for the Messianic Jewish community as a whole to launch a concerted attack on the question. Not that there needs to be uniformity of opinion—the words of *Beit-Hillel* and of *Beit-Shammai* were both said to be the words of the living God—but that the issues need to be understood in depth.

Why is the issue crucial? Informed and committed Orthodox and Conservative Jews will immediately see why, for they consider obedience to *Torah* the central distinctive of Judaism. Since they probably believe that Christianity teaches Jews "to apostatize from Moses, telling them not to have their sons circumcised and not to follow the traditions,"[12] they are likely to consider it impossible for Messianic Judaism to be Jewish. (Some Orthodox Jews reject Conservative and Reform Judaism on the same ground.) Jews who define their Jewishness differently, emphasizing ethics and God's unity (Reform) or

---

11 See Chapter III, Section B-4.

12 Acts 21:21. These words expressed a false accusation against Paul.

identity with the Jewish people (some Conservative, Reconstructionist), may not find obedience to the *Torah* so crucial in delineating a position vis-a-vis Messianic Judaism. Christians who have a simplistic attitude that "faith is more important than works" may be insensitive to the glories and nuances of *Torah* as understood by those who uphold it; such Christians may therefore fail to deal with the matter of primary concern to a substantial percentage of Jews, and their Gospel of faith without *Torah* (which falls short of being the true Gospel) will pass committed Orthodox Jews like a ship in the night, failing to make contact at all.

2. *What Is Meant By* "The Torah"?

Before deciding whether Messianic Jews should keep the *Torah,* we must ask what is meant by "the *Torah.*" Here are five possible answers.

Orthodox Judaism considers the *Torah* to be the body of teachings and legal rulings produced over more than three millennia by the Jewish people. It begins with the Five Books of Moses and continues with the rest of the *Tanakh* and the Oral Law, which the Orthodox say was revealed by God to Moses on Mount Sinai. The Oral Law is set forth in the *Talmud,* the Halakhic *Midrashim,* and the writings of later sages—the *Savora'im, Pos'kim, Rishonim* and *Acharonim*—in their codes and responsa.

Within this framework, depending on the context, the term *Torah* can mean: (1) the five books of Moses; (2) that plus the Prophets and the Writings, *i.e.,* the *Tanakh;* (3) that plus the Oral *Torah,* which includes the *Talmud* and later legal writings; or (4) that plus all religious teaching from the rabbis, including ethical and aggadic materials.

An overview of what Orthodox Jews consider legally binding may be found in the *Shulchan Arukh,* a comprehensive code written in the sixteenth century; this, in turn, has been summarized in a book available in English, Solomon Ganzfried's *Code of Jewish Law.*" The Orthodox admit that the Law can adapt to changing circumstances, but in practice it adapts very slowly; there was greater flexibility centuries ago, before the Oral Law had been committed to writing. The Orthodox categorically deny that anyone outside the stream of Orthodox Judaism has authority to make rulings affecting the Law.

Conservative Jews hold generally to the overall framework of thought developed in Orthodoxy but differ on specific judgments, generally in the direction of adapting the Law to the needs of modern society and removing what they consider cruel, obstructive or meaningless aspects. Of course they disagree that only the Orthodox may make binding rulings.

Reform Judaism, as opposed to the Orthodox and Conservative positions, generally holds that only the ethical commands are binding Law; the ceremonial and civil components are optional. Their position, curiously enough, is not very different from that of many Christians who consider the moral law eternal and binding, but the Jewish ceremonies and rules of civil procedure abrogated by the New Testament.

Biblical Law, that is, the Written Law, is what some Messianic Jews and certain groups of Christians believe should be followed; they consider the Oral Law not inspired and not binding. This is why Seventh-Day Adventists are vegetarians—it's their version of keeping *kosher.* There are Messianic Jews who say they keep "biblically *kosher*" They don't eat pork and shrimp, but they do serve milk and meat at the same meal, since that aspect of *kashrut* is not taught in the Bible. In Yeshua's time the Sadducees held to a somewhat similar position, rejecting the oral tradition of the Pharisees. In the eighth century C.E. the Karaites broke away from rabbinic Judaism over the same issue.

My own view is that the *Torah* is eternal, and the New Testament has not abrogated it. But in its totality the *Torah* must be understood and interpreted in the light of what Yeshua

13. Solomon Ganzfried, Code of Jewish Law (New York: Hebrew Publishing Company, 1961).

the Messiah and the rest of the New Covenant Scriptures have said about it.

3. *Should Messianic Jews Keep The Torah As Understood In Orthodox Judaism?*

Since discussions of whether Messianic Jews should observe the *Torah* generate more heat than light when there is disagreement over what is meant by "the *Torah*" we shall for the purpose of this section define *Torah* arbitrarily as what Orthodox Judaism understands it to be, so that we can progress to analysis. Here are five possible answers ranging the spectrum from Yes to No.

Absolute Yes. Messianic Jews should keep the Orthodox Jewish Law. This was the view of certain sects the Church regarded as heretical, for example, the second-century Ebionites. One can find New Testament support for compulsory Law-keeping.

- At Mattityahu [Matthew] 5:17-20 Yeshua says he did not come to abolish the *Torah,* and that anyone who disobeys its least commands and teaches others to do so will be counted least in the Kingdom of heaven.[14]
- When castigating the religious establishment for majoring in minors he does not denigrate any part of the *Torah:* "Woe to you hypocritical Torah-teachers [scribes] and *P'rushim* [Pharisees]! You pay your tithes of mint, dill and cumin; but you have neglected the weightier matters of the *Torah*—justice, mercy, trust. These are the things you should have attended to—without neglecting the others!"[15] Without taking away from

14. Whether or not this argues for compulsory obedience to the *Torah,* the prospect of being counted least in the Kingdom of Heaven still ought to discourage Christian and Messianic Jewish leaders from publicly teaching tfoobedience to it.

Yeshua's emphasis on justice, mercy and trust, we note that he adds the phrase, "without neglecting the others," in order to affirm that the less weighty commandments are still in force.

- At Mattityahu 23:2-3 he says, "The *Torah*-teachers and the *P'rushim* sit in the seat of Moses," meaning that they have authority to determine how to apply the Law in specific instances. "So," he continues, "whatever they tell you, take care to do it."
- At Romans 7:12 Sha'ul [Paul] calls the *Torah* "holy, just and good."

Nevertheless, it is unlikely that Yeshua's remarks were meant to apply throughout history, especially in the light of Mattityahu 16:19 and 18:18-20, where he establishes his *talmidim* [disciples] as the fount of binding authority in interpreting the *Torah.*[16] And the fact that the Law is holy, just and good does not necessarily make it compulsory; moreover *"Torah"* at Romans 7:12 does not necessarily include the Oral Law.

I am unaware of any modern movement of Jewish believers in Yeshua which takes the position that Messianic Jews must keep the Orthodox Jewish Law or else lose their salvation.

It is Desirable. It is desirable that Messianic Jews observe the Orthodox Jewish Law but not essential. Why desirable? Three reasons.

First, the Law (at least its biblical portions) was given by God to the Jewish people and never abrogated; it is God's guide to godly behavior and worthy of being followed. We are Jews, so we will follow it.

Second, those who know Jewish history cannot be unaware that the Law has kept the Jewish people more than the Jewish people have kept the Law. It is God's will that the Jewish

15. Mattityahu [Matthew] 23:23, *Jewish New Testament.*
16. For further discussion see Section B-5 below.

people be preserved—we can know this not only from the Jews' astounding history of survival despite two thousand years of dispersion and persecution, but also from both the *Tanakh (e.g.,* Isaiah 49:6) and the New Testament (Romans 11). Therefore Messianic Jews should support one of the chief means God has used to preserve us.

Third, it is a way for a Messianic Jew to identify with his fellow Jews, some of whom may consider him excluded from the Jewish community. Here's how it works: a Jewish believer says to a non-Messianic Jew, "I believe in Yeshua, and I'm still Jewish." The response: "You say you're Jewish, but tell me, do you keep *kosher!* Do you avoid driving on *Shabbat."* A Messianic Jew who can answer in the affirmative supposedly removes a potential barrier to the Gospel, rendering both himself and the Gospel more credible. Some might support this approach with 1 Corinthians 9:20, where the King James Version has, "And unto the Jews I became as a Jew, that I might gain the Jews." However, in the *Jewish New Testament* it is translated differently, bringing out that Sha'ul was not changing his behavior like a chameleon changes colors, but empathizing with, putting himself in the position of, the people with whom he was sharing the Gospel. (As we shall see, this third reason is a poor one.)

But then, why, if it is so "desirable," is the Law "not essential"? Because salvation, the proponents of this position would answer, is based on trust alone, on faith, on repentance from sin and turning to God through his Messiah Yeshua. The behavior pleasing to God can be suggested in a written code, but if it is interpreted by the letter and not by the Holy Spirit, it will bring death not life.[17] The only "essential" is to love God and one's neighbor—with the proviso that love implies acts, not just feelings.

It is Indifferent. Messianic Jews may keep the Jewish Law if they wish, or they may not. Whether Messianic Jews

---

17. 2 Corinthians 3:6.

obey the Law is a matter of individual conscience, neither required nor forbidden. The New Testament, the Church and Christianity have nothing to say on the subject one way or another and should remain neutral. The guiding principles for the Church in such "*adiaphora*" (matters of indifference) are set forth in Romans 14 and 1 Corinthians 8. The single proviso that proponents of this position might want to make explicit is that obedience to the Jewish Law does not count with God for salvation.

This stance is taken by many Christian denominations and by many Messianic Jews. It is more *pro-Torah* and is less inhibitive of Jewish identity within the Body than the remaining two stances, which have dominated the Church throughout most of its history. But is *God* satisfied to have his *Torah* ignored? Is it a matter of indifference to *him!* Having given us a holy, just and good *Torah,* whose ways are peace, does he leave to our choice whether to obey it or not? Is this really what the New Testament says?

It is Undesirable. It is undesirable for Messianic Jews to keep the Orthodox Jewish Law, but it is not prohibited. Why undesirable? Because Messianic Jews should realize that they are now "free from the Law," with its "deadness of letter" and are now "alive in the Spirit." 2 Corinthians 3 and Romans 7-8 give plausible support to this position.

Then why "not prohibited"? Because the Jewish believer who wants to keep following the Jewish Law is to be thought of as "weak in faith" in the sense of Romans 14:1-2, someone who is to be indulged until he grows strong enough to give up his "crutch of legalism." This position is more often expressed as social pressure than articulated clearly. Jews who come to believe in Yeshua are made to feel they are outsiders in the Church if they continue—let alone begin—to follow Jewish customs alien to the Gentile Christian majority.

Absolutely not. Messianic Jews should not observe the Orthodox Jewish Law, because if they do they will regard it, rather than trust in Yeshua, as their means of salvation. Texts to support this position are usually brought from Romans, Galatians and Hebrews. A key element here involves equation of Torah-observance with legalism, an equation we disproved earlier.[18]

This attitude is present, consciously or unconsciously, in the Christian who tells a new Jewish believer (and it has happened), "Now that you're a Christian, you're free from the Law. Have a ham sandwich!"—Without realizing that "Gentilizing" a Jew violates the spirit of Galatians 2:13-14 as much as Judaizing a Gentile. They consider Messianic Jews who keep Jewish customs to have "weak faith" in the sense of Romans 14:1-2 (even though that text speaks of Gentiles, not Jews), but they don't obey Sha'ul's caution in the verses following not to judge one's brother for observances done "unto the Lord."

These five positions should be evaluated not only on the basis of their content, but also on the basis of the hidden agendas behind them. For the Church's opposition to a Messianic Jew's observing the *Torah* seems to be based on fear either that he might leave his Messianic faith altogether and return to non-Messianic Judaism,[19] or that he might set up an elite of Law-keepers within the Body and thus "rebuild the middle wall of partition."[20]

Similarly, why would Messianic Jews who do not consider the Oral Law divinely inspired favor keeping it, if not in the hope of bolstering their claim to be still Jewish? But any Messianic Jew who thinks that following the Orthodox or Conservative Jewish version of the *Torah* will increase his credibility before non-Messianic Jews ought to disabuse himself of the idea at once. He will never be "Jewish enough" to prove that Yeshua is the Messiah, and there is a risk that he himself will become the issue, rather than Yeshua. Furthermore, non-Messianic Jews who consider him no longer Jewish

18. See Section A-2-b above.
19. This is clear from the confession quoted in Chapter III, Section B-4.
20. Ephesians 2:11-16.

will not be convinced otherwise by his Law-keeping. Rather, they will say, "You have left Judaism, and it really doesn't matter to us whether you keep the Law or not." Or they will say, "You are keeping it only in order to deceive us, to have us fall prey to your wiles."

Other non-Messianic Jews will not deny the Jewishness of a Jew who accepts Yeshua, but they will say he is deluding himself, on the ground that the Law *ipso facto* precludes belief in Yeshua and the New Testament. And they will not allow that a Messianic Jew has authority to reinterpret the Law in a way that permits him such a belief.

However, that is precisely what needs to be done, so we now abandon the assumption that the *Torah* is what Orthodox Judaism (or any other form of non-Messianic Judaism) says it is. Instead, let us see what we Messianic Jews say it is.

* * * * *

In order to turn the discussion in this new direction, I want to begin by saying that I think the question, "Should Messianic Jews obey the *Torah*?" is not quite on target. I would rather re-phrase it, "Should all Jews and all Gentiles observe the *Torah*?" Revealing the end from the beginning, I say that the answer will be, "Yes!" But it will depend on answers to four subsidiary questions:

- What, at this point in history, really is the *Torah*?.
- Who has the right to determine what the *Torah* asks from us?
- What is meant by "keeping" ("observing," "obeying") the *Torah*?
- What are the different responsibilities of Jews and of Gentiles?

In the rest of Section B we will attempt to make progress in framing these issues, even though we cannot expect to resolve them. We shall examine the questions in turn.

4. *The* Torah *Today Is The* Torah *Of The Messiah*

We said that within traditional Judaism the word *"Torah"* can have four meanings: (1) The five books of Moses, (2) the *Tanakh;* (3) that plus the Oral *Torah;* and (4) all religious teaching from the rabbis. All of these meanings can be found in the New Testament. Some of the references are to *Torah* as understood by non-Messianic Judaism. Others are to *Torah* within the framework of New Covenant truth. Specifically, in the New Testament, (1) *Torah* is to be understood as the Messiah understands it,[21] (2) it includes the Messiah's *mitz-vot,*[22] (3) it includes the New Testament itself,[23] and (4) it names a new group of people as having authority to interpret the *Torah.*[24] Besides such general principles arising from the "change of *Torah"*[25] brought about by the Messiah, the New Testament contains actual *diney- Torah* ("legal decisions about the *Torah")* concerning specific applications of the Law.[26] The phrase in the New Testament which best encompasses all of these new elements is "the *Torah* of the Messiah."[27]

Some Christian theologians seem to think that the *Torah* of the Messiah can be virtually divorced from its Jewish context. There are those who throw out the Jewish *Torah,* claiming that the only thing left of *Torah* after the New Testament gets through with it is love.[28] The *Torah is* fulfilled by love, but this fact does not constitute a command to replace the wisdom God gave us in his *Torah* by a vague instruction to "love."

---

21. As, for example, in the Sermon on the Mount (Mattityahu [Matthew] 5-7); see discussion of Mattityahu 5:17 in Chapter IV, Section E-4-c.
22. Yochanan [John] 14:15; *mitzvot* means "commandments."
23. Messianic Jews [Hebrews] 8:6; see Section A-2-d above.
24. Mattityahu [Matthew] 18:18-20; see Section B-5 below.
25. Messianic Jews [Hebrews] 7:12; see Chapter IV, Section E-l-b.
26. See Section C-2 below.
27. Galatians 6:2.
28. Romans 13:8-10, Galatians 5:14.

Others retain only the Ten Commandments, although theological gymnastics are required in dealing with the command to observe *Shabbat.* Others retain the moral aspects of the *Torah* but discard the ceremonial and civil portions as "for the Jews under the old dispensation, and therefore not in force today."

Since most theologians have been Gentile Christians, and Gentiles are not Jews, they have had little incentive to grapple with the enormous number of detailed issues raised by taking *Torah* seriously. Messianic Jews cannot afford to be so cavalier. We will not only fail in our goal of bringing the Gospel to our people but we will be both proclaiming and living "another gospel"[29] if we do not interact on an intellectually serious level with the specifics of *Torah* as religious Judaism understands it. "Free from the Law" is head-in-the-sand.

What the *Torah* is, in Jewish thought, is intimately connected with who has the right to say what it is; so we will deal with both together in the next section.

5. Who Has The Right To Determine What Is Torah?

Traditional Judaism is based not only on the Old Testament, but on the Oral Law. Within Judaism, the Oral Law, which corresponds more or less to what the New Testament calls "the tradition of the elders,"[30] is supposed to have been given to Moses at Sinai along with the Written Law. The Written Law was, of course, made part of the Hebrew Bible; but the Oral Law was not committed to writing until the *Mishna* compilers began their work in the second century C.E. Of the Oral Law, the *Mishna* says:

> Moses received the *Torah* from Sinai and handed it down to Joshua, and Joshua to the elders [the Judges

29. Galatians 1:6-9.
30. Mattityahu [Matthew] 15:2 ff., Mark 7:3 ff.

> or other early leaders], and the elders to the prophets, and the prophets handed it down to the men of the Great Assembly [120 leaders who returned from exile with Ezra].[31]

The common Christian idea that Judaism became "degenerate" because human tradition was added to God's Law is mistaken. The five books of Moses have rightly been called the constitution of the Jewish nation, but a nation needs more than a constitution. There could never have been a time when tradition of some sort was not a necessary adjunct to the written *Torah*—for the written *Torah* simply does not contain all the laws and customs needed to run a nation.

For this there is evidence even in the Pentateuch. Moses wrote in Deuteronomy 12:21 that the people of Israel could slaughter animals "as I have commanded you," but no commands concerning how to slaughter are found anywhere in the written *Torah.* Something external is implied—legislation, tradition, an oral *Torah.* God could announce his will from heaven whenever uncertainty arises, but this is not his normal means of guidance either in the Old Testament or in the New. Nothing in the Bible suggests that God opposes accumulating knowledge and experience or creating guidelines and rules. It is only when these are misused that they become wrong. Yeshua did not object to "tradition" as such when he criticized the *P'rushim,* but to "your" tradition: "By *your* tradition you make null and void the word of God!"—and he gave a specific example of what he meant.[32]

For traditional Judaism the scriptural basis for an authoritative system of *Torah* interpretation is Deuteronomy 17:8-12, which says that Israel is to consult and obey the priest or judge "who is in office in those days." This is made the ground for the entire system of rabbi-created law—which is understood not as being created anew but derived from what Moses re-

31. *Pirkey-Avot* 1:1.
32. Mark 7:8-13.

ceived at Sinai and handed down to the elders. As Saul Kaatz, a German Jewish scholar explained it,

> Every interpretation of the *Torah* given by a universally recognized authority is regarded as divine and given on Sinai, in the sense that it is taken as the original divinely willed *(gottgewollte)* interpretation of the text; for the omniscient and all-wise God included in His revealed *Torah* every shade of meaning which divinely inspired interpretation thereafter discovered. . . . Therefore, every interpretation is called *derash,* "searching" for what God had originally put there. . . . Every interpretation given by the scholars of the Talmud, Moses had received on Mt. Sinai, for he had received the *Torah,* and the interpretation was contained in it, not mechanically, but organically, as the fruit of the tree was contained in the seed from which the tree had grown. . . .[33]

The New Testament sets up a different system of authority, although there is a question of whether it is entirely independent of the older system. At Mattityahu [Matthew] 18:18-20, after Yeshua has given authority to congregation leaders to excommunicate rebels, we read:

> Yes! I tell you [disciples] that whatever you bind [that is, prohibit] on earth will be bound in heaven, and whatever you loose [permit] on earth will be loosed in heaven. To repeat, I tell you that if two of you here on earth agree about anything people ask, it will be for them from my Father in heaven. For wherever two or three are assembled in my name, I am there with them.[34]

33. Saul Kaatz, *Muendliche Lehreundlhr Dogma,* Berlin, 1923, p. 48, as quoted in George Horowitz, *The Spirit of the Jewish Law* (New York: Central Book Company, 1973), p. 92.
34. Mattityahu [Matthew] 18:18-20, *Jewish New Testament.*

The last sentence is commonly regarded as assurance that Yeshua is present with believers when they pray—I have heard it said that a Messianic *minyan*[35] consists of "two or three" assembled in Yeshua's name, plus Yeshua himself, who is "there with them." That is true, but not on the basis of this verse. Yeshua here is speaking to people who have authority to regulate Messianic communal life (see the preceding three verses). He says that they—and presumably subsequent leaders—have the right to establish *halakhah,* because the terms "bind" and "loose" were used in first-century Judaism to mean "prohibit" and "permit." Yeshua is teaching that when an issue is brought formally to a panel of two or three Messianic Community leaders, and they render a halakhic decision here on earth, they can be assured that the authority of God stands behind them.

The battle-lines are thus clearly drawn. Traditional Judaism claims that the rabbis determine the *halakhah.* The New Testament transfers this authority to Yeshua's disciples, and, according to Mattityahu [Matthew] 28:20, to believers in positions of leadership afterwards. The Roman Catholic Church uses this passage and Mattityahu 16:19 to establish the Petrine succession of the Pope and the authority of its hierarchy. Protestants, in reaction, have virtually deprived these verses of their plain meaning and import. Messianic Jews should understand them as an enormously significant grant of authority but must determine the form and pattern of use of that authority based on a Jewish understanding of the text.

In the State of Israel today there is a conflict which is described as being over the issue of "Who is a Jew?" but actually it is over "Who is a rabbi?" The Orthodox in Israel refuse to acknowledge as valid the conversions of Gentiles to Judaism made by Conservative and Reform rabbis, even when these conversions are done according to the procedures laid down in the Orthodox *halakhah.* If this is so, imagine how much

35. A *minyan* is a quorum sufficient for public prayers, ten in traditional Judaism.

greater will be the conflict when there begin to be Messianic Jewish halakhic authorities who presume to issue *diney-torah* (halakhic judgments). Till now Messianic Jews have steered clear of such a conflict, not out of fear but by default, because of the mistaken theological view that *ha-lakhah* is irrelevant to New Testament living. That era is about to pass away. When Messianic Jews (and perhaps informed Messianic Gentiles) begin to deal with *Torah* in a Jewish way, issuing decisions based on the authority granted by Yeshua but ignored until now, the proclamation of the Gospel will have entered a new era.

But how will these decisions affect the lives of believers? Or will they at all? That is our next question.

6. *What Is The Role Of Halakhah? Or: Why The Oral Law Was Oral. Or: What Does It Mean To "Observe" The Torah?*

As I said, *halakhah* means "the way to walk," and it can refer broadly to the whole system of how to live within the framework of *Torah,* or to a specific rule meant to guide behavior in a particular situation. It was only when the Jewish nation was being dispersed throughout the world and there was no longer a Temple to unite the people that the rabbis realized it would be necessary to write down the Oral Law containing the *halakhot*.

Many of them had misgivings about doing this, and not without reason. So long as the Oral Law remained oral, judgments tended to be more spontaneous, decisionmaking more flexible, more responsive to the needs of a given situation. It was easier to consider changes in social life without feeling hidebound by precedents established centuries earlier when conditions were different. But when case law began to be written down, there were disadvantages as well as advantages. It was no longer necessary to re-invent the wheel, but sometimes the available wheels didn't fit the new vehicles.

And this is precisely the criticism the revisionist branches of Judaism make of Orthodox Judaism today. For example, the Bible itself says that a Jew is not to light a fire on *Shabbat.* The rabbis have interpreted this to mean that a Jew is prohibited from operating an elevator on *Shabbat,* Because when he presses the elevator button, the elevator is activated by a spark of electricity, a fire. But if a "*Shabbat* elevator" is provided which automatically goes up and down all day, stopping on each floor, an Orthodox Jew is permitted to enter when it stops at his floor and leave when it arrives where he wants to go, because he is not himself lighting a fire on *Shabbat* (or even causing one to be lit).

The majority of Jews, even those who understand the above logic, think that something is peculiar about a system that produces this rule, that such a rule neither enhances human spirituality nor expresses God's will. There is a *halakhic* principle that a *halakhah* unacceptable to the majority is not valid, but Orthodox Judaism does not see fit to apply it to themselves (they say a ruling must be unacceptable to the majority of *halakhically knowledgeable Orthodox* Jews to be invalid).

Most Jews, in a spirit of pluralism, certainly would not prohibit Orthodox Jews from obeying their own rules, but they would not care to have them imposed on themselves against their will. In my judgment this attitude is less due to rebellion against the authority of the rabbis than to a gut sense that Orthodoxy for centuries has failed to deal satisfactorily with the realities of life. In the Diaspora this conflict between the Orthodox and the majority of Jews makes no headlines, because the Orthodox Jews do not wield political power. But in Israel it has produced a full-scale *kulturkampf* between "secular" and "religious" Jews, a conflict in which Messianic Jews are not at present involved—except for being convinced that if both religious and secular Jews would put their trust in Yeshua the Messiah, the *kulturkampf would* end.

When the Oral *Torah* was truly oral, not fixed as it has been since the compiling of the *Talmud,* there was more room for flexibility. Conservative Judaism tries—albeit in a very limited way, since its rule-making bodies are controlled by its right wing—to modernize certain *halakhot.* A well-known example is the rule concerning the *agunah,* the woman whose husband has disappeared and whose whereabouts is unknown. According to Orthodox *halakhah,* the woman cannot obtain a divorce, because the husband is not there to write her a *get,*[36] nor can she be regarded as a widow, since there is no definite evidence the husband has died. Therefore she cannot remarry. This can cause great hardship—a young *agunah* who never learns the fate of her husband must stay single all her life. Conservative Judaism has developed a different *halakhah* which allows remarriage under certain conditions and thus alleviates the hardship.[37]

All of this is by way of background to considering what the role of *halakhah* might be in the light of the New Covenant. According to the New Testament, every believer has in him the Spirit of God.[38] It is written that the letter kills, but the Spirit makwS alive.[39] It does not say that the *Torah* kills, for the *Torah* is holy, just and good. It does say that love fulfills the *Torah,* which I see as another way of saying that obedience to the *Torah* by the Spirit makes the *Torah* come alive.

It is clear that people need guidance in ethical behavior. But Christian ethics tends to float above specific rules to a Platonic world of general principles. This can be seen in the writings of Dietrich Bonhoeffer, who led an ethical life (even unto death at the hands of the Nazis) but whose books on ethics tended to soar into spiritual realms—inspiring, but far from the brass tacks. Messianic *halakhah* can provide specific guidance for those who seek it. It can provide a basis for discussion, for

---

36. A *get* is essentially what the *Tanakh* and the New Testament call a "bill of divorcement;" see Deuteronomy 24:1-4, Mattityahu [Matthew] 19:3-9.
37. For a discussion of the *agunah* problem, see *Encyclopedia Judaica,* Volume 2, pp. 429-433.
38. Romans 8:9.
39. 2 Corinthians 3:6.

probing in the direction of finding godly solutions to ethical questions, as well as for ceremonial situations, helping to establish communal norms—*norms,* not hard-and-fast rules! A balance must be struck between heavyhandedly imposing halakhic decisions on the believing community and carelessly failing to give adequate guidance, with the result that each must fend for himself.

So we have our answer: "observing" the *Torah* of the Messiah means accepting the guidance of New Testament *halakhah* for our lives, while remaining sensitive to the Holy Spirit. Whether the Spirit wants us to obey the rule or to break it will be decided within a communal, congregational framework in which our respected leaders and colleagues help us determine the mind of the Messiah, which "we"—as a community, not each individual—have.[40]

7. Torah *For Gentiles?*

Because Gentiles are included in the New Covenant, they are subject to New Covenant *Torah,* the *Torah* of the Messiah. Since *Torah* itself is a medium through which God expresses his grace toward his people, it is not surprising that if through Yeshua God has poured out his grace equally on Gentiles and Jews (this is the main point of Romans 1-11), he has also made requirements of Gentiles as well as of Jews (some of them are detailed in Romans 12-15).

What God initially requires of Gentiles who accept Yeshua as their Messiah is spoken of in traditional Judaism as the Noachide Laws, which the *Encyclopedia Judaica* says are:

> the seven laws considered by rabbinic tradition as the minimal moral duties enjoined by the Bible on all men *(Talmud, Sanhedrin* 56-60; Maimonides: *Mishneh Torah, Yad Chazakah, Melakhim,* 8:10, 10:12). Jews are obligated to observe the whole *Torah,* while every

---

40. 1 Corinthians 2:16: "For *we* have the mind of the Messiah."

non-Jew is a "son of the covenant of Noah" (see Genesis 9), and he who accepts its obligations is a *ger-toshav* ("resident stranger" or even "semi-convert"; see *Talmud, Avodah Zarah* 64b; Maimonides, *op. cit.,* 8:10). Maimonides equates the "righteous man *(hasid)* of the [gentile] nations" who has a share in the world to come even without becoming a Jew with the gentile who keeps these laws. Such a man is entitled to full material support from the Jewish community ... and to the highest earthly honors ... The seven Noachide laws as traditionally enumerated are: the prohibitions of idolatry, blasphemy, bloodshed, sexual sins, theft, and eating from a living animal, as well as the injunction to establish a legal system *(Tosefta* tractate *Avodah Zarah* 8:4; *Sanhedrin* 56a). Except for the last, all are negative, and the last itself is usually interpreted as commanding the enforcement of the others (Maimonides, *op. cit.,* 9:1). They are derived exegetically from divine demands addressed to Adam (Genesis 2:16) and Noah (see *Midrash Rabbah* on Genesis 34; *Sanhedrin* 59b) *i.e.,* the progenitors of all mankind, and are thus regarded as universal ... Noachides may also freely choose to practice certain other Jewish commandments (Maimonides, *op. cit.,* 10:9-10). Jews are obligated to try to establish the Noachide Code wherever they can *(ibid.,* 8:10). Maimonides held that Noachides must not only accept "the seven laws" on their own merit, but they must accept them as divinely revealed. This follows from the thesis that all ethics are not ultimately "natural," but require a theological framework ... Views differ as to whether the ultimate stage of humanity will comprise both Judaism and Noachidism, or whether Noachidism is only the penultimate level before the universalization of all of

> the *Torah* (see Jerusalem *Talmud, Avodah Zarah* 2:1) . . .[41]

Many commentators have noted the resemblance between the Noachide laws and the requirements placed on Gentile Christians in Acts 15:20. The Jerusalem Council, a kind of Messianic *Sanhedrin,* was convened to determine under what conditions Gentile believers were to be accepted into the Messianic Community (that is, into the Church). It was decided that they need not convert to Judaism but should initially observe four *mitzvot*—"to abstain from things polluted by idols, from fornication, from what is strangled and from blood."

This teaches us that the elements of *Torah* which apply to Gentiles under the New Covenant are not the same as those which apply to Jews. (The Jerusalem Council made no change whatever in the *Torah* as it applies to Jews, so that a number of years later there could still be in Jerusalem "tens of thousands" of Messianic Jews who were "zealots for the *Torah*"*2) It should not surprise us if New Covenant *Torah* specifies different commandments for Jews and Gentiles. First, the Five Books of Moses have commands which apply to some groups and not others—to the king but not to his subjects, to *cohanim* ("priests") but not to other Jews, to men but not women. Second, the New Testament too has different commands for different categories of people, for example, men and women, husbands and wives, parents and children, slaves and masters, leaders and followers, widows as distinct from other women.[43]

41. *Encyclopedia Judaica* (Jerusalem: Keter Publishing House, Ltd., 1971), volume 12, p. 1189.
42. Acts 21:20, *Jewish New Testament.*
43. See 1 Corinthians 11:2-16, 14:34-36; Ephesians 5:22-6:9; Colossians 3:18-4:1; 1 Timothy 3:1-13, 5:3-16; Messianic Jews [Hebrews] 13:7, 17; 1 Kefa[1 Peter] 3:1-7.

However, Acts 15 also teaches that although Gentiles were *required* to observe only four laws upon entering the Messianic Community, they were *permitted* to learn as much about Judaism as they wished[44] and presumably to observe as many Jewish laws and customs as they wished. This feature too corresponds to Noachidism. The only proviso added in the New Covenant (in Galatians) is that Gentiles should not suppose that their self-Judaizing will earn them "salvation points" with God.

Moreover, it should not be thought that the only requirement the New Covenant makes of Gentiles is to obey these four commands. On the contrary, there are hundreds of commands in the New Testament meant as much for Gentiles as for Jews. Nor should it be thought that the New Covenant does away with moral, civil, ceremonial or any other category of law. There are New Testament commands for Jews and Gentiles in all of these categories. To give but a few examples, Romans 13:1-7 and Acts 5:29 touch on civil obedience and disobedience, Mattityahu [Matthew] 28:19 and 1 Corinthians 11:17-34 deal with matters of ceremony, 1 Corinthians 5:1-6:7, 14:26-40, 2 Corinthians 2:5-11 and Mattityahu 18:15-17 deal with order in the Messianic Community, and there are so many moral, ethical and spiritual commands that there is no need to cite them (1,050 commands of all kinds, according to one enumeration).[45]

We conclude that under the New Covenant the *Torah* remains in force and is as much for Gentiles as for Jews, although the specific requirements for Gentiles differ from those for Jews. We will now examine some implications of this conclusion in greater detail.

---

44. Acts 15:21.
45. Finnis Jennings Dake, *Dake's Annotated Reference* 5/6/e(Lawrence-ville, Georgia: Dake Bible Sales, Inc., 1961), New Testament, pp. 313-316.

C. HALAKHIC ISSUES IN MESSIANIC JUDAISM

1. *Introduction*

A Messianic Jew who realizes that the *Torah* still is in force under the New Covenant ought to be full of questions. How is the *Torah* to be applied? What is the *halakhah* under the New Covenant? What ought to be done, and what ought not to be done in particular situations?

One can imagine creating a body of New Testament case law much like the *Talmud,* the Codes and Responsa of Judaism. It would take into consideration Jewish *halakhah,* which has, after all, dealt with nearly every sector of human existence; yet everything would have to be reexamined in the light of New Covenant truth. It would be created by both Jewish and Gentile scholars and judges familiar with the Bible and the halakhic process, with the prime text on which to base such a procedure being Mattityahu 18:18-20.[46]

But what good would it do? Who would listen to it? Who would obey it? Is anyone demanding it? Who needs it? Who cares? Are we not guided in all things by the Holy Spirit? Do we require a set of rules or guidelines? Does the New Testament even allow taking a halakhic approach?

Well—that's how the discussion begins. We will pursue it a short distance in the remainder of this chapter; there is no finishing it. We will ask a few of the questions and try to think about them. Nothing here is meant to be taken as a "ruling" on any subject, since no one has authorized me to make rulings.

2. *New Testament Halakhot*

One of the questions raised in the preceding section was: Does the New Testament allow taking a halakhic approach? The only possible answer to this is: Yes, because the New Testament itself actually states a number of *diney-torah* (specific

46. See discussion of this passage in Section B-5 above. In writing, "One can imagine" creating Messianic *halakhah* I am not *advocating* doing it in a style imitative of the *yeshiva* world, or even doing it at all.

judgments as to how to apply the *Torah)* or *halakhot* (applications of Law), and these are generally arrived at by thoroughly rabbinic ways of thinking. Here are four instances:

a. *Yochanan [John] 7:22-23*

In this passage Yeshua presents a *din-torah* that the *mitzvah* of healing takes precedence over that of refraining from work on *Shabbat.* In making this decision as to which of two conflicting laws holds in a particular situation, he was doing much the same thing as did the rabbis who developed the Oral *Torah.* In fact, Yeshua referred in this passage to a well-known such decision which can be found in the *Talmud,* tractate *Shabbat,* pages 128aff.

The rabbis were confronted with the conflict between the law against working on *Shabbat* and the commandment that a man should circumcise his son on the eighth day of his life. The conflict arises from the fact that cutting and carrying the tools needed to perform *ab'rit-milah* through a public domain are kinds of work forbidden by the rabbis on *Shabbat.* They decided that if the eighth day falls on *Shabbat,* one does the necessary work and circumcises the boy; but if the circumcision must take place after the eighth day, say, for health reasons, it may not be done on *Shabbat* in violation of the work prohibitions; one waits till a weekday.

Yeshua in defending his ruling used what Judaism calls a *kal v'homer* ("light and heavy") argument, known in philosophy as reasoning *a fortiori* ("from greater strength"). Its essence is in the phrase "how much more...!" Yeshua's point at Yochanan 7:23 is: "You permit breaking *Shabbat* in order to observe the *mitzvah* of circumcision; how much more important it is to heal a person's whole body, so you should permit breaking *Shabbat* for that too!"

b. *Galatians 2:11-14*

Sha'ul [Paul] pronounced an important *halakhah* at Galatians 2:11-14. It too is a decision as to how to proceed when two valid principles conflict, but in this case the conflict was between an Old Testament command and a New Covenant necessity. His conclusion was not, as some suppose, that the Jewish dietary laws no longer apply, but that Jewish believers' observance of *kashrut* must not be allowed to impede their fellowship with Gentile believers. Communion in the Messiah is more important than eating *kosher.* But when a Jewish believer's eating *kosher* does not break such fellowship, then nothing in Galatians 2:11-14 can be construed to imply that the Jewish dietary laws should not be observed.

c. Mark 7:1-23

While on the subject of *kashrut* we will look at two other passages commonly cited to prove its abolition and show that this is not their purpose. Mark 7:1-23 is concerned not with *kashrut* but with ritual washing before meals *(n 'tilat-yadayim),* a practice observed in traditional Judaism today.[47] Therefore when Yeshua "declared all foods clean"[48] he was not declaring *treif* foods *kosher,* but saying that *kosher* food is not rendered ritually unclean when hands not ritually washed touch it. Although in our age it is hard for anyone not an Orthodox Jew to think intelligently about ritual impurity, its importance in Yeshua's time can be roughly measured by the fact that one of the six major divisions of the *Talmud (Tohorot,* "Purities") is almost entirely devoted to this subject.

However, the important *halakhah* for us to note has nothing to do with eating. In this passage Yeshua does not give zero weight to the "tradition of the elders," as do many Christians. Rather, what he does insist on is that human traditions should not be used to "make null and void the word of God." This is a key halakhic ruling by the Messiah himself which can guide us in creating New Testament *halakhah* today. It says that we must keep our priorities straight: only

47. See Mark 7:2-5.
48. Mark 7:19.

God's word commands absolute obedience. Our *halakhot* may be useful, suggestive, edifying, valuable as guidance, but they are still only "tradition of men," hence fallible and less important. The Messiah's *halakhah* contrasts with the prevailing view in Orthodox Judaism, which, being descended directly from the Pharisaic position Yeshua criticized, can punish violation of a rabbinic ruling more severely than violation of a biblical precept.

d. Acts 10:9-17, 28

Kefa [Peter] had a vision in which three times he saw *treif* animals being lowered from heaven in a sheet and heard a voice telling him to "kill and eat." Unlike those interpreters who instantly assume the passage teaches that Jews need not eat *kosher* food any more. Kefa spent some time "puzzling over the meaning of the vision." Only when he arrived at Cornelius' home did he get the pieces of the puzzle put together, so that he could state, "God has shown me not to call *any person* unclean." The vision was about people, not food. It did not teach Kefa—who had always eaten *kosher*—to change his eating habits, but to accept Gentiles equally with Jews as candidates for salvation.

For it must be remembered that the sheet lowered from heaven contained all kinds of animals, wild beasts, reptiles and birds; yet I know of no Bible interpreters who insist that eagles, vultures, owls, bats, weasels, mice, lizards, crocodiles, chameleons, snakes, spiders and bugs must now be considered edible. God specifies in Leviticus 11 what Jews are to regard as "food." Even if there were a secondary message in this vision about eating, it would not totally overthrow the dietary laws but would state the same rule we found above in Galatians 2:11-14, that preserving fellowship between Jewish and Gentile believers might at times supersede observance of *kashrut.*[49]

---

49. For more on this subject, see my notes on Galatians 2:11-14 in the *Jewish New Testament Commentary.*

3. *Other Materials To Draw On In Creating New Covenant Halakhah*

What might Messianic Jewish halakhists wish to consult as they prepare for their task? We have just seen that the New Testament is one such source, and it should go without saying that the *Tanakh* is another. In addition to the Bible, Messianic Jewish halakhists must know how to deal with the vast amount of halakhic material that has arisen within Judaism. This includes not only the the *Mishna* (220 C.E.) and the two *Gemaras,* each of which with the *Mishna* equals a *Talmud*—the Jerusalem *Talmud* (4th Century) and the Babylonian (5th century)—but also the *Tosefta* (composed of 2nd-3rd century codifications similar to the *Mishna),* the halakhic *midrashim (Mekhilta* on Exodus, *Sifra* on Leviticus, *Sifrei* on Numbers and Deuteronomy, all compiled in the 4th or 5th centuries) and the opinions of the *Savoraim* (6th-7th centuries), *Gaonim* (7th-10th centuries), *Poskim* (1 lth-14th centuries), *Rishonim* (14th-17th centuries) and *Acharonim* (18th-20th centuries) contained in codes, responsa (case law) and other writings. There are no shortcuts to familiarity with this large body of material; if Messianic Judaism is going to undertake seriously the creation of New Testament *halakhah,* it will have to prepare its scholars for the work.

Other Jewish materials touch on *halakhah* from without rather than from within. For example, there is Jewish philosophy, Jewish ethics *(musar),* and an interesting literature on *ta'amey ha-mitzvot,* "the reasons for the commandments."[50]

---

50. See [Ascribed to] Rabbi Aaron HaLevi of Barcelona (Charles Wengrov, translator), *Sefer HaHinnuch* (Jerusalem & New York: Feldheim Publishers, 1978); Gersion Appel, *A Philosophy of Mitzvot* (New York: Ktav Publishing House, 1975); Abraham P. Bloch, *The Biblical and Historical Background of Jewish Customs and Ceremonies* (New York: Ktav Publishing House, 1980); Abraham Chill, *The Mitzvot: The Commandments and Their Rationale* (New York: Bloch Publishing Co., 1974); Abraham Chill, *The Minhagim: The Customs and Ceremonies of Judaism, Their Origins and Rationale* (New York: Sepher Hermon Press, 1979); Alfred J. Kolatch, *The Jewish*

We should research the Conservative, Reform and Reconstructionist writings on *halakhah,* since these movements have had to explain to their own constituencies why they adopt a view different from that of the Orthodox, and have therefore pioneered some paths we should explore, even though we will not wish to end up where they lead.

The leaders called "scribes" in the New Testament were actually Torah-teachers Jews well educated in Judaism. Yeshua, at the close of his teaching on the Kingdom of Heaven, says something very interesting about them: "So then, every Torah-teacher who becomes a disciple in the Kingdom of Heaven is like a homeowner who brings out of his storage room both new things and old" (Mattityahu [Matthew] 13:52). This means that the *talmid chacham* ("wise student"), the Jew well trained in rabbinic literature, who comes to faith in Yeshua the Messiah is uniquely positioned to help Messianic Judaism develop its *halakhah.* Yeshua thus contradicts the Jewish community's claim to find no place in the Body of the Messiah for a Jew educated in his Judaism. On the contrary, as we have said before, being Messianic is the most exciting way to be Jewish!

4. *Areas Of New Covenant* Halakhah *For Jews*

Judaism concerns itself with all areas of life. In this section I will talk about these areas and raise some of the questions Messianic Jewish *halakhah* might wish to deal with, touching especially on how Messianic Jews ought to live.

a. Individual And Family Life

Should Messianic Jews make use of the *mikveh* (the ritual bath), and if so, when, for what and why? Should Messianic

---

Book of Why (Middle Village, New York: Jonathan David Publishers, 1981); Alfred J. Kolatch, *The Second Jewish Book of Why* (Middle Village, New York: Jonathan David Publishers, 1985); Abraham 1. Sperling, *Reasons for Jewish Customs and Traditions* (New York: Bloch Publishing Co., 1968).

Jewish couples observe the biblical command of *niddah* (separation of husband and wife during and after the wife's menstrual period)? Should Messianic Jews recite the daily blessings? Should we observe *kashrutl* Should we put *mezuzot* on our doors? Should we leave an unplastered wall in a home we build to remind us of the destroyed Temple? Should Messianic Jewish men wear *tzitziyot*? lay *t'fillin*? wear a *kippah*?

b. Calendar And Holidays

Judaism sanctifies time by its requirements for observing various events tied to the calendar. Synagogue services are tied to the day, *Shabbat* to the week, *Rosh Chodesh* to the month, the festivals to the year, *shmittah* (letting agricultural land lie fallow) to a seven-year cycle, the Jubilee to a fifty-year cycle, and various important events to the life cycle.

We can say categorically that Messianic Jews have as much right to to these celebrations as non-Messianic Jews. Whether we *must* observe them is already a matter for debate. And *how* to celebrate them opens a huge can of worms! Should we simply accept non-Messianic Judaism's way of celebrating? Or should we attempt to infuse Messianic meaning into them? Should we eliminate elements that are not biblically based? Or can we include rabbinic elements without compromising our faith? Should we add evangelistic elements? What does our celebrating mean—to us, to non-Messianic Jews, to Gentile Christians and to God?

We will consider the synagogue service in the subsection on liturgy,[51] but here are some questions connected with observing *Shabbat.* Should one refrain from lighting fires on *Shabbatl* We noted that this is not a rabbinic but a biblical prohibition.[52] How should the principle, "*Shabbat* is for man, not

51. Section C-5-f.
52. Exodus 35:3.

man for *Shabbat,"*[53] which has parallels within rabbinic Judaism, be applied here and generally? Should a Messianic Jew light *Shabbat* candles? If he does, should he recite the traditional *b'rakhah* ("benediction"), "Praised be thou, *Adonai* our God, king of the universe, who has sanctified us by his commandments and commanded us to kindle the light for *Shabbat"* even though no such command can be found in Scripture? I have heard the word "permitted" substituted for "commanded"; but in Judaism God is blessed for his commands, not his permissions, so that this modification sounds strange. I have also heard ". . . who has commanded us to be a light to the nations" substituted for the final phrase. Although the substitute is biblically based, it is not immediately relevant to *Shabbat* candles and therefore may conflict with the sensible principle that *b'rakhot* are to be said when specific acts are actually performed; otherwise they are considered to have been spoken "in vain."

While on the subject of *b'rakhot* we may note the phrase found in many blessings, ". . . who has sanctified us by his commandments." Some object to it on the ground that New Covenant believers are sanctified (separated for God) by Yeshua, by his blood *(i.e.,* his death), and by the Holy Spirit,[54] but not by the commandments. A possible resolution lies in metonymy: the commandments stand for him who commands. Another resolution: since both the *Torah* and the Holy Spirit were given at *Shavu'ot,*[55] the commandments symbolize, represent or express the Holy Spirit.

Since the Jewish believer Victor Buksbazen published *The Gospel in the Feasts of Israel*[56] a number of books have appeared pointing out the Messianic significance of the festivals, including one encouraging Gentile Christians to experience the

53. Mark 2:27.
54. 1 Corinthians 1:2, Messianic Jews [Hebrews] 13:12, Romans 15:16.
55. Exodus 19:1 ff., Acts 2:1 ff.
56. Victor Buksbazen, *The Gospel in the Feasts of Israel* (WestCollings-wood, New Jersey, The Spearhead Press, 1954).

blessing of observing them.[57] The manner of observing the festivals in Messianic Judaism is still unsettled. Three principles to keep in mind when working in this area are that we want to honor the Messiah, retain the Jewish meaning, and keep things sufficiently spontaneous and in the Spirit (the two are not necessarily identical!).

The major life-cycle events are *b'rit-milah* (circumcision), *pidyon-ha-ben* (redemption of the firstborn son), *bar-mitzvah,* marriage, and death. I took a course at the University of Judaism in Los Angeles with Harold Schulweis, a noted Conservative rabbi, in which he made the following assignment for a term paper: "The life-cycle events attract many Jews who have little connection with their religion. If you were the officiating rabbi, what kind of sermon would you give at each life-cycle event to win back these strays to a more Jewish life?" I used the opportunity to explain how I would preach to make Yeshua known in the Jewish ceremonies (I got an "A" on the paper but no comment on its content). Rabbi Schulweis's point ought to be well taken by Messianic Jews interested in using these events for evangelistic purposes. We should also use them to knit our community closer together in the Lord. For more on this see below in the discussion of liturgy.

This is a good place to note the Jewish principle of performing *mitzvot* beautifully. Much of Jewish art centers around the ceremonial objects needed to perform *mitzvot,* and in recent years Messianic Jewish artists have begun developing these themes in the production of Messianic Judaica. There are well-designed Messianic *ketubot* (wedding contracts), *aronot-Torah (Torah* arks), *kippot, afikoman* covers and other ritual items. There is room for taking any of the celebrations and traditional art forms and using them to reflect our faith with both joy and beauty.

57. Martha Zimmerman: *Celebrate the Feasts* (Minneapolis: Bethany House, 1981); Barney Kasdan, *God's Appointed Times* (Clarksville. MD: Lederer/Messianic Jewish Publishing, 1989)

c. *Ethics And Morals*

Messianic Judaism will wish to deal with such topics in the area of moral life as charity, kindness, justice, filial love, humility, purity, holiness, good citizenship, forgiveness, temperance, and *derekh-eretz* (literally, the "way of the Land," *i.e.,* how to behave toward others). It will consider practical life questions such as the dignity of labor, study, responsibilities of laborers and employers; matters of civil law such as taxation, duties to rulers, unlawful gain, wrongs in deeds and words; issues affecting relations between social classes, private and public charity, justice, truth, and peace; and it will want to address specific current issues such as minorities, abortion, euthanasia, genocide, war, ecology, smoking, and so on without end. My leaving these topics to one short paragraph does not mean they are unimportant! Messianic Judaism at present seems preoccupied with rituals because we are groping for our identity. But we also know that these deeper issues demand our attention and must not be put off.

5. *Congregational Life*

Many halakhic questions arise in the area of congregational life. We will delay to a later section dealing with how Messianic Jews and Messianic Gentiles are to interrelate in the public life of a Messianic Jewish congregation[58] and address other problematical matters here.

a. *Messianic Synagogues.*

Should one speak of a Messianic Jewish congregation as a Messianic synagogue? There is scriptural warrant for doing so in Ya'akov [James], 2:1-2 which reads,

> My brothers, practice the faith of our Lord Yeshua, the glorious Messiah, without showing favoritism.

58. See Sections C-6-c and C-6-d below.

> Suppose a man comes into your synagogue wearing gold rings and fancy clothes, and also a poor man comes in dressed in rags . . .

Ya'akov is writing to "the Twelve Tribes in the Diaspora,"[59] that is to say, Jews. Moreover, as we see in the passage quoted, these Jews are Messianic Jews whom he calls "brothers" and exhorts to "practice the faith of our Lord Yeshua, the glorious Messiah." The word rendered "synagogue" in the *Jewish New Testament* and which Gentile-oriented Bible versions usually translate "assembly," "church" or "meeting," is Greek *suna-gôgê,* which means nothing but "synagogue" when the context is Jewish (the word appears 57 times in the New Testament). Finally, Ya'akov speaks of "*your* synagogue," the one which you Messianic Jews are in charge of and therefore in which you should not "show favoritism." In the light of this New Testament precedent, I see no reason not to speak of Messianic synagogues today and to establish them in greater numbers—keeping in mind that Messianic Gentiles must be made welcome in them.

The problem with this term comes not from the New Testament but from the expectations a Jewish person has when told he is going to a "synagogue." We will not be surprised if he objects to our Messianic emphasis, for that we can expect. But we would not like to be embarrassed by using Jewish materials ignorantly. A Messianic synagogue ought not to be merely a church service with a few Jewish words, clothes and symbols. If the materials of Judaism are used, they should be used properly; or, if we change the normal ways of using these items, we should do so intentionally and not out of indifference or ignorance.

For example, I knew of one congregation that owns a *sefer-Torah (Torah* scroll for public reading)—so far, so good. But what do they do with this *Torah* scroll? They recite the

59. Ya'akov [James] 1:1, *Jewish New Testament.*

blessing, *"noten ha-Torah"* ("Praised be thou, *Adonai,* giver of the *Torah")* but then read from the King James Version of the Bible, because no one knows Hebrew well enough to read from the scroll (or even from a pointed Hebrew text). To a knowledgeable Jewish observer this looks ridiculous. One can defend this parody of synagogue procedure by saying that God judges hearts and is not concerned with ritual details or whether people can read Hebrew. True enough, so far as the believers themselves are concerned; their salvation is not in question. But we are taught by Sha'ul to be concerned with what "uninstructed people or unbelievers"[60] will think if they come to our meetings. Our object is not to amuse or offend them but to win them to the Lord; we need not add the offense of the ignorant believer to the offense of the Gospel. No one expects a *Torah* reading in a church service, and there are synagogue services without *Torah* readings too. But if a *Torah* scroll is taken out in a Messianic synagogue, it should be read properly. If no one knows how, it may be better not to do it at all.

It isn't that everything has to be done perfectly. There are many synagogues where people don't do things right. The difference is that frequently the Messianic Jewish congregations have little desire to go beyond what I call "the Jewishy veneer" to greater authenticity. Often the reason for the Jewishy veneer is to impress unbelievers (relatively ignorant ones, of course), not to express the Messianic Jewish faith of the congregants. This is a mistake. Nothing good can come from putting up a front. Congregations who do this will be accused of trying to deceive, and rightly so. Only the congregations whose members are seriously trying to express the Jewishness which is in fact theirs will be able to weather such criticism; they will weather it because they are doing something real, not acting in a show.

60. 1 Corinthians 14:23.

b. Meeting Time

When should services be? In the United States it is common for Messianic Jewish congregations to meet on Friday nights and Saturday mornings. In Israel, at least one congregation meets on Saturday evening *(Motza'ey-Shabbat),* after the busses start running again; moreover, it seems that this is when the New Testament believers met—on "the first day of the week," which in the Jewish calendar commences after sundown on Saturday.[61] Does *Shabbat* represent unity with Jews and Sunday with Gentile Christians? If so, is there a sort of schizophrenia, and how does one handle it? Or is the meeting-day a minor point for us?

c. Kippah

A Jewish man is not compelled by *halakhah* to wear a *kippah;* there is no mention of it anywhere in the *Talmud.* But it is certainly an identification tag, since it has become such a universal custom among religious Jews that it nearly carries the weight of an halakhic requirement. It is interesting that what the *kippah* identifies in the Diaspora is different from what it identifies in Israel. In the Diaspora it says "Jew;" but in Israel it says *"dati"* (religious), and its style (knitted, black, embroidered, etc.) tells what kind of Orthodox Jew is wearing it.

Because of 1 Corinthians 11, an issue has arisen as to whether a Messianic Jewish man may wear a *kippah* when he prays. My answer, as it appeared in my "Response" to Arnold Fruchtenbaum's "A Quest for a Messianic Theology" in *Mishkan* is:

---

61. This seems quite~clear from Acts 20:7-11, where the church of Troas met on "the first day of the week" in the evening, presumably in the afterglow of the Jewish day of rest, and Paul stayed on until the following morning. This seems more likely than that the Jewish believers in the local body would disperse to their places of work for one day and then return for a meeting on Sunday night.

It is *not* unscriptural for Messianic Jewish men to wear *yarmulkes* when worshipping, as is evident from the meaning of the Greek words used in 1 Corinthians ll:4-5a, 7a. A literal translation of this passage is: "Every man praying or prophesying having [something] down over his head shames his head, but every woman praying or prophesying with head unveiled shames her head ... For a man indeed ought not [to have] the head to be veiled." Paul is writing about veils, which come down over one's head. A *kippah* is not a veil, and it does not come down over one's head. Therefore there is no conflict between 1 Corinthians 11 and a man's wearing a skullcap.[62]

d. Misusing Jewish Sancta?

Messianic Jews are accused by some in the Jewish community of "misusing Jewish sancta." We have spoken of this somewhat above, in relation to reading from a *Torah* scroll. I said the sancta are ours to use, since we are Jews too; but they are not ours to misuse out of ignorance, nor are they ours to put on a show with; rather, they are ours with which to express and enhance our Messianic faith.

So if we use the found half of the *afikoman* and the third cup of the Passover *Seder* for communion, non-Messianic Jews may object; but we can defend ourselves on the ground that this is what the Messiah did. If we point out that the three *matzot* represent Father, Son and Holy Spirit, and that the broken middle *matzah* represents Yeshua's body, broken for us, we have theological grounds for what we do. In fact, there is a good chance we have historical grounds; many scholars believe that these customs were started by Messianic Jews and invested with the meanings we have noted here, but somehow the customs were absorbed into non-Messianic Judaism and

62. Arnold Fruchtenbaum, "The Quest for a Messianic Theology: Statement," and David H. Stern, "Response" in *Mishkan*, Issue No. 2 (Winter 1985), pp. 1-23. The quotation is from p. 22.

stripped of their Messianic significance. It would be wise for us to make such modifications only after much thought and prayer. For we are dealing with ceremonies weighted with intellectual, emotional and spiritual meaning. *Ad hoc* changes are likely to prove tasteless, offensive, theologically erroneous, or all three.

e. Messianic Rabbis

Starting with the Christian side of this issue, we have Mattityahu [Matthew] 23:8, where the Messiah warns his disciples, "But you are not to let yourselves be called "Rabbi'; because you have one Rabbi, and you are all each other's brothers." But a literalistic approach here seems inappropriate, since he also warns against being called "father" or "leader." The context leads me to believe that Yeshua here prohibits believers from allowing themselves to accept unearned honors generally rather than outlawing three titles forever.

What would a "Messianic rabbi" be? Merely a pastor under another name? It seems to me again that as with "synagogue" the term "rabbi" sets up Jewish expectations which ought to be fulfilled. Therefore, someone who calls himself a Messianic rabbi, or who permits his congregation to call him that, ought to have training commensurate with that which would enable him to qualify as a rabbi in a non-Messianic Jewish setting. (But in which setting—Orthodox, Conservative or Reform?—or is that a wrong question?) Should a Messianic rabbi have *smikhah* (ordination)? If so, should it be Messianic or non-Messianic? If Messianic, who is qualified to give it? Where can an aspiring Messianic rabbi get the necessary training? In any case, in order not to embarrass the Messianic Jewish movement, I urge leaders without rabbinic training to resist letting themselves be called "Rabbi."

f. Messianic Jewish Liturgy

Since many in the Messianic Jewish movement have received much of their Messianic experience in Protestant churches with an anti-liturgical approach to worship, we must begin by pointing out that Judaism is a liturgical religion. This is true not only of Judaism in its rabbinical forms, but of Judaism in the *Tanakh* as well. The Levites in the Temple sang the Psalms, apparently in antiphonal choirs. The *Tanakh* contains many formulas to be repeated verbatim. There are also liturgical elements in the New Testament. Moreover, the Protestant denominations which favor "free" worship generally develop formats just as rigid as the liturgical approaches they oppose. Suffice it to say that liturgy, properly used, does not keep the Holy Spirit from having his way in the worship service.

The main liturgies in Judaism are:

- The *Siddur*, the prayerbook for the daily and *Shabbat* synagogue services, as well as certain other synagogue and home services.
- The *Machzor*, for the High Holydays, containing the synagogue prayers for *Rosh-HaShanah* and *Yom-Kippur.*
- The *Haggadah*, containing the service to be read at home during the Passover *Seder*.
- Home and synagogue liturgies for other festivals, *e.g., Sukkot, Chanukah, Purim, Shavu'ot* (the term *machzor* is also used for these).
- Liturgies for the life-cycle events.

A number of efforts have been made to "Messianize" these liturgies, but none have reflected the concerted effort or won the general approval of the Messianic Jewish community as a whole. Therefore, I want to suggest a few principles for those who wish to develop Messianic Jewish liturgy:

First, the Messianic Jewish version of a liturgy should be based on the Orthodox Jewish version. The Conservative and Reform liturgies are derived from the Orthodox one, and we don't need a modification of a modification. (Actually there are several Orthodox versions because the ethnic communities have evolved minor variations, but these pose no significant obstacles.)

Second, a Messianic Jewish version should consist of the Orthodox version with additions and subtractions. The additions will express specifically Messianic aspects of our faith in the framework of the given prayers; these additions could be, for example, New Testament citations, affirmations of New Testament theological truths, or expressions of unity with the Body of the Messiah. The subtractions will be words, phrases, and perhaps even entire prayers that are inconsistent with or irrelevant to Messianic Jewish faith.

Third, the published Messianic version of a liturgy should include the entire Orthodox version, with the subtractions included but clearly indicated, and the additions also indicated. Thus anyone will be able to tell at once how the Messianic version differs from the Orthodox one. The reason for doing this is to set up a basis for discussion with non-Messianic Jews, as well as to educate our own people. The published version should be well indexed (this will be a welcome change from most published liturgies), and coded to indicate optional elements for those who wish shorter services. Some commentary should be included, for many people want to understand the origins and functions of the prayers they are being asked to recite. Related songs and readings will be appreciated. In most instances the published version should be in both Hebrew and the vernacular language.

One question remains: who will use Messianic Jewish liturgy? Is there a demand for it? If I am right that Messianic Judaism will not make significant inroads in the Jewish community without interacting seriously with the Judaism that exists today, then we have no alternative to creating Messianic Jewish liturgy. Even if it should turn out that there is no demand for this liturgy for worship purposes, it would be needed just for the sake of interacting with the Jewish liturgical materials.

Actually I think the Gospel can be well communicated through the medium of Messianic Jewish liturgy. Moreover, such liturgy can express our faith and who we are as Messianic Jews. It is a shame to miss the opportunity, and I believe God will bless the work.

Related to liturgy but not exactly the same are devotional anthologies and songbooks. In connection with songwriting, I will say that in Israel more than a hundred songs in Hebrew have been written and published in recent years and are in use by the local congregations. However, most of them are brief and use Bible texts, although some draw from the *Siddur.* As yet we have very few original hymns in Hebrew, but we do have translations of traditional Christian hymns into excellent Hebrew by Moshe I. Ben-Maeir and Amikam Tavor. However these are characteristically sung to the traditional Christian melodies, which convey no Jewish flavor at all. I suggest that talented composers set these translated hymns—whose words are superb—to more Jewish or Israeli melodies.

6. *Gentile Christians And Messianic Judaism*

Does Messianic Judaism rebuild the middle wall of partition between Messianic Jews and Gentile Christians? or between Messianic Jewish congregations and Gentile-oriented churches? Are Gentile Christians in Messianic Judaism being offered second-class citizenship? Does separatism lurk in the wings? We will explore several issues related to this question.

But first let us reaffirm that Messianic Gentiles and Messianic Jews are equal before God in the Body of the Messiah. There is no room in the Messianic Community for invidious comparisons between Jewish and non-Jewish believers. This is basic. On this foundation we can build.

a. Conversion Of Gentile Christians To Judaism

Recall that a Messianic Jew was defined as a person born of a Jewish mother or who converted to Judaism, who is a genuine believer, and who positively acknowledges his Jewishness.[63] We asked whether a Gentile member of a Messianic Jewish congregation may call himself a Messianic Jew and concluded that he should not. Suppose, however, that a Gentile Christian who knows he is not a Jew wants to become one. We then have the conversion issue—and it's a touchy one.

Given that no Gentile needs to become Jewish in order to be saved,[64] why would a Gentile Christian want to convert to Judaism? One can imagine conversions of convenience for the spouse of a Messianic Jew, or for a Gentile Christian living or wanting to live in the State of Israel; but no religion, Judaism included, looks favorably on converts with ulterior motives. Judaism rightly considers *yirat-HaShem,* "fear of God," as the only legitimate reason for converting. If a Gentile Christian's fear of God includes not only commitment to the Messiah, but also an equal commitment to the Jewish people, including the desire to serve God and his Messiah as a Jew, then it would seem that he qualifies for conversion.

Or does he? Does Scripture allow a Gentile Christian to convert to Judaism at all? Sha'ul wrote,

> Let each person live the life the Lord has assigned him and live it in the condition he was in when God called him. This is the rule I lay down in all the congregations. Was someone already circumcised when he was called? Then he should not try to remove the marks of his circumcision. Was someone uncircumcised when he was called? He shouldn't get circumcised. Being circumcised means nothing, and being uncircumcised means nothing; what does mean some-

63. See Chapter II, Section B-3.
64. Acts 15:1-29.
65. 1 Corinthians 7:17-20, *Jewish New Testament.*

> thing is keeping God's commandments. Each person should remain in the condition he was in when he was called.[65]
>
> What the Messiah has freed us for is freedom! Therefore, stand firm, and don't let yourselves be tied up again to a yoke of slavery. Mark my words—I, Sha'ul, tell you that if you [merely] get circumcised [without going on to do what joining the Jewish people entails], the Messiah will be of no advantage to you at all! Again, I warn you: any man who gets circumcised is obligated to observe the entire *Torah* [as Judaism understands it]! You who are trying to be declared righteous by God through legalism have severed yourselves from the Messiah! You have fallen away from God's grace! For it is by the power of the Spirit, who works in us because we trust and are faithful, that we confidently expect our hope of attaining righteousness to be fulfilled. When we are united with the Messiah Yeshua, neither being circumcised nor being uncircumcised matters; what matters is trusting faithfulness expressing itself through love.[66]

For years I understood these two texts as prohibiting Gentile Christians from converting to Judaism, but an article by an Orthodox Jewish philosopher named Michael Wyschogrod changed my mind.[67] (Incidentally, he also co-authored a book against "Jewish Christianity."[68]) In his article he notes that rabbis are required by *halakhah* to discourage potential converts in order to winnow out those who are insincere and suggests that Sha'ul's remarks are of this character, not absolute prohibitions.

Since Wyschogrod is a philosopher and not an historian, I had doubts. This "normal discouragement" is known from

---

66. Galatians 5:1-6, *Jewish New Testament.*
67. Michael Wyschogrod, "Judaism and Evangelical Christianity," in Marc H. Tanenbaum, Marvin R. Wilson and A. James Rudin, *Evangelicals and Jews in Conversation* (Grand Rapids, Michigan: Baker Book House, 1978), pp. 34-52.
68. David Berger and Michael Wyschogrod *(op. cit.* in Chapter IV, footnote 55).

third-to-fifth century sources,[69] but Sha'ul was writing in the first century. In that century Yeshua spoke of the *Torah*-teachers and *P'rushim* who "compass sea and land to make one proselyte,"[70] which is the opposite of "normal discouragement." Was there any first-century precedent for discouraging Gentiles from converting to Judaism? Yes, there was. According to Josephus, Izates, King of Adiabene (near the Persian Gulf) from 36 to 60 C.E., was convinced of the truth of Judaism by a Jewish merchant named Ananias [Chananyah]; his mother, Helena, however, feared that if he got circumcised the people would not bear his rule. Chananyah reassured him "that he might worship God without being circumcised, even though he did resolve to follow the Jewish law entirely; which worship of God was of a superior nature to circumcision." He was persuaded for the time being, but he had not lost his desire to convert completely; so when another Jew named El'azar (who evidently was more missionary-minded) saw him reading from the *Torah* and chided him for not doing what the *Torah* says, he had himself circumcised. This took place before he became king in 36 C.E.[71]

This evidence convinces me that if a Gentile Christian wants to identify fully with the Jewish people, the New Testament allows him to become a Jew. He should accept the whole *Torah* as understood in the form of Judaism to which he is converting (this is implied by Galatians 5:3, where "*Torah* "seems to include Oral *Torah*), except where it conflicts with the New Covenant.

However, because of the reservations any non-Messianic Jewish converting agency would be likely to have about accepting into Judaism a Gentile who continues believing in Jesus, there remains a problem about Gentile Christian conver-

69. *Ruth Rabbah* 2:16, *Yevamot* 47a-47b.

70. Mattityahu [Matthew] 23:15.

71. Josephus, *Antiquities of the Jews*, 20:2:3-4; *Encyclopedia Judaica*, Volume 1, pp. 267-268, 924; compare *Genesis Rabbah* 46:10.

sion to Judaism. If the convert conceals the fact that he continues to believe in Jesus, the ethical issue is obvious. However, I know of an instance in which a Gentile Christian studied Orthodox Judaism for over a year; when he was about to enter the *mikveh* for the conversion ceremony he informed his rabbi that he still believed Yeshua is the Messiah. The rabbi was taken aback but allowed the ceremony to continue, and eventually (after an unusual delay and several requests) mailed him a conversion certificate. Another Jewish believer commented that even though this man had not concealed his faith, the rabbi had not really understood him; instead of realizing he was serious, the rabbi had probably thought he was making a casual remark and that in the light of his year of Jewish study and practice his vestigial Christianity would soon drop away. In other words, the person spoke, and the rabbi heard, but there was no real communication. I will leave the discussion here, unfinished as it is, adding only that while some Jews would regard any Gentile Christian conversion to Judaism as fraudulent if the convert continues to believe in Jesus, others respect whoever voluntarily and sincerely throws in his lot with the Jewish people, even if he retains his faith in Yeshua.

Messianic Judaism has another problem with regard to conversion of Gentile Christians by non-Messianic Jewish rabbis, namely, that if we honor their conversions we are thereby recognizing the authority of these non-Messianic Jewish rabbis in our own community. Doing that is something which ought to be discussed, not assumed.

In principle there is no reason why Messianic Judaism could not perform conversions. But until Messianic Judaism has a clearer idea of what being Jewish in a Messianic setting means, it seems premature to convert Gentiles, enjoining them to "observe the entire Torah" (Galatians 5:3) before we ourselves are sure what the "entire *Torah,*" understood from a New Testament viewpoint, is!

For Messianic Jews there is one final point, a sociological one: if many Gentile Christians were to convert to Judaism (whether through Messianic or non-Messianic rabbis), their numbers could overwhelm the born Jews in the movement, adding another problematic dimension to the relationship between Messianic Jews and the non-Messianic Jewish community.

b. Intermarriage Between Messianic Jews And Gentile Christians

Should a Messianic Jew marry a Gentile Christian? On the one hand, the New Testament permits it—any two believers may marry, according to 1 Corinthians 7:39.

One aspect of such a marriage is the potential for positive witness: the couple's common faith in Yeshua should help them to have a successful marriage even if others have contrary expectations.

On the other hand, Orthodox Judaism does not recognize the marriage of a Jew to a Gentile, and many nonreligious Jews feel uneasy about it as well. This is because intermarriage is considered a major threat to the survival of the Jewish community. Intermarriage rates in some areas run as high as 50%, and dire predictions are being made that if this continues (along with low birthrates), the American Jewish community will dwindle from six million to one million in the twenty-first century. In such a context, any Jewish-Gentile marriage is considered a contribution to catastrophe.

Moreover, Messianic Jews are sometimes told by non-Messianic Jews, "You may stay Jewish yourself, but what about your children? Growing up in a Christian environment they will lose their Jewish identity." And in the past this has been a cogent accusation. We can only hope that by developing the Messianic Jewish community we will at last be able to overcome this criticism. But intermarriage certainly makes the task more difficult, not easier!

There is an asymmetry between the Gentile Christian husband with a Messianic Jewish wife and the Gentile Christian wife with a Messianic Jewish husband. Since the mother's influence on young children tends to be stronger than that of the father, and since the children of a Jewish mother are halakhically Jewish, their children may have a stronger Jewish identity. But the family's life and ministry, being determined more often by the husband, will tend to be Gentile-oriented—except in the rare instance of a Gentile Christian man who really wants to be involved in Messianic Judaism. A Messianic Jewish husband and a Gentile Christian wife can be expected, in most instances, to be involved in a Messianic Jewish lifestyle, as determined by the husband; but the children may grow up with less Jewish knowledge, unless the husband takes an active part in the children's education. Of course there are many exceptions to these generalizations.

Summing up, in regard to intermarriage (another touchy subject!): how should New Covenant *halakhah* weigh the varying claims of Jews, Gentiles, Messianic Judaism, the couple and their families—not to speak of God?

c. Gentile Christian Participation In Messianic Jewish Congregations

A number of interesting issues arise for relationships between Gentile Christians and Messianic Jews in Messianic Jewish congregations.

Let us return to the fact that Jews and Gentiles are equal before the Messiah. The question is whether this equality should be expressed in all Messianic Jewish congregational activity. For example, should a Gentile Christian be given an *aliyah* (a call-up) to read from the *Torah* scroll in a Messianic synagogue? Equality would say yes, but the Jewishness of reading from the *Torah* scroll might say no. The fact that the *Torah* requirements under the New Covenant are different for Jews and Gentiles might lead to an outcome in which Gentiles are not involved in specifically Jewish activities. Yet equality (no middle wall of partition, no second class citizens in the Kingdom) might dictate that he (or she, following the pattern of Conservative Judaism) be allowed.

Should Gentile Christians be elders in Messianic Jewish congregations? A more cogent question is whether there is any scriptural ground whatever for excluding them. Indeed, wouldn't excluding them vitiate the unity of Jew and Gentile under the New Covenant, since eldership is specifically a New Covenant mandate? Yet isn't there a risk, if they become elders or join Messianic Jewish congregations in great numbers, that the Jewish witness will be spoiled? But is that a proper consideration? Perhaps they should be pastors and elders only temporarily, until Messianic Jewish leadership can be found? If so, when should responsibility be relinquished to the Messianic Jews? Is there a tendency for Gentile Christians in such a situation to hang on to leadership too long?—and if so, is this merely an example of the "missionary syndrome" found throughout the world, in effect a kind of colonialism which quashes and enervates local development? I have heard the view expressed that Gentile Christians should be on tap, not on top, serving the Messianic Jews, not telling them what to do. But such an attitude seems far from scriptural, for all of us are to serve one another.

d. Legislation Of Jewish Practices In Messianic Jewish Congregations

Congregations sometimes put requirements on their members. In a Messianic Jewish congregation some of these requirements may be to adopt certain Jewish practices. Should Jewish practices legislated by a congregation be demanded of Gentiles as well as Jews? Is this Judaizing, which Scripture prohibits?[72] Or do Gentile Christians in a Messianic Jewish congregation—even if they constitute a majority—implicitly agree to conform to Messianic Jewish patterns? What about practices not offi-

72. Galatians2:ll-21.

cially "legislated" but understood by all to be "how we do things around here"?

As a specific example, what about circumcision of Gentile believers in a Messianic Jewish congregation? Would it be for children only? If for adults too, it can only mean for conversion to Judaism—on which, see above. If Gentile babies are circumcised, would the same ceremony be used as for a Messianic Jewish baby—including coming under the covenant of Abraham? I would think not.

Should Gentile Christians be involved in making decisions on what practices shall be followed by a Messianic Jewish congregation? It seems odd to have Gentiles telling Jews what is Jewish to do, yet equality must be preserved and discrimination avoided.

To what degree may or should Gentile members of Messianic Jewish congregations imitate or take on Jewish practices by choice? Should they wear *kippotl tallitotl tzitziyotl* lay *teflllirf!* My gut reaction is that their doing so would be peculiar. What does it signify when Gentiles do these things? What would it signify if Gentile Christians in Gentile congregations began doing these things? What does it signify when Messianic Jews do these things? When non-Messianic Jews do them?

e. Ways In Which Gentile Christians Can Help Messianic Judaism

Gentile Christians, including those not directly involved in the Messianic Jewish movement, can help the movement. How? Organizationally, with personnel, financially; by teaching; by correcting Gentile Christian theology and ideology in the light of Messianic Judaism; by advising, encouraging and helping those attempting to create Messianic Jewish theology and practices different from those usually found in the Church; by evangelizing non-Messianic Jews; by learning more about Jewish culture, Judaism and the Jewish roots of Christianity—and by encouraging Messianic Jews to minister to the Church.

7. *Messianic Judaism And The Jewish Community*

a. Can Messianic Judaism Be a Fifth Branch of Judaism?

Do we want to be? Some of us do, others are satisfied to be more separatist with respect to the unsaved Jewish community. Does the idea of our being a branch of Judaism violate New Testament canons? If the overlapping circles of Figures 3 and 5F are our model, then the answer is: No, because we do not leave the Messianic circle when we call ourselves a branch of Judaism. Will the Church object? Some parts won't, other branches which understand Messianic Judaism less well will. Will organized Jewry object? Absolutely; they will do all they can to stop us, at every step of the way. If so, in what sense would Messianic Judaism be a fifth branch and not a fifth wheel? Answer: in a scriptural sense; for Scripture can't be changed by mere human opposition. It was God, not the Jewish community, who made us Jewish; so the Jewish community lacks both the authority and the power to make us not be a branch of Judaism if that is what we want to be.

b. Relating To The Jewish Community Structure

What should Messianic Jews do in relation to the institutionally organized Jewish community structure, e.g., the United Jewish Appeal, Jewish community centers, Jewish philanthropies, Zionist organizations? Can Messianic Judaism be supportive of them? Should we be? When? How? Which conditions that might be asked of us should we be willing to submit to, and which not? Sometimes we find ourselves in this bind: we wish to be pure, not conditioning our support on a *quid pro quo* from the Jewish community—such as allowing us to be public about our faith. On the other hand, ought we to agree to be silent? "If you will not confess me before men, I will not confess you before my Father in heaven."[73] But if we consent to silence, are we allowing ourselves to be used? And if so, is that bad? Etc.

73. Mattityahu [Matthew] 10:33.

c. *Behavior Of Messianic Jews In Non-Messianic Jewish Settings*

I commissioned someone to knit me several *kippot* with *"Yeshua HaMashiach* " written on them. I wear them on the streets of Jerusalem and to meetings of my congregation. Once, without thinking much about it, I wore one to a Messianic *bar-mitzvah* at the *Kotel* (the Western or "Wailing" Wall). It attracted the unfavorable attention of some Orthodox Jews, one of whom snatched it off my head and burned it. Initially I was angry and pursued him, but (with a little help from my friends) I remembered that the *Kotel* area is officially regarded as a synagogue—and indeed, not just any synagogue, but the holiest one in the world. In such a place religious law is enforced as the law of the State of Israel, and since *halakhah* probably has something to say about a *Yeshua kippah,* it seemed wise to finesse the matter and return to the *bar-mitzvah* (someone loaned me a more conventional *yarmulke).* Having told that story on myself, I will say that as a rule I don't cause problems in synagogues and don't recommend it; better to follow the expected canons of behavior, praying, learning and letting the Spirit reveal opportunities for personal evangelism.

However, I continue to wear a *Yeshua kippah* in nonreligious settings, where, of course, it stimulates interest and encourages good conversations. I suppose the key is to create interest in the Messiah Yeshua—and this can include unfavorable interest, which is generally better than none—without violating legal, moral or ethical standards. The organization "Jews for Jesus" has been in the front lines in pioneering the art of making Yeshua known to a public not especially interested in hearing about him, without violating the aforementioned legal, moral and ethical limits.

d. *What Kind Of Judaism Should Messianic Judaism Look To For Standards?*

There might be purists (of a sort) who would say, None—we should develop our own standards, or, We should look to God for standards. But we do not live in isolation. Judaism is not simply whatever a group of Jews decide to do. Should we look to Diaspora Judaism, Israel Judaism, rabbinic Judaism, secular Judaism, ethnic Yiddishkeit (which originated in the Diaspora)? Or should we develop a Judaism based on the Bible alone? This has already been discussed.[74] In a recent issue of *The Hebrew Christian,* the Israeli Jewish believer Baruch Moaz had an article called "How We Should Celebrate Passover,"[75] in which he suggested several novel practices, some of which could be quite striking but so differ from what is customary that we must ask: would they isolate us from what other Jews can recognize as Jewish? Or could we hope to bring forth our customs into the world and have them understood and appreciated? It remains to be seen.

e. Topics Of Special Interest To The Jewish Community

Among the topics Messianic Judaism ought to explore which would be of special interest to the Jewish Community are: the Holocaust; antisemitism in Christianity and in Messianic and non-Messianic Judaism (self-hate); the Jewishness of the New Testament; and the role of the State of Israel (on this see more in Chapter VII).

f. The Evangelistic Imperative

No matter what is said about our relating to the Jewish community, Messianic Judaism can never ignore the evangelistic imperative. On the one hand, our love and help is genuine and not merely a means to an end; on the other, our desire to bring people to salvation is itself an expression of our love. This is a delicate balance; in the end only God, who knows our hearts, can judge our honesty and integrity.

---

74. See Section B-2 above.
75. Baruch Moaz, "How We Should Celebrate Passover," in *The Hebrew Christian,* Volume 60, Number 1 (March-May 1987), pp. 14-24.

8. *Conclusion: Torah! Torah! Torah!*

What I have written here does not read like a rabbi writing about *halakhah.* That is for a very simple reason: I am not a rabbi. However, by writing about the issues *of halakhah* as best I can, I hope to stimulate others to advance thought on these subjects. For the key to reuniting the paths of the Church and the Synagogue is the role of the Law. Our rallying cry must be: Torah! Torah! Torah!—understood in the Spirit of the Messiah.

But the Spirit of the Messiah is the Spirit of Holiness. Without holiness Messianic Judaism must fail altogether. To this we now turn.

CHAPTER VI
HOLINESS

A. THE WEIGHT OF HOLINESS

The most important element in a Messianic Jewish vision is holiness. Not self-righteousness, not a "holier-than-thou" attitude, but "holiness, without which no one will see the Lord."[1] My chapter on it is the shortest, but I compare holiness with the last two verses of Ecclesiastes, where the Preacher writes,

> The end of the matter, all having been heard, is: Fear God! And keep his commandments! This is what being human is all about. For God will bring every deed into judgment—even every hidden thing—whether it is good or evil.[2]

Ecclesiastes is like a seesaw balanced askew, with a very heavy stone on the short end, more than offsetting all the light weights on the long end. The Preacher made wonderful plans, did marvellous works, exercised great wisdom, and yet concluded it was all vanity and striving after wind—when done apart from fearing God and his judgment, so that one keeps his commandments.

Likewise with this or any other vision for Messianic Judaism. I appreciate Herzl's epigram which inspired the Zionist

1. Messianic Jews [Hebrews] 12:14.
2. Ecclesiastes 12:13-14, my translation.

movement: “If you will it, it is no dream.” But in the case of Messianic Judaism, neither dreaming it nor willing it is enough. Unless we have the mind of God, our own dreamings and willings are mere striving after wind. In attaining the goals of Messianic Judaism holiness outweighs all dreams, efforts and ambitions.

B. PLANNING VERSUS HOLINESS?

In the final chapter I will set forth a sketch of a plan for action, complete with goals for Messianic Judaism and indications of how to achieve them. I will say we need such-and-such a program, such-and-such research, such-and-such books and materials, places and buildings, organizations, institutions and personnel. Well—do we really need them? Or do we need to live lives of holiness, fearing God and keeping his commandments?

It’s a bad question. I have set up a false dichotomy, pitting two alternatives against each other as if they were mutually exclusive. They are not. Holiness and planning can go together, as was clear to the author of the book called *God’s Purpose, Man’s Plans.*[3]

Holiness means doing everything in life in the fear of God and in obedience to his commands. This includes planning, programming, building, administering, researching, writing, working, playing.... There are clearly times to retreat from the bustle of daily activity and “wait upon the Lord,” as we learn from the lives of Yeshua, Elijah, Moses and Joseph among others. But these retreats prepare us for advances. The Bible teaches that progress comes in conjunction with human planning and willing participation, not from passive indecision. The planning must be done with a willingness to set the plan aside in order to follow God’s immediate instruction—we worship God, not the plan. But when we don’t hear such an instruc-

3. Ed Dayton, *God’s Purpose, Man’s Plans* (Monrovia, California: MARC, rev. ed. 1974).

tion, we follow the plan. God's blessing may come in a manner unrelated to the plan, yet the planning itself will have been in obedience to God.

C. THREE LEVELS OF HOLINESS

1. *Individual Holiness*

Individual holiness is loving God with all your heart and with all your soul and with all your strength.[4] Others have written so well about holiness in a person's private life that I have nothing to add. We should pray, repent, forgive; commit ourselves to God and to one another and to spreading the Gospel; be discipled and disciple others; be involved with a local congregation; love God and our neighbor and love not the world—except like God, who "so loved the world that he gave his only Son, in order that everyone who trusts in him may have eternal life, instead of being utterly destroyed."[5] We should avoid selfish concerns, pride, fleshly methods, abuse of power; we should set aside our differences, regarding other above self; we should make real on earth the unity that is already ours in the heavenlies; we should, by faith do the good works that God has prepared for us to do; we should keep close to God.

2. *Interpersonal Holiness*

I call it interpersonal holiness, the New Testament calls it loving one's brother,[6] and the Jewish community calls it being a *mentsh.* The word comes from the German *Mensch* (man), but a *mentsh*—either a man or a woman—is more than just *homo sapiens:* a *mentsh* is a real person, what a human being ought to be, upright, ethical, caring, soft at the right time and firm at the right time—as in Rudyard Kipling's "If":

---

4. Deuteronomy 6:5, Mark 12:30.
5. Yochanan [John] 3:16, *Jewish New Testament (op. cit.* in chapter II, footnote 20).
6. 1 Yochanan [1 John] 4:7-21.

"If you can keep your head when those about you
Are losing theirs and blaming it on you,
If you can [manifest a long list of other noble
character traits],
Then yours is the world and all that is in it,
And what is more, you'll be a man," a *mentsh,* "my
son."

Being a *mentsh* also means getting along with each other, allowing that on many matters of doctrinal and practical difference we can have our own opinions and still treat as brothers and sisters those with whom we disagree.

For example, consider the charismatic movement, a cross-denominational subgrouping. Messianic Jews can be found on both sides of the charismatic issue. My experience is that charismatics and non-charismatics can get along well with each other, but that anti-charismatics and hyper-charismatics have problems. What do I mean? Charismatics say that the gifts of the Holy Spirit[7] are being manifested in the Body of the Messiah today as promised in the Bible, and say they are experiencing them. Non-charismatics generally believe the gifts are real but are not being manifested in the way the charismatics claim, and say the experiences may be from God but are not identical with the gifts as God gave them in the first century. The two disagree but respect each other. They can worship together in a charismatic or in a non-charismatic service, so long as each observes the order prevailing in the meeting. Anti-charismatics find the charismatic phenomena, attitudes and doctrines offensive and not of God and cannot abide them. Hyper-charismatics in effect treat anyone who is not charismatic as an inferior Christian or perhaps not even saved. Both usually hold their views so strongly and gratingly that others must exercise great forbearance to suffer their company. Holiness implies both having correct doctrine and being able to get along with our brothers, but a sharp conflict like this makes holiness hard work! Perhaps it could not be otherwise, and

7. As listed, for example, in 1 Corinthians 12:29-30.

shouldn't be—so that we will rely on God's grace to lead us to harmony, conforming us more and more to the pattern of Yeshua.

The Messianic Jewish movement is divided by this issue and also by the tensions between Messianic Jews (in the narrow sense) and Hebrew Christians, as well as by conflicting loyalties.[8] In all these areas study and forbearance are needed. But more than that, we should not permit these differences to turn us away from one another. Yeshua prayed that we would be one.[9] It is easy to be united with those with whom we agree, but the real miracle is when we can have genuine love for those with whom we disagree, enabling us to work harmoniously with them. This is possible through Yeshua: "Lo, I am with you always"[10]—with you-plural—even when you disagree with each other.

Actually, most conflicts in the Messianic Jewish movement (and all other movements) revolve around neither doctrines nor practices but personalities and power struggles. Sha'ul's letter to the Galatians lists fifteen sins which exclude a person from the Kingdom of God; the majority reflect bad interpersonal relationships—"feuding, fighting, jealousy, anger, selfish ambition, factionalism, intrigue and envy."[11] My impression is that in the last several years the Messianic Jewish movement has matured, and its leaders have become more willing to approach each other lovingly to deal with differences. We have a long way to go, but with the Messiah as our model we will keep running with endurance in the contest set before us.

A common vision and a common awareness of the dangers facing Messianic Jews can help unite us. My hope is that this book will contribute to such unity. But I am aware that a book of this kind can just as easily be used in the service of causing division as in the service of expressing singleness of mind and heart. So my prayer as I write is that that will not

8. See Chapter VII, Section A-3.
9. Yochanan [John] 17:20-21.
10. Mattityahu [Matthew] 28:20.
11. Galatians 5:19-21.

happen, and instead, that we will all keep close to God, and through him close to each other.

3. *Communal Holiness*

We are indeed each of us singly connected with God, yet we are collectively a Body and individually members thereof.[12] Our holiness must be expressed corporately in a way which singles us out as a community from the communities organized in the world's way. Group holiness implies social action, Gospel witness and, as a community, remaining close to God.

D. HOLY IMPLIES SAVED—AND VICE VERSA

Only saved people can be holy. No one is saved from sin and its consequence, eternal separation from God, apart from Yeshua the Messiah. But standards have been lowered—not God's but man's. Many people think they are born again when they are not. Here is reality: one can have extraordinary, supernatural experiences and still not be saved. One can be miraculously healed of a fatal disease and know that God did it and still not be saved. One can experience the very presence of God and still not be saved.

In recent years some have come to confuse experiences and feelings with salvation. The criteria for salvation are clear in Scripture: repent; accept God's grace and forgiveness by trusting in Yeshua as Messiah, Savior and Lord; acknowledge him publicly; be immersed; and by the power of the Holy Spirit live a holy life. "Lord" means "commander." When Yeshua is your Lord, he tells you what to do, and you do it. "By their fruits shall ye know them."[13]

A person who is not totally dedicated to living a holy life is not saved. That is what being saved means. God's making you

12. 1 Corinthians 12:27.
13. Mattityahu [Matthew] 7:16, King James Version.

righteous in *his* sight *(not self-righteous!)* means that you are being conformed daily to the righteous image of the Messiah himself. He does not produce halfway dedication. Halfway holy is no-way born-again. Only saved people can be holy, but only holy people are saved.

As this book goes to print, tawdry scandals and stories of self-seeking greed have rocked the Christian community in America, bringing shame to the Gospel. There can be only one reaction from genuinely saved people, who are the only kind of people who can build a Messianic Jewish movement—a yet stronger commitment to "holiness, without which no one will see the Lord."

E. POWER

> "But you will receive power when the *Ruach HaKodesh* comes upon you."[14]

We need the power of God! Without it Messianic Judaism will be dead, dry, incapable of doing anything useful in the world. With God's power Messianic Judaism will change history, ministering God's life, holiness, beauty, love, mercy and righteousness—just as in New Testament times.

But how can we have this power? Not by aiming at power, but by seeking God! "Seek first his rulership and his righteousness, and all these things will be given to you as well."[15] We must reach out boldly with faith that God will fulfill his promise of Holy Spirit power for us, personally.[16]

Power? "I tell you that whoever trusts in me will also do the works I do! Indeed, he will do greater ones"[17]—such as witnessing to what God has done through Yeshua in history and in personal lives, showing forth God's love, praying in the Holy Spirit, and exercising the gifts of the Holy Spirit, so that

14. Acts 1:8, *Jewish New Testament.*
15. Mattityahu [Matthew] 6:33, *Jewish New Testament.*
16. 1 Corinthians 14:1.
17. Yochanan [John] 14:12, *Jewish New Testament.*

when God's truth is perceived, his love felt, our prayers answered, and his healings, signs and wonders experienced, people repent and are saved. "And [Yeshua's disciples] went out and proclaimed [the Gospel] everywhere, the Lord working with them and confirming the message by the accompanying signs."[18]

One caution: not all spiritual power is from God. Though limited by God,[19] the Adversary (Satan) and his demons are God's enemies in the spirit realm offering their own ungodly kind of power. The core of our faith is love. As we build our movement, we incorporate or adapt elements from non-Messianic Judaism and Christian tradition that can enhance this core of faith and love. But since non-Messianic Judaism is not submitted to Yeshua the Messiah, and much Christian tradition is of merely human origin, we must guard against the spiritual powers of darkness[20] which attach themselves to these systems. For example, when we study the *Talmud,* we must not open ourselves to a spirit of religiosity, or of legalism, or of ethnic pride, or to any other demonic spirit that would use our interest in expressing our Jewishness to quench the Holy Spirit, who alone can guide us into all truth. We cannot allow Jewishness, or even the Messianic Jewish movement, to become an idol. "Thou shalt have no other gods before me."[21]

So I conclude the chapter on holiness with this final exhortation and caution: seek God's power, because without it the Messianic Jewish movement will amount to nothing; yet, do not seek power for its own sake or even for the sake of the movement, but for the sake of glorifying God.

---

18. Mark 16:20, *Jewish New Testament.*
19. Job 1-2.
20. See Galatians 3:1-3, Ephesians 6:10-18, 2 Corinthians 10:3-5.
21. Exodus 20:3.

CHAPTER VII
PROGRAM

In this outline of an action program for Messianic Judaism I have tried to paint a very quick sketch on a very large canvas. I hope I haven't left too many blank spots. I will be pleased if some correct the sketch and others add color and texture. I will not be disappointed if the entire canvas has to be discarded and another used. I am certain that the Messianic Jewish movement will progress and that it will need to think about how.

A. THE MESSIANIC JEWISH COMMUNITY TODAY

1. *Numbers, Structure*

Before presenting this program, I must paint another picture, also quickly, of today's Messianic Jewish Community.

It is difficult to give numbers, partly because of definitional problems (Who is Jewish? Messianic? a Messianic Jew?),[1] and partly because the Jewish believers, however defined, are often hard to locate and count. In recent years I have heard estimates in the 50,000-100,000 range for the number of Jewish believers in America, but some would say fewer and others more. In Israel there may be 1,000-3,000 Jewish believers in 25-30 congregations, some three to twelve of which are more or less Jewishly oriented. In Great Britain the figure I hear is 3,000-

---

1. See Chapter II, Section B. On earlier Messianic Jewish history see Chapter III, Section F.

5,000 Jewish believers, and in other western countries 1/2 to 1% of the Jewish population might be a good first approximation. According to Richard Wurmbrand, the Jewish believer ransomed from Communist Romania after fourteen years in prison for his faith, there are at least six thousand Jewish believers in Moscow; by extrapolation Russian Jewry must include several tens of thousands. Call all these figures guesstimates, and let it go at that.[2]

There are in the United States over 120 Messianic Jewish congregations, mostly independent but some affiliated with Christian denominations. There are missions focusing on Jewish evangelism; some sponsor congregations, others have regular fellowship meetings. There are radio and television ministries, publishers, schools and camps associated with our movement. There are many Jewish believers in Gentile-oriented churches (more than 200 in one large California church), and other Jewish believers who are virtually isolated. There is an umbrella organization for individual Messianic Jews, the Messianic Jewish Alliance of America. For congregations there are four organizations: the Union of Messianic Jewish congregations, the International Alliance of Messianic Congregations and Synagogues, the Association of Messianic Congregations, and an intradenominational grouping within the Assemblies of God.

The International Hebrew Christian Alliance, founded in 1925 in Great Britain, where it is still headquartered, has thirteen affiliated national alliances—in Argentina, Australia, Brazil, Canada, France, Germany, Great Britain, Holland, New Zealand, South Africa, Switzerland, the United States and Uruguay. Israel has recently organized an alliance; as of this writing it is not yet affiliated with the IHCA. A number of missions to Jews are headquartered in these and other countries.

2. David Barrett, editor of the *World Christian Encyclopedia,* writes, surprisingly, "Some 2% of all Jews (350,000) are believers in Jesus Christ." *(AD 2000 Together,* Fall 1988 issue, p. 21.)

2. *What Unites Us*

What unites us Messianic Jews is being committed to God, with the Messiah Yeshua and his Holy Spirit in us; being part of his Body, the Messianic Community, brothers in spirit to all Messianic Jews and Gentiles; being Jewish, brothers in the flesh to all Messianic and non-Messianic Jews; being concerned for evangelism generally, and for the Jewish people in particular; having in common a measure of tension as well as brotherhood in relating to both the Church and the Jewish Community; and having a sense of our future (to which this book is intended to contribute).

3. *What Divides Us*

What divides Messianic Jews from each other? Theological differences can do it, such as where we stand on Messianic Judaism (in the narrow sense) vs. Hebrew Christianity; assimila-tionism vs. Jewishness; Messianic Jewish congregations or not; charismatic or not; distinctive doctrines related to where we happen to have studied or whom we happen to have associated with; our approach to ecumenism (some Jews whose Messianic experience has been in a Protestant environment question whether it is possible for Jewish Catholics to be brothers in the Lord); differences about end-time prophecy. The remedy is to keep in mind Sha'ul's [Paul's] words:

> "For now we see obscurely in a mirror, but then it will be face to face. Now I know partly; then I will know fully, just as God has fully known me."[3]

Differences in practice and method can do it. A leading Messianic Jew was once asked to leave a Hebrew Christian congregation because he wore a *kippah* at the meeting. Jewish believers differ over whether, in what measure and how to

---

3. 1 Corinthians 13:12.

evangelize Jews. The remedy is to let a hundred flowers bloom, but water them with living water.[4]

Conflicting loyalties can do it, whether to denominations, congregations, para-congregational organizations (missions, fellowship groups, ministries), or individuals. The remedy is to put God first.

Power struggles and personality differences can do it. "'I'm for Sha'ul!' 'I'm for Apollos!' 'I'm for Kefa.' 'I'm for the Messiah!'" The admonition, "Don't touch God's anointed!"[5] is frequently a danger signal that someone is grasping for power. The remedy is in Philippians 2:4, "Let each of you look not only to his own interests, but also to the interests of others," with the verses that follow.

Finally, isolation can do it. A group retreats from the marketplace and from the spiritual battle to pietistic platitudes in its own small protected turf, fragmenting our movement and depriving us of each other. The remedy is to "Be strong and of good courage!"[6]

B. PROGRAMMATICS AND MESSIANIC JUDAISM

The word I use for theology-constrained planning is "programmatics." By it I mean the theological discipline of setting forth a program for all or part of the Body of the Messiah. It involves stating for a group of people or an institution purposes, goals, means of attaining the goals, priorities among the goals, determination of necessary resources for reaching the goals, inventorying available resources, and scheduling—in short, the basic elements of planning—but all in a theological and ideological context. Theology (that is, the organized arrangement of biblical truth for a particular people, culture

4. Yochanan [John] 7:38.
5. 1 Corinthians 1:12; see Psalm 105:15.
6. Deuteronomy 31:6, 7, 23; Joshua 1:6, 9, 18. On the need for holiness in resolving our conflicts, see Chapter VI, Section C-2.

and time) and ideology (a coordinated body of ideas about human life and culture, coupled with integrated assertions, theories and aims constituting a social, political and spiritual vision) become the sieve through which goals, means and priorities must pass.

The leaders in the Messianic Jewish movement are not unaware of programmatics. The progress the movement has made since the 1960's can be understood partly in terms of breadth of vision and realization of plans. Most of the leaders are pragmatists, constantly revising their plans in accordance with experience, new knowledge, newly perceived needs, feedback from what has happened so far, external sources of information, and better understanding of Scripture; and may it so continue.

Why is programmatics important? Because "without a vision the people perish." According to George Ladd, this verse, exegetically, means that without a prophetic vision inspired by God the people perish. Therefore what I mean is that programmatics must spell out such a prophetic vision.

Most prophetic visions are contingent. That is, they detail "blessings" if one course of action is followed, and "curses" (unpleasant consequences) if another course of action is followed. Modern decision theory does the same.

Scripture contains an overarching prophetic vision of the Kingdom of God; with this vision we will not perish. Any vision or plan of ours must find its place in this grand plan of God's. The key verse from this grand vision, encouraging us in every contingency, is: "We know that all things work together for good to them that love God, to them who are the called according to his purpose."[7]

Messianic Judaism is unique. No other community is in the position of mediating between, and at the same time belonging to, both parts of the one people of God. Consequently, models appropriate to various church situations do not necessarily fit here. Messianic Judaism is not merely another culturally

7. Romans 8:28.

distinct branch of the Church, like the Korean church or that of the Berber tribe. No ethnic church is faced with passages like Ephesians 2:11 ff.; Galatians 2:1-21, 3:28; Romans 9-11. There is a theological stratum in understanding Messianic Judaism that is nowhere else present.[8] Nothing less than a comprehensive approach to planning, in the light of theology as well as ideology, can clarify the vision of Messianic Judaism so that may aspire to its destiny in the life of the Jews, the Church and the world.

C. INSTITUTIONS WE NEED

1. *Do We Need Institutions At All?*

The importance of having a vision and a plan for creating institutions—and working tirelessly to realize it—is demonstrated by Rabbi Isaac Mayer Wise (1819-1900), the key figure in making Reform Judaism a major component of American Jewry. He arrived in America in the 1840's, and as soon as he oriented himself to conditions he began insisting that American Judaism needed three institutions—an organization for congregations, a rabbinical training institution and a fellowship for rabbis—and a new prayerbook suited to the American environment. The results of his insistence were the Union of American Hebrew Congregations (1873); Hebrew Union College (1875), of which he was the first president; the Central Conference of American Rabbis (1889), of which he was also the first president, an office he held till he died; the Union Prayerbook (which was not the one he favored but which still fulfilled his vision); and a movement which at present claims about a million members and whose infrastructure exists because of this man's indefatigability.

---

8. The theological stratum explains why Jewish evangelism is different from all other kinds, why "contextualization" of the Gospel is inadequate, and why "Type IV evangelism" is needed. See Appendix, Section B.

Many believers are suspicious of institutions. They are suspicious on principle—people are warm and caring, but institutions are cold and heartless, easily becoming vehicles for domination of the many by the few. Although there is a kernel of truth behind this attitude, in what follows I assume that people can stand to think about creating institutions and organizations and can see them more as tools to be used than as monsters to be feared.

In fact, when I talk about a program for creating and developing institutions, I have in mind an environment of community; and by nature, community must be organic, built on interpersonal relationships. Not that the ultimate community must exist before the institutions are created; on the contrary, the purpose of the institutions is to foster community. They are also meant to foster the development of Messianic Jewish identity within the framework of Messianic Jewish community.

My approach will be abstract, rather than historical. What I mean is that I will discuss institutions needed as if nothing existed today filling or partially filling the need. In other words, I will mostly ignore the material I presented in Section A; those involved in the Messianic Jewish movement will know how to fit my outline to the situation as it exists.

For Messianic Judaism to become what it ought to be, we need a "broad movement" ("denominational") organization, we must meet communal needs, and we should develop educational and professional institutions.

2. *Broad Movement ("Denominational") Organization*

I know that the word "denomination" scares people, so I have cooped it up in parentheses and inverted commas where it can do no harm and instead used the awkward term "broad movement" to describe Messianic Judaism in its most wide-ranging sense. The organization is needed to catalyze activities at various levels and foster participation in the community (the currently "in" word for this is "networking"). It should not have authority over congregations and individuals but should facilitate their desire to cooperate. It should have several tiers or categories of membership, like the National Association of Evangelicals (to name an organization familiar to some of my readers). In particular, it should allow for:

Individuals:

- Jewish believers (Messianic Jews) and their spouses (*i.e.,* "regular members").
- Gentile Christians who share our viewpoint and want to encourage us ("supporting members").
- People who may not agree with us but are interested in being kept informed and willing to be associated ("associates"). These could include Christians who are not especially sympathetic to Messianic Judaism, as well as some non-Messianic Jews and secular Gentiles.

Organizations:

- Messianic Jewish congregations.
- Gentile churches with many Jewish members, whether independent or denomination-affiliated.
- Missions and other outreaches to Jewish people, whether independent or denominational. Examples: Chosen People Ministries, Messianic Jewish Movement International, Jews for Jesus.
- Gentile Christian churches with few or no Messianic Jews, but which support our aims.
- Christian organizations, other than churches and Jewish missions, which support our aims.

- Interested synagogues and Jewish community organizations; it would be made clear that their association with us would not necessarily imply sympathy with our aims (compare the category of "associates" for individuals).

Super-organizations:

- Organization for individuals: the Messianic Jewish Alliance of America.
- Organizations of Messianic Jewish congregations (at present there are four).
- Fellowship organization for pastors; at present this function is carried on within the congregational organizations.
- Fellowship organization for missionaries; the Fellowship of Christian Testimonies to the Jews has filled this role.
- Jewish evangelism clearinghouse: to be specific, the Lausanne Consultation on Jewish Evangelism.
- Gentile Christian denominations active in Jewish work, such as the Assemblies of God.

Other Kinds of Entities:

- Organizations of subgroups of Jewish believers, e.g., of charismatic or of non-charismatic Messianic Jews, or of Messianic Jewish doctors.
- Journals, magazines, radio and television broadcasts, film companies connected with the movement.
- Educational institutions connected with the movement.
- Special-purpose Messianic Jewish organizations, such as Maoz, Inc.
- Special-purpose committees, e.g., on theology, liturgy, social action, fostering unity.

3. *Communal Needs*

The following list of needs our community should try to meet is by no means exhaustive.

- Caring for Messianic Jews who are poor, elderly, disadvantaged, handicapped. "The religious observance that God the Father considers pure and faultless is this: to care for orphans and widows in their distress and to keep oneself from being contaminated by the world."[9]
- Promoting *aliyah,* demonstrating support for the State of Israel, and promoting Messianic Judiasm there. (See Section E below.)
- Promoting and operating a Messianic Jewish seminary.
- Establishing a library for Messianic Jewish materials and for materials related to Jewish-Christian relations. (The library of the late Elie Cleaveland went to Northeastern Baptist College, partly because Jewish believers had not established an institution capable of dealing with his 20,000-plus volumes.)
- Promoting theological, historical, philosophical and liturgical scholarship in Messianic Judaism.
- Providing educational materials on Messianic Judaism for Messianic synagogues, Messianic Jewish schools and seminaries, the general public, non-Messianic Jews, Gentile Christians.
- Training teachers.
- Developing journals and magazines in Messianic Judaism and Messianic Jewish education.
- Promoting presentations in other media: television, radio, drama, film, music, etc.

---

9. Ya'akov [James] 1:27.

- Holding seminars for interchange of scholarly opinions and views on particular topics—for Messianic Jews only, and/or for Messianic Jews with other Jews and Christians.
- Developing materials for improving Jewish-Christian relations, holding seminars, forums, meetings, and promoting scholarship in this area.
- Dealing with public relations and apologetics, answering attacks against us, speaking on our behalf to Jewish, Church and secular misunderstandings and accusations.
- Mediating—resolving conflicts between various components, factions and individuals within the Messianic Jewish movement. Conceivably this function might extend to doing the same for relationships between Messianic Jewish groups and Jewish or Christian groups outside our movement.
- Cooperating with the Jewish community where possible, e.g., helping to bring Jews out of Russia, supporting the State of Israel, helping the elderly—but not, for example, supporting*yeshivas* that teach against Yeshua the Messiah.
- Cooperating with the Church—locally, denominationally, nationally, internationally.

To deal with these and other purposes one can imagine a number of institutions or just one. There is no shortage of material written to describe how the Jewish community has organized itself; it may suggest areas needing attention in the Messianic Jewish community.

4. *Educational Institutions*

In order to assure that the identity we gradually develop for ourselves as Messianic Jews and the knowledge we gain through researching Judaism and Christianity will be passed on to others, including our own children, we need specialized educational institutions. For although the primary responsi- bility for education in the faith, after the family itself, rests with the congregations, they rarely have the capacity to organize what is needed by the movement as a whole.

For our children we need not only "Sunday schools," *i.e.*, once- or twice-a-week classes, but day schools, where the full range of secular and religious studies can be combined in a faith-enhancing environment. One key to the success of these schools is developing Messianic Jewish children's materials; another is having teachers who themselves are examples of Messianic Jewish identity and living. Otherwise one has just another Christian Sunday school that uses a few Jewish words, or a Jewish Sunday school with a few Christian words. The Messianic Jewish congregations in Philadelphia, the Washington D.C. area, and elsewhere have made more than a promising start in this direction; they are already conducting successful programs.

For young adults we could contemplate developing a college or university, but the most pressing need is a seminary or *yeshiva* where those researching Judaism and Christianity and helping develop the intellectual side of our Messianic Jewish identity can pass on to others what has been learned; and potential Messianic rabbis, pastors and other workers can be trained. This need has begun to be met in the Washington area by Messiah Yeshiva under the leadership of Dr. Michael Brown.

The most economical way to begin a Messianic Jewish seminary would employ (you should excuse the expression) the piggyback system. The students are sent to a Jewish institution for their Jewish studies and to a Christian institution for their Christian studies, so that only the specifically Messianic Jewish studies and comprehensive overview need to be taught by the seminary staff. (Note the contrast between what is suitable for children and for adults. Adults can chew and digest Gentile Christian and non-Messianic Jewish materials, discarding what is irrelevant and culturally inappropriate. Children are not generally mature enough to do this; that is why it is so important to develop Messianic Jewish teaching materials for them.)

The curriculum of such a seminary should begin with Jewish and Christian courses such as can be found in the catalogs of existing seminaries, drawing from them material to be digested into Messianic Jewish courses, while discarding what is irrelevant. The overall viewpoint should focus individually on discipleship and socially on the four audiences. The curriculum should include:

Bible: Old and New Testaments
Bible introduction
Biblical and intertestamental history

Biblical theology Systematic theology
Apologetics to Jews, apologetics to the Church Ethics, including issues of both private morality and social conscience

Hebrew

Talmud
Midrash
Other rabbinic literature
Halakhah and the halakhic process
Jewish philosophy
Other Jewish literature

Jewish history since the Bible, including the current scene Church history, including the current scene Messianic Jewish history, important figures

Fundamentals of spiritual living
Jewish and Christian worship practices; liturgy
Jewish practice for Messianic Jews
Evangelism
Relating to Jews, Church and World: social action
Year of study and experience in Israel

Other education projects might include education by extension for isolated Messianic Jews, adult education and summer camps for children, and short tours of Israel involving the Jewish believers there.

5. *Professional Institutions*

Institutions to facilitate professional activity include:

- An association for congregation leaders, a pastors' association. At present there are already at least two such collegial associations in which pastors can share problems, pray for one another, learn from one another, and help one another.
- A Messianic Jewish Theological Society for theologians, scholars and halakhists. Its purpose would be to enable Messianic Jewish theologians to know which among their number would be best able to criticize and comment on their work and provide encouragement, correction and cooperative effort. It could publish a journal, hold conferences, and be a focus for Jewish believers who want religious and theological education. Perhaps it could foster exploration of a variety of theological, philosophical, ideological and practical questions peculiar to Messianic Judaism. Perhaps it could assume a role of leadership in developing and speaking up for a distinct Messianic Jewish viewpoint to the four audiences.
- An association for Messianic Jewish seminarians studying in various kinds of institutions, in which they can focus together on Messianic Jewish issues. This might be a project of the previous institution.

D. LITERATURE WE NEED

If I had a hundred Messianic Jewish scholars at my disposal, I could keep them all busy researching and writing for the rest of my life. Among the materials I would have them produce are the following:

1. *Bible Translations And Commentaries*

Ten years ago I had all the material for this book, but the Lord would not let me write it. Instead, he had me look over my list of everything Messianic Judaism needed (I have based this chapter on that list), and my eye fell on "Messianic Jewish commentaries to New Testament books." He said, "You do that."[10] I began my commentary on the book of Acts but soon found that half of it was occupied with objecting to the English translation I was using. As an experiment I tried translating the first few chapters of Acts myself and was pleased with the result. Thus the *Jewish New Testament* was born.

The *Jewish New Testament* (see Chapter II, footnote 20) is my own translation, from the original Greek into English, of the New Testament. It expresses the New Testament's original and essential Jewishness in three ways which I call cosmetic (or superficial), cultural-religious, and theological. Cosmetic elements—using "execution-stake" instead of "cross" or "Ya'akov" instead of "James"—are the most obvious; their frequency produces a collective effect. Cultural-religious elements embed the Gospel more securely in its Jewish setting; an example is my use of the word *tzitzit* instead of "fringe" at Mattityahu [Matthew] 9:20 to describe what the woman with a hemorrhage touched. Theological elements include what was pointed out earlier in the analysis of Messianic Jews [Hebrews] 8:6, that the New Covenant has not been merely "established" but "given as *Torah.*"The *Jewish New Testament Commentary* deals with questions Jewish people have about the New Testament, Yeshua and Christianity; questions Christians have about the Jewish roots of their faith and about Judaism; and questions Messianic Jews have about their own destiny and role. *The Complete Jewish Bible* offers the *Jewish New Testament* bound together with my version of the Tanakh.

---

10. For the curious: God didn't say it in words, but he gave me peace about doing it, and he took away the writer's block that had affected me when I was trying to write this book.

Since I began my work two adaptations of existing Gentile Christian translations have appeared—Sid Roth's *The Book of Life,* which is a modification of the New King James Version, and the late David Bronstein's Messianic Edition of *The Living Bible.* An actual translation by the Jewish believer Heinz W. Cassirer (1903-1979) was published by Eerdmans in 1989 under the title *God's New Covenant.*

Jehiel Zvi Hirschensohn-Lichtenstein (1827-1912) wrote a commentary in Hebrew on the entire New Testament which was published in installments by the Institutum Delitzschianum in Leipzig, Germany, between 1891 and 1904, with the text in block print and the comments in Rashi script. He had followed in the footsteps of Joiachim Heinrich Biesenthal (born Raphael Hirsch, 1800-1886), who wrote commentaries on the Gospels, Romans and Hebrews, as well as on Psalms and Isaiah. In this century Victor Buksbazen, Charles Lee Feinberg and Moshe I. Ben-Maeir are among the Jewish believers who have written commentaries to one or more books of the Bible. There remains a need for Messianic Jewish commentaries on all of the books of the Bible, both *Tanakh* and New Testament. The "Netivyah" organization in Jerusalem, under the direction of Joseph Shulam, is preparing a Hebrew commentary on the New Testament which draws on Jewish sources and tries to recover Jewish understandings.

2. *Other Informational And Academic Books*

We need Messianic Jewish research and writing in the areas of biblical and systematic theology, ethics, liturgy, apologetics, Jewish-Christian relations, and antisemitism. We need research and writing in the history of Messianic Judaism.[11] We need books explaining what Messianic Judaism is; they should be written with the various audiences in mind. And we need bibliographical materials for the researchers.

---

11. A worthwhile new contribution is Robert I. Winer, M.D., The Calling: The History of the Messianic Jewish Alliance of America, *1915-1990* (P.O. Box 417, Wynnewood, PA 19096, USA: MJAA, 1990). Gershon Narel is currently preparing his doctoral

3. *Biographies And Testimonies*

Everyone wants to know how God is working in other people's lives, and everyone who has had that experience wants others to know. Therefore we have many autobiographies, testimonies, and testimony collections.[12]1 mentioned earlier the biography collection by Bernstein[13] and suggested that a modern update including the lives of this century's believers would be welcome. Otherwise we will forget them.

For example, there was Rabbi Daniel Zion (1883-1979). Having translated the *Siddur* into Bulgarian, he was Chief Rabbi of Bulgaria when he had a vision of Yeshua and came to faith in him. Because of his faith and his position he had the ear of King Boris II at the critical time in 1943-1944 when the Nazis wanted the Jews deported—to the death camps. *Rav* Daniel strenuously urged the king not to do this, and he assented. As a result, 86% of Bulgaria's 50,000 Jews were saved, a better record than in any Nazi-affected country except possibly Denmark. After World War II he made *aliyah* with nearly all of Bulgarian Jewry. On *Shabbat* he would officiate in his Jaffa

---

dissertation at the Hebrew University, Jerusalem, on the history of the Jewish believers in Israel, 1925-1988. Ruth Fleischer Snow is doing hers at Kings College, University of London, on the emergence of a uniquely Jewish expression of faith in Yeshua, 1925 to the present. Also see Chapter III, footnotes 43-45.

12. Three anthologies of the testimonies of Jewish people who have come to Messianic faith in recent decades are: Ruth Rosen, ed., *Jesus For Jews* (San Francisco: A Messianic Jewish Perspective, 1987); Mike Evans with Bob Summers, *Young Lions of Judah* (Plainfield, New Jersey: Logos International, 1974); and James Hefley, *The New Jews* (Wheaton, Illinois: Tyndale House Publishers, 1974). Three anthologies of testimonies of Jewish people who came to faith mostly 50 to 150 years ago are: Henry and Marie Einspruch, eds., *Would I? Would You?* (Baltimore, Maryland: The Lewis and Harriet Lederer Foundation, 1970); Jacob Gartenhaus, *Famous Hebrew Christians* (Grand Rapids, Michigan, Baker Book House, no date); and Zola Levitt, *Meshumed* (Chicago: Moody Press, 1979).

13. *Op. cit.* in Chapter III, footnote 46.

synagogue in the morning and teach New Testament in the afternoon. He also wrote nearly 200 Messianic Jewish songs, some of which are in use in Israel.[14] His story is one of many that will be lost unless researchers and writers get busy!

Two books I personally would love to read, if someone would write them—and if no one does, I'll be tempted to do it myself—would be one on miracles in the lives of Messianic Jews, and one on how Messianic Jewish couples met and married (but it has to include how Martha and I met at the MJAA's "Messiah 75" conference!).

4. *Other Books*

Here are some suggestive titles:

The Messianic Jew and the State of Israel (See Section E.)

A Messianic Jew Looks at the Talmud.

The Jewish Attitude Toward Christianity and Messianic Judaism. There are a number of summaries by non-Messianic Jews,[15] but no extensive ones by Messianic Jews. The book should cover the range from the period of the Talmud through the Middle Ages to modern times. In modern times it is useful to distinguish Orthodox from Reform and secular views.

A Messianic Jewish Understanding of the Bible. Compare, on the Gentile Christian side, W. D. Davies' *Invitation to the New Testament* and, on the non-Messianic Jewish side, Samuel Sandmel's *A Jewish Understanding of the New Testament.*

A Messianic Jew Looks at the Halakhah.

---

14. This information comes largely from Joseph Shulam, who belongs to the Bulgarian Jewish community in Israel. I met *Rav* Daniel in 1974 and heard his testimony.

15. See, for example, Walter Jacob, *Christianity Through Jewish Eyes* (Hebrew Union College Press, 1974); F. E. Talmage, ed., *Disputation and Dialogue: Readings in the Jewish-Christian Encounter,* Trude Weiss-Rosmarin, ed., *Jewish Expressions on Jesus: An Anthology* (New York: Ktav Publishing House, 1976).

Messianic Judaism and Mysticism.

Issues in Messianic Judaism, to stimulate thought on current controversies.

Varieties of Messianic Judaism. The idea would be to depict a range of possibilities, using a comparative approach illustrated by testimonies and biographical sketches. One might try to document observant Orthodox Jews who believed in Yeshua secretly or openly, complete apostates from Judaism who joined Gentile Christians in persecuting Jews, assimilated Jews who become Gentilized church members, assimilated Jews who rediscovered their Jewishness, Messianic Jews who were raised as such, Messianic Jews who for ideological reasons held back from joining congregations or getting immersed—and so on.

Messianic Jewish Encyclopedia. I can't even imagine what this could become, but it's an exciting title!

5. *Children's Books*

Children's books are a popular way to instill faith in the young. How important it is, then, to be able to do so in a Messianic Jewish way! We desperately need Messianic Jewish children's books to convey Messianic Jewish identity to our young children. Above all we need Messianic Jewish children's Bibles for various ages, both abridged and unabridged.

6. *Periodicals*

Journals, magazines, newspapers, digests, and yearbooks can range from popular to scholarly. The purposes are explaining ourselves and the Gospel, doing apologetics and evangelism, interacting with and responding to those who write about us in Jewish, Christian and secular media, setting goals and priorities, spurring action and exchanging ideas. Again, the publications should be aimed at the several audiences. Existing publications include *The Interpreter, The Hebrew Christian* (published by the International Hebrew Christian Alliance), the

Jewish Alliance Quarterly (published by the Messianic Jewish Alliance of America), *Mishkan* (a theological forum published by the United Christian Council in Israel), and a variety of publications by missions, such as *Issues* (from Jews for Jesus, dealing with issues of concern to nonbelieving Jews), *Jewish Voice* (published by "Jewish Voice"), *The Chosen People* (Chosen People Ministries), and a number of less well known publications. Hebrew language publications in Israel include *B'Shuv* and *Me'et Le'et,* edited by Menahem Benhayim and Baruch Maoz respectively.

7. *Fiction, Poetry, Drama*

This is an open field. One need only recall novels like *The Robe* and *Ben Hur* or a poem like "The Hound of Heaven" to appreciate the value of these forms.

8. *Other Media*

Let us note other media, including music and art. Messianic Jewish music can be for congregational use, for stage use, for concerts, for recordings. Fine art, graphic art and craft skills can be put in the service of the Kingdom. Dance too, both for stage and for folk participation, has potential for Kingdom service. All these are at present being done, and we can expect them to continue.

A final request: quality. When Dr. Henry Einspruch produced his translation of the New Testament into Yiddish, he set out to do it beautifully. The elegant graphics illustrating the text are by Ephraim Lilien, one of the founders of the Betzalel School of Art in Jerusalem; and it is just an outstandingly produced book.[16] Let us not be satisfied with mediocrity. This is especially important in children's books, where the art work conveys much of the meaning.

---

16. Henry Einspruch, *The New Testament in Yiddish* (6204 Park Heights Avenue, Baltimore, Maryland: The Lewis and Harriet Lederer Foundation).

E. MESSIANIC JUDAISM AND ISRAEL

1. *Israel The Center Of Messianic Judaism*

In this section we will discuss Israel as the potential world center for Messianic Judaism, and, in consequence, how Messianic Judaism should relate to the Land of Israel and to the State of Israel.

We laid some theological groundwork in Chapter IV, Sections E-4, E-5 and E-6. There we concluded that God will fulfill his promise to give the Land of Israel to the Jewish people, although the rights of Arabs willing to live peacefully in the Land are to be preserved. We noted that Messianic Judaism will eventually be centered in Israel, first, because Scripture prophesies it—"For out of Zion shall go forth *Torah* and the word of *Adonai* from Jerusalem;"[17] second, because no major movement which stays centered in the Diaspora when the Jewish State exists can hope to affect significantly the Jewish people; and third, because there is a strong grass-roots feeling among Messianic Jews that that's the way it ought to be. It means that ultimately, when "all Israel shall be saved," that Israel's establishment will be Messianic Jewish.

We laid the attitudinal groundwork in Chapter III, Section A-l, where we pointed out that Israeli Jews are more sensitive than Diaspora Jews to the Jewish people's role in history, which is likely to sensitize them to the message that only through Yeshua can that role be fulfilled.

In Chapter II, Section A-4 we said that while Messianic Judaism in the Diaspora is a valid expression of New Testament faith, the most natural place for it to take root is Israel. This is because being Jewish is *normal* in Israel. A Jew in the Diaspora, Messianic or not, has real difficulty seeing how distorted his life as a Jew is outside of Israel. A measure of this distortion is the tendency for Messianic Jews in the Diaspora to focus on their Jewishness as something they have to "do."

---

17. Isaiah 2:3.

In Israel, a Jew doesn't have to "do" his Jewishness or prove it. Almost everyone is Jewish, so he is accepted as Jewish whether he does anything about it or not. Therefore a Messianic congregation in Israel is, at least in principle, free to focus on the Messiah and not on being distinctively Jewish. It doesn't free us from the responsibility of determining appropriate Jewish expressions of Messianic faith, but it does free us from the need to feel that unless we "behave Jewishly" we will be absorbed into some other way of being. We can just be ourselves. That is normal.

2. *The Messianic Jewish Community In Israel Today*

What is the situation of the Messianic Jewish community in Israel today? Is it strong enough to bear the weight of being tapped to lead a world movement with the key role in history we claim it has? The answer must be that although the Israeli Messianic Jews struggle under many burdens, God, by his grace, is preparing us here in Israel in ways both obvious and not so obvious for the task that will certainly fall to us eventually.

A Spiritually Underdeveloped Country. I find it convenient to begin my analysis with concepts drawn from my training as an economist. I see Israel as a spiritually underdeveloped country. The thing about economically underdeveloped countries, beside the obvious fact of low income levels (which too has its spiritual analogy), is that they lack a good economic infrastructure. The grocery stores run out of staples because of inadequate transport; electricity is supplied to only half of the country, with outages frequent; traffic signals are rare and often not working due to unavailability of spare parts and competent repairmen; business skills, especially in management, are lacking.

A similar thing happens spiritually. Countries with many believers and a long history of belief in Yeshua have a well-developed spiritual infrastructure. There are churches on every other streetcorner. Schools, seminaries, Bible camps and counseling centers abound. The Gospel is proclaimed to old and young, rich and poor, athletes and handicapped, businessmen and street people. Tens of thousands of books based on New Covenant truth can be bought in easily accessible religious bookstores or checked out of well-stocked libraries. Above all, there are well-trained, experienced pastors and leaders.

Western Christians take these things for granted, but Israel has virtually none of them. It is estimated that there are between one and three thousand Jewish believers in the country, which is less than one-tenth of one percent of a Jewish population nearing four million. The largest congregation in the country (measured by non-tourist attendance at the largest weekly meeting) has around 200 people, while most of the 25 or so congregations that include significant numbers of Jewish believers are attended by 15-50. New-Covenant based books can be bought from perhaps eight or ten bookstores in the whole country. Theological education is just beginning; anything one would call a seminary or Bible college is for the future. In fact, there is not one comprehensive biblical- or systematic-theology book in Hebrew. Outreach is weak, scattered and not consistently directed at any target subgroup.

Economies of Scale. "Economies of scale" refers to advantages that accrue to a large enterprise simply because of its size. Our congregations are small, and for this reason we do not have economies of scale. A church in America with a thousand people drawing on its membership for counselors, teachers, bus-drivers and janitors can still have plenty of troops left to participate in prayer meetings, evangelize, sing in the chorus and organize potlucks. But a *kehillah* of twenty-five carrying on a comparable range of activities lives in a constant state of exhaustion. Everyone in a small congregation is hard-pressed just to maintain the group's ongoing existence. Any new plan that requires an output of energy is met with groans.

This is especially true in Jerusalem, where vast numbers of tourists visit the city's few small congregations in order to experience the blessing of attending a service in the city where the Church began. Often there are more visitors at a meeting than locals, and we can expect this to continue every week until the Messiah returns (and probably then too). Hospitality demands that we treat this never-ending flood of visiting brothers and sisters courteously, since for many of them a pilgrimage to the Holy Land is a high point in a lifetime of faith. Still, it adds to the pressure on the Body of the Messiah in Israel.

The Messianic Community of Israel. One good thing we have in Israel is a sense of the Body, nationwide. That is, one can speak of "the Messianic Community of Israel" in a way that would not apply to "the Church of America." Through traveling, attending conferences and sharing with others, a believer here will, within two or three years, have friends all over the country. I can expect to visit any congregation "from Dan to Beersheva" and see people I personally know, have prayed for, have heard about, or who know people I see all the time. When the Tiberias congregation had its meeting place destroyed, brothers and sisters throughout the country felt it and acted. There is a deep unity transcending doctrinal and personality differences which stems from the awareness that "we're all in it together." Some of this closeness is, of course, due simply to the fact that the Body here is so small—about as big as one moderately large church in the United States.

National Conferences. We have a number of country-wide conferences which draw 100-200 people; and the believers need these conferences in order to survive spiritually; for if one's fellowship is limited to the 15 or 30 in one's own congregation, Messianic life easily becomes ingrown, flat, ghetto-ized. The Messianic Assembly and its sister congregations host conferences at a modern facility on Mount Carmel in Haifa. Netivyah holds seminars twice a year. During the last eight years a series of music conferences has brought out a lot of talent among Israelis, with over a hundred Hebrew songs now recorded on cassettes, printed in songbooks, sung throughout the Land, and many of them used around the world. Another conference which began as a meeting for youth during Passover Week, 1981, drew 200 adults and children annually for seven years. But no believer-owned conference center in Israel can hold more than this number, although Baptist Village plans to expand.

The first gathering having a narrow-sense Messianic Jewish focus was organized in 1986 by Ari Sorko-Ram and the Ramat-HaSharon congregation; its main speaker was Daniel Juster. Two follow-up conferences were topped by "Shavu'ot '88," held at Jerusalem's Diplomat Hotel and attended by 700 Messianic Jews from Israel, America and elsewhere, with an equal number of Gentile believers; it drew national media attention.

"Selections. "Until 1989 Menahem Benhayim prepared and the United Christian Council in Israel published a 6-to-10-page English digest of the local press's reportage on Messianic Judaism, Christian missions, anti-missionary activity, positive and negative Jewish reactions, Jewish-Christian dialogue, and cults. Unfortunately this excellent service is no longer available; perhaps the newly formed Messianic Jewish Alliance of Israel will undertake to resurrect it.

Jewish Evangelism and Fear. Over the last several years there has been great growth in fearless public evangelism. One still sees the old-style "hit-and-run" approach—leaving tracts in mailboxes or on car windshields. But since 1984 more than a million evangelistic "broadsides" written in Hebrew have been handed out personally in cooperative intercongregational street campaigns held three or four times a year in Israel's major cities. Jacob Damkani has pioneered the placing of full-page advertisements in Israel's leading Hebrew newspapers; the first, published just before *Yom Kippur,* 1988, pictured a slain lamb on the Temple altar, was headlined "Who Is The Sacrifice?" and explained to half the population of Israel how Yeshua the Messiah atones for sin.

When we made *aliyah* eleven years ago, fear was the main impediment to evangelism. Here is an example. In 1980 Martha and I were flying on El Al for our first visit to the "old country."

The lady behind us noticed that Martha was reading a book about a Jewish family who had found their Messiah. The woman, a Christian living in Jerusalem, struck up a conversation by remarking that she knew the author. Martha replied, "I know her too, I met her when I was working with Jews for Jesus," whereupon the lady, glancing at the other Jewish passengers, whispered, "Shhh! Someone might hear you!" Martha, true to form, raised her voice to reply, "What? Why shouldn't they know I worked for JEWS FOR JESUS?"—as the lady shrank back into her seat.

What are believers afraid of? Quite simply: of men rather than God. Some don't want to lose Jewish friends by supposedly antagonizing them with the Gospel. Often they do not realize that Israeli Jews are far more open to hearing the Gospel than most Jews in the Diaspora. This is because the Gospel does not threaten the Israeli Jew's identity. The Diaspora Jew, belonging to a small minority in a Gentile society, is constantly alert to maintain his Jewishness against odds; often the only "Jewish" act an assimilated Jew can think of is rejecting Yeshua. But here, in a Jewish society, a Jew doesn't have to prove he's Jewish—everybody is. So he can listen to the Gospel on its merits without automatically having to oppose it.

Many Gentile Christians here on temporary visas are afraid that if they evangelize openly, they will be kicked out of the country. Our response is: so what? Suppose even 100 of the reputedly 3,500 missionaries in Israel were to get out on the streets, go door to door, or do whatever kind of evangelism the Lord gave them to do, openly, fearlessly and full-time. If the opposition succeeded in persuading the government not to renew the visas of only ten of them, it would quickly become a worldwide cause for lifting up the name of Yeshua. Does God praise fearful, non-evangelizing "missionaries" for reposing their bodies in the Holy Land? Some claim they are "planting seeds." Maybe—but if so, where are the trees? My guess is that less than 100 Jewish Israelis per year come to faith (less than one for every thirty-five missionaries).

Jewish believers may have different fears. Sometimes they are fired from their jobs (or not employed in the first place) because of their faith, or their children have a rough time at school, or they encounter some form of discrimination or intimidation. But no one promised us a rose garden—except for thorns in the flesh.

The ultimate way for a Messianic Jew to express his fear is to remain a so-called "secret believer." I am asked how many there are in Israel. Well, how can I know? Moreover, what good do they do anyone—themselves, the Body, or the Lord? As I said earlier, on the basis of Luke 12:8-9 they should not be called believers at all.[18] I hear of secret believers and, worse, of Christians who encourage them to stay that way. But our prayer is that they will have the courage to "come out of the closet" and stand openly for their faith.

A historical factor responsible for much of the fear is the flight of Jewish believers following the establishment of the State in 1948. At that time Christian denominational leaders, expecting a purge of Jewish believers when the British mandate ended, evacuated many of them to Europe and America. The purge did not materialize, but the local body was left depressed and decimated of leadership. This trauma affected attitudes here for thirty years; only now is a new generation of *sabras* growing into the faith free of paranoia and able to evaluate the opposition realistically.

The Opposition. Outside Israel rumors are rife about persecution of believers. Let us say once and for all that compared with Communist and Muslim countries, there is nothing worthy of the name "persecution" happening to Gentile Christians or Messianic Jews in Israel. No one is killed, sent to prison or tortured for his faith.

Nevertheless, there is real opposition to the believers and to the Gospel. Personal physical attacks are rare, but there is social, economic and psychological intimidation—including

18. Chapter II, Section B-4.

wiretapping, bugging, spying and interfering with mail (to what degree is difficult to assess). There is occasional vandalism—the Baptist Church auditorium was burned to the ground, thugs gutted a hotel where the Tiberias congregation used to meet, a piano was destroyed at the Messianic Assembly in Jerusalem. And there is a continuous stream of verbal abuse heaped upon Yeshua, the Gospel and the believers by a tiny minority of "anti-missionaries." Moreover, although in principle there is freedom of religion, the government does not always stand behind it with the vigor Americans are used to; instead, anti-missionary activity receives at least tacit approval from certain branches of the government and sometimes covert financial support.

"But," people ask me, "isn't it illegal in Israel to tell Jews about Jesus?" No, it isn't. A law was passed in 1977 against bribing someone to change his status, as officially recorded on his identity card, from one religion to another; but no one has ever even been accused of doing this, let alone convicted (a recent case in preparation, which would have stood no chance in court, was quietly dropped by the government). Moreover, most Jews who come to believe in Yeshua as Israel's Messiah don't change their official status and would oppose doing so on principle, for they have not stopped being Jews.

"Suppose *YadL'Achim*finds out."(*YadL'Achim,* literally, "A Hand for Brothers," also known as the *Peylim,* "Activists," is the best-known anti-missionary organization.) This brings us back to the subject of fear, and our answer is: Well, suppose they do—who cares? It is far more important to spread the Gospel than to waste time second-guessing a bunch *of nudniks.* The *Peylim* produce reports on missionaries and Jewish believers, generally full of lies, innuendoes and misinformation. To give an example from some years ago: a Christian worker was described in one of their publications as having been forced out of the country, the implication being that the *Peylim* had pressured him to leave. In fact the man had died years before.

Moreover, not only is their own constituency small, but their "anti-constituency," the secular and other Jews who despise narrow-minded religious extremism of any variety, is large. A Messianic Jew can gain a sympathetic hearing in Israel by appealing to secular Jews who, though not about to accept Yeshua, favor civil rights and oppose rigid Orthodoxy.

In sum, those who spread the Gospel should expect opposition—read the book of Acts. But nothing worthy of the name "persecution" happens here—no one here has been driven out of town and left for dead because of preaching the Word, as was Sha'ul (Acts 14:19). Should I say, "Praise God!" or "Shame on us!"?

Responding to Opposition. It is worth noting that—like Sha'ul relying on his Roman citizenship in defending his right to preach—the believing community here is beginning to respond to opposition in mature and measured ways, rather than retreating behind closed doors "for fear of the Jews" (as most versions translate Yochanan [John] 20:19).[19] Our friends Ari and Shira Sorko-Ram brought suit against the mayor of Ramat HaSharon for slandering them in a city council meeting, describing them as "missionaries" who "bribe children to convert to Christianity;" he was forced to print a retraction. The *Peylim* pestered the City of Jerusalem into filing a case against the Netivyah organization for holding public meetings in a building zoned for residences (even though the City had sent warning letters to dozens of similar zoning violators but had not brought them to court); we fought this nuisance case, asking the judge to throw it out on the ground of religious discrimination, with the result that the City seems to have let the matter drop. But we still do not have a clearinghouse for responding to public defamation of Yeshua and his Body.

Using the Opposition to Further the Gospel. The opposition expects the believers to be cowed and frightened, and unfortunately their expectations have too often been fulfilled. We

19. The *Jewish New Testament* renders it "Judeans" and the *Jewish New Testament Commentary* makes the case for so doing *(op. cit.* in Chapter II, footnote 20).come against this, having learned the importance of boldness and strategy. Here is an instance.

come against this, having learned the importance of boldness and strategy. Here is an instance.

Every so often the *Peylim* launch a campaign against Christians generally and Messianic Jews in particular. This helps them convince contributors abroad that they are doing something. In 1985 they demonstrated and plastered posters all over Jerusalem warning Jews to have nothing to do with Netivyah, the Messianic Assembly, the Caspari Center (which engages in theological education for Hebrew-speaking believers) and the Baptist Church (which has a number of Jewish believers). Usually the believing community would not have reacted publicly at all; at most someone might have sent a letter to the editor of *The Jerusalem Post.* In this case, we took the initiative and wrote the text for the following poster, which was printed in Hebrew:

> THE MESSIANIC JEWS
>
> THANK THE PEYLIM/YAD L'ACHIM!
>
> *We want to thank this small group of ultra-Orthodox extremists for the publicity which their posters and demonstrations have given four groups of Christians and Messianic Jews who teach about*
>
> **YESHUA THE MESSIAH!**
>
> *The Messianic Jews and their friends invite anyone who wants to know about the New Testament and about Yeshua, Israel's Messiah, to come to [names, addresses and phone numbers of the four groups].*

Probably not more than 20 of these posters were put up, and they were all ripped down within hours; nevertheless, they had a profound effect on the opposition. Our response was reported in at least three Hebrew newspapers and even noted in one Jewish paper abroad. Why? Because it conveyed a hidden message very clearly: "We are not afraid. We will not be silent. We will use opposition to the Lord's advantage." So far as I know, the *Peylim* have not put up any more posters against the believers since then and seem to have found other ways to do fundraising.

Conclusion. In sum, if being Messianic is the most exciting way to be Jewish, Israel is the most exciting place to be a Messianic Jew. Which leads to our next topic.

3. *Messianic Jews And Aliyah*[20]

The logical step for anyone who thinks that Israel is the Jewish country would be to "make *aliyah*" that is, to immigrate to Israel. (The literal meaning *of aliyah* is "going up." The spiritual geography of the world is such that from anywhere, even Mount Everest, one ascends to Israel.) But very few American Jews, Messianic or otherwise, do make *aliyah.* In the depths of my soul I am convinced that there ought to be more Messianic Jews in Israel. Two ways we Messianic Jews who are already in Israel can help bring that about are by encouraging our children to follow the faith, and by evangelizing the Israeli Jewish population. The third way, of course, is to increase the number of Messianic Jews who make *aliyah.*

The Challenge. Only after coming here ourselves and returning to the United States on visits did we discover how much indifference and even opposition there is among Jewish believers to making *aliyah.* The clearest demonstration of it was when I was invited to give a report from Israel to a group of Messianic Jews some years ago. About a hundred people were present. I asked who was Jewish, and about half the

20. Except for the subsection "Law of Return", Section 3 is printed as in the 1988 edition, when, prior to the Beresford verdict, I could state in good faith that I believed the Law of Return allowed Messianic Jews to make *aliyah* as Jews. Since Israel's Supreme Court in 1989 decided otherwise, I must now write that I think the judges erred, and that Messianic Jews and their supporters must pray and work to change the situation. Therefore read Section 3 together with "*Aliyah* Update 1990" on pages 265 ff.

audience raised their hands. I told those who hoped to live in Israel some day to keep their hands in the air, and 90% did so. I then asked, "How many of you who hope to come have begun planning your *aliyahT*"[1] and all but three or four put their hands down.

I told the group, "My guess is that you're like most of the Jewish believers in America I talk to—they usually say that the reason they have not begun planning is that they don't yet 'feel called'to make the move. But," I said, "you don't need a special call, because as Jewish believers you have been called already—by God, in Scripture! You know that God gave *Eretz-Yisrael* to the Jews, and if that doesn't include *you,* why call yourself a Messianic *Jew]* Isaiah 51:11 says that 'the redeemed of the Lord shall return and come with singing unto Zion, and everlasting joy shall be upon their head. They shall obtain gladness and joy, and sorrow and sighing shall flee away.' In context, 'the redeemed of the Lord' are the remnant of Israel, which in the present era means Messianic Jews. At Ezekiel 36:26-28, after God says, 'A new spirit will I put within you,' which is fulfilled in an individual sense when a Jew comes to faith in Yeshua, then God continues, 'And ye shall dwell in the land that I gave to your fathers,' which is fulfilled when he moves to Israel.

"So if you're waiting for God to 'call' you to make *aliyah,* you've got it backwards! You need a call from God to know that you are to remain in the *Galut* In Scripture *galut* is regarded as a curse, not a blessing. There are those who have such a call and are serving God productively in America or elsewhere. But if you have not been personally called by God to remain in the Diaspora, you should be thinking seriously about *aliyah,* not waiting for God to give you a special word. You don't wake up in the morning and say, 'I wonder if God will show me that I should rob a bank today, or kill someone.' You already know God's will, since he expressed it in the Ten Commandments, so you don't need a special 'call' not to steal or commit murder. Likewise, God's desire for Jews, both believers and non-believers, concerning *aliyah* is crystal clear, even though it is not stated as a command.

"The Jewish state exists in the Promised Land. Come and live in it, be *chalutzim,* pioneers. David Ben-Gurion and Golda Meir restored the Land physically, but you will be spiritual *chalutzim* bringing the Word of Life to a very thirsty people! Or encourage your whole congregation to make *aliyah* as a group, like the early pioneers. Plan your *aliyah* now! Come with singing unto Zion, and everlasting joy shall be upon your head!"

Practical Advice. If you are thinking about personally fulfilling God's promise that "the redeemed of the Lord *[i.e.,* Messianic Jews] shall return and come with singing unto Zion, and everlasting joy will be upon their head," here is some practical advice.

The first and most important thing to do is to be thoroughly convinced that Messianic Jewish *aliyah* is in God's will and is a good thing for you personally. As I said, most Jewish believers in America, like most Jewish nonbelievers in America—and like me before God changed my mind—expect to live out the rest of their lives in what they consider the land flowing with milk and honey, namely, the good old U. S. of A. But once the possibility, or, rather, the normalcy, of Messianic Jewish *aliyah* is brought to their attention, along with the scriptural basis, many Messianic Jews are interested and challenged.

Second, be in touch with people who can advise and encourage you. Without doubt, changing countries is stressful; but the only way to have your particular worries addressed and your questions answered is to communicate. In the meanwhile, here are a few general pointers:

- *Law of Return.* The State of Israel has a "Law of Return" which allows all Jews to "return home" to Israel and become citizens here (American Jews need not forfeit their U.S. citizenship). Originally this law defined "Jew" as "a person born to a Jewish mother or converted to Judaism." But in 1961 Oswald Rufeysen ("Brother Daniel") attempted *aliyah,* stating on his application that he was a Jew by nationality and a Roman Catholic by religion. This case reached the Supreme Court *("Bagatz")*, which ruled against him, stating that a Jew could not separate religion from nationality. As a result of this and the Shalit case (1970), over whether a (non-Messianic) Jew with a Gentile wife could register their son as Jewish, there was added to the Law of Return's definition of "Jew" the phrase, "who is not a member of another religion and did not voluntarily change his religion." In 1978 *Bagatz* decided that Eileen (Esther) Dorflinger, a believer in Yeshua born to a Jewish mother, who said she had not changed religion and had been baptized not into a church but, as a Jew, into the universal Body of the Messiah, could not make aliyah under the Law of Return on the ground that she was, in spite of herself, "a member of another religion." In 1989 it ruled similarly against Gerald and Shirley Beresford, professing Messianic Jews, even though, according to a reliable poll, 78% of the Israeli Jewish public opinion would gladly have accepted them. For details of this public opinion survey and for discussion of other legal and ethical aspects of Messianic Jewish *aliyah* in the post-Beresford era, see "Appendix: *Aliyah* Update" on pages 265 ff.

Incidentally, if your mother is not Jewish, then, according to both *halakhah* and the Law of Return, neither are you. However, if you have a father or grandparent who fits the Law of Return's definition of "Jew," then, even if you are openly known as a Christian, you have the undisputed right to immigrate to Israel under a special provision of the Law of Return dealing with non-Jewish descendants of Jews.

- *Money.* Come with money if you can. If a year or two of hard work will significantly build up savings, it may be worthwhile postponing the big move, because it's much easier to accumulate money in America than in Israel. (Israeli joke: How do you make a small fortune in Israel? Bring a large one.)

- *Work.* Come with a profession if you can. But before investing years in training, check to see if your skills will be needed, and how well such work pays, and whether you will be able to work without broad knowledge of Hebrew, and whether it might be better to gain your particular job skills in Israel rather than in the *Galut.*

- *Hebrew.* Start learning Hebrew *now.* Every bit helps. If possible, take a course that gives you an overview of the linguistic structure and grammar, because Israel's *ulpanim* (Hebrew-language training programs) never do that. Since most Americans, deep in their hearts, believe that English is the only "real" language in the world, learning Hebrew is their greatest single barrier to getting adjusted in Israel.

- *Marriage, Children.* If you are single, it doesn't matter whether you marry here or there, although the marriage pool of Jewish believers in Israel is very small. But if you're married, childless, and thinking about whether to have your children in Israel or abroad, come to Israel and have them here later; because the time and energy needed for family maintenance will slow down your learning Hebrew and adjusting to the culture, both of which are essential to successful *aliyah* and require a minimum of 2-3 years. Still, if you have kids already, come anyway! They'll soon be teaching you Hebrew, since they'll learn it faster than you. As the saying goes, Israel is the only country where mothers learn their mother-tongue from their children.

- *Spiritual Needs.* Plan for your spiritual needs. Start by consulting with your elders and your congregation, so that you will be covered spiritually as you plan a very important step in your life, so that you won't depart in a disorderly manner, and so that you will be spiritually prepared when you arrive. You should make contacts in Israel and plan to be connected with other believers, so as not to become a spiritual orphan. If you don't, then the excitement, difficulties and shocks of life in the Jewish state will probably cause one of three outcomes, all of them bad: you will become spiritually isolated and thus useless for the Kingdom, or you will fail to adjust and leave the Land, or you will fall away from the faith. I know of several instances of each, and all might have been prevented had the people been less paranoid and more zealous about joining up with the believers here.

- *Visit.* If you can afford it, and especially if you have never visited Israel, do so for four to six weeks, in order to get a feel for the Land. Contact the believers in Israel, so that we may point you in useful directions and answer your questions. Then return home to plan your *aliyah* on the basis of direct personal knowledge. For if a picture is worth a thousand words, a visit is worth a million pictures.

- *Ask Advice.* It's easier in person, but even across an ocean you can be advised about what to bring, where to live, where and when to buy which appliances, housing, jobs, finances, learning Hebrew, making friends, spiritual matters—in short, about all the details which, taken together, will eventually make or break anyone who comes. The believers who have gone ahead of you will help you. In that way you will avoid pitfalls and be prepared for difficulties—there are many, but they are worth it.

Third, put fear aside. Recall that when Moses sent twelve men to spy out *Eretz- Yisrael* (Numbers 13-14), two—Joshua and Caleb—returned with good reports, encouraging the people to go in and conquer the Land; but ten gave bad reports, describing the inhabitants as too strong to be defeated. As we know, the people believed the ten and refused to enter, even though God wanted them to. Why did they refuse? Think about it. They had a choice. They chose to cater to fear rather than faith. I am giving you a good report about the Land of Israel. Go in and conquer it!

Finally, we and other Jewish believers who have made *aliyah* from America and elsewhere can be for you a home away from home, a little piece of the "old country" for Messianic Jewish tourists considering *aliyah* and for culture-shocked Messianic Jewish *olim* (immigrants), encouraging you when you're lonely, depressed or frustrated. Since most of us are still on the ladder of getting absorbed into Israel, we are well placed for reaching down a rung or two to you. Whether you come for a visit or a permanent stay, we will say to you: "*Barukh ha-ba ba-shem Adonai* (Blessed be he who comes in the name of the Lord)."

4. *Messianic Jewish Program in Regard to Israel*

The Messianic Jewish movement should create suitable institutions for promoting Messianic Jewish *aliyah* and for promoting and assisting Messianic Judaism and Jewish evangelism in the State of Israel.

There should also be institutions designed to cooperate with the non-Messianic Jewish community in connection with supporting the State of Israel, although this should be done with careful oversight. I know of a church that has given large sums of money to the State of Israel, which distributes it in such a way that some of the funds arrive in the hands of Orthodox *yeshivas* that teach people to hate Ye.->hua. This is not wise stewardship. Better to designate funds for aiding the elderly, planting trees or other neutral activities.

The Messianic Jewish movement should be cautious when cooperating with (Gentile) Christian Zionist organizations, since they may be working toward somewhat different goals, with somewhat different motives, and under somewhat different constraints. Organizational separation may serve best.

Regardless of what the Messianic Jewish movement as a whole does, Messianic Jewish individuals can support Israel, visit Israel, or make *aliyah*.

F. WHICH DIRECTION?

I have never seen a drawing like figure 6 in a theology book. Being an economist, however, I see about twenty diagrams like it in every issue of the *American Economic Review.* Yes, I know Thomas Carlyle dubbed economics the dismal science, but try to bear with me.

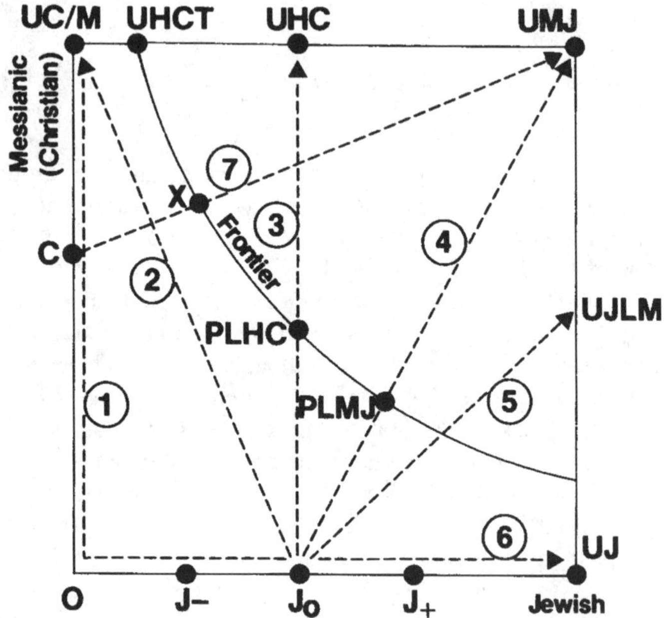

Figure 6

Which Direction?

On the horizontal axis is measured "Jewish." It could include involvement in Jewish community life, regular synagogue attendance, ethical living, doing *mitzvot,* "learning" (as the *ye-shiva backers* call rabbinic studies), eating lox and bagels, etc. Whatever mixed bag of things "Jewish" involves, if you're farther to the right, you've got more of it. You start as a baby with none (at 0, for "origin" or "zero"), and as you grow you learn and get more and more "Jewish," passing through J-mi-nus *(am-ha 'aretz,* literally "people of the land," but it means someone Jewishly ignorant), up to J-zero, "your average Jew." Then, if you go on, you pass to J-plus and if you ever get to UJ (for "ultimate Jew"), you've "got it all." Maybe I should have called this exalted state "TC," for *talmid chacham* ("scholar, wise man"), or "LV," for *lamed-vavnih,* one of the supposedly 36 righteous men for whose sake, according to Jewish tradition, God preserves the world.

Vertically one measures "Messianic" or "Christian" (and here I use the terms loosely as synonyms). Points actually on the vertical axis are Gentile Christian (since the Jewish component is zero). "Messianic" or "Christian" involves trusting in Yeshua as Savior, Messiah and Lord, displaying the fruit of the Spirit, having theological understanding, leading a good prayer life, caring for widows and orphans, etc.—but in what mix and with what other elements, I leave to the reader's judgment. The farther up you are the more you've got of it, and at UC/M (for "Ultimate Christian/Messianic") you've "got it all."

Obviously "having it all" is absurd in both cases, since God is infinite and we are finite. On the other hand, our potential for becoming like him, conforming more and more to the image of the Messiah, or developing along the lines of being Jewish or Messianic/Christian, is not explicitly limited. But since we can't draw infinite diagrams, we will make do with the one we have.

Non-Messianic Jews stick to the horizontal axis, and Gentile Christians generally remain on the vertical axis, but Messianic Jews wander off upward from the horizontal axis into the space below and to the left of the "Frontier" line. That space represents forms available now, today, for expressing Jewish and Messianic faith together. Beyond the Frontier, above and to the right, are forms as yet unachieved.

The Ultimate Messianic Judaism (UMJ) would be in the upper right corner, "100% Jewish and 100% Messianic" to a degree unknown at present. As I understand Hebrew Christianity, its ultimate expression (UHC) would be less Jewish but fully Christian. For the sake of conceptual completeness there is also shown a range of ultimately Jewish but limited Messianic possibilities (UJLM) that do get people born again but somehow stunt their growth in the Lord.

Now take your typical Jew, J-zero; call him Jo. God does the greatest miracle he can do in Jo's life: saves him. What happens to him then? Where does Jo go from here?

As we have seen, in the fourth century he would have been required to follow Path (1), back to 0, and up the vertical axis, conforming entirely to Gentile standards and renouncing his Jewishness completely. And since the fourth century this has been an acceptable, even the normal, path for a Jew to follow in the Church.

But the Church has not always been so uptight, and frequently it was glad to let Jo be who he was. However, it did nothing to help preserve Jo's Jewishness; and since he was in a Gentile Christian church, with mostly Gentile Christian friends, his behavior and attitudes would gradually become less Jewish and more Gentilized as he grew in faith, following a path more like (2).

Along came Hebrew Christianity in the 19th century, with the notion that a Jewish person can stay Jewish while being Christian. There was no concern to *increase* Jo's Jewishness, but there was no pressure to decrease it either, to have him become more Gentilized. His Jewishness was a matter of indifference, so far as his faith was concerned. So he embarked on a path (3), neither gaining more Jewishness nor losing what he had. If this diagram, with its Frontier, is drawn in a way that reflects any reality, he reaches a point PLHC (the present limit of Hebrew Christianity), where it becomes difficult to proceed straight ahead (straight up). That is, for him to grow in faith either he must pioneer beyond the Frontier, or he must give up some of his Jewishness. Why so? Perhaps there are so few Hebrew Christians maintaining Jewishness at even Jo's level that in order for Jo to grow in his faith he necessarily finds himself adding more Gentile experiences to his life and so moves along the Frontier itself as he becomes more Messianically expressive, ending up on the Frontier at UHCT (the ultimate Hebrew Christianity of today).

The target of Ultimate Messianic Judaism (UMJ) offers another possibility, namely, that Jo can grow both Messianically and Jewishly, moving along path (4). But again, at PLMJ (the present limit of Messianic Judaism), he reaches the Frontier; and, as I have drawn the Frontier, PLMJ is at a lower level of Messianic faith but a higher level of Jewish expression than PLHC. Whether a Frontier so shaped (sloping down to the right) reflects reality is itself a question to be examined.

I hope Jo doesn't get sidetracked onto path (5) which leads him to a limited form of Messianic faith, even though he grows in Jewish knowledge.

And if he had never gotten saved, he might have followed path (6) toward being a (non-Messianic) *talmid chacham.*

IF YOU ARE A MESSIANIC JEW, Jo IS YOU. IN WHICH DIRECTION ARE YOU HEADED?

We need not exclude Gentile Christians from the picture. C is a Gentile Christian who, without trying to Judaize himself, decides to support the Messianic Jewish movement. He heads out on path (7) toward UMJ. His experience along his path will be very different from Jo's, but if Jo is on path (4), both have the same goal. C, however, would get to the Frontier at X, which stands for "Present limit for Gentile Christians supporting the Messianic Jewish movement;" it is less Jewish and more Christian than PLHC. And this is to be expected, because

C is not Jewish. He absorbs Jewishness as an outsider, and his background probably includes Christian cultural elements which Jo does not share. Even at the Frontier (as drawn) his "Jewish" is about the same as that of J-minus, the *am-ha'aretz.*

But should Jo look down on C for that? Never! In the Lord we love one another, count others better than self, do nothing from selfishness or conceit, are of the same mind and of one accord. The American melting pot has long since evolved into a stewpot, so we can appreciate one another for who we are, without wishing Gentiles more Jewish or Jews more Gentile. UMJ is a target at which both Jews and Gentiles can aim without becoming clones of each other.

We could talk longer about Figure 6, finding meanings for other points, paths and regions on the graph. Another interesting thought experiment is to analyze what it means to shape the Frontier differently or move it.

But—there is another dimension, a dimension that rises up, off the graph, out of the book, and on into heavenly places with God. That dimension cannot be shown on paper, it must be lived. Without this dimension, "Ultimate Messianic Judaism" is earthbound and dead, words in a book, charts on a page. With it, with the dimension of the living God, with *him,* Messianic Judaism will achieve its ultimate destiny, and the God who made us all and who gave us our *Torah* and our Messiah Yeshua will bring us all to his promised goal.

O the depth of the riches
    and the wisdom and knowledge of God!
How inscrutable are his judgments!
    How unsearchable are his ways!
For from him and through him
    and to him are all things.
To him be the glory forever!
    Amen.[21]

21. Romans 11:33, 36, *Jewish New Testament.*

APPENDIX 1: RESTORING THE JEWISHNESS OF THE GOSPEL

A. INTRODUCTION

This appendix brings one simple message, namely, that unless the Church does everything in her power to restore the Jewishness of the Gospel, she lacks a key element of God's message. In consequence she cannot fulfill the Great Commission properly, and the Jewish people cannot be the right kind of "light to the nations."

The seven chapters of the main part of this book examine what the aforementioned "Jewishness" entails, and the point is made there that the burden of developing Messianic Judaism necessarily must fall in the main on the Messianic Jews. This appendix, however, is primarily for Gentile Christians, the vast majority in the Church; and the point I am making here, that the Jewishness of the Gospel needs to be restored, is the *one* idea I want to communicate to *all* believers. I am asking non-Jewish Christians to share some of the responsibility for restoring the Gospel's Jewishness and to do whatever they can to convey this concept to those in the Church who can be instrumental in its accomplishment.

When the Church proclaims a Gospel without its Jewishness restored, she is at best failing to proclaim "the whole counsel of God" (Acts 20:27). At worst she may be communicating what Sha'ul [Paul] called "another Gospel" (Galatians 1:6-9). Moreover, not only Jews suffer from this off-target preaching—Gentiles suffer too. Therefore I believe I am focussing on an extremely serious problem which has not received from Christians the attention it deserves.

Instead of "restoration," what is being taught in missiological circles is "contextualization" of the Gospel. Contextualization falls short of restoration. Section B examines why this is an inadequate approach to Jewish evangelism.

In Section C, I explore three propositions with which I assume my readers will agree. They are not themselves part of the restored Jewishness but are presupposed by it: first, Christianity is Jewish; second, antisemitism[1] is un-Christian; and third, refusing or neglecting to evangelize Jews is antisemitic. Also in this section I examine whatSha'ul meant when he said at Romans 1:16 that the Gospel is God's power for salvation "to the Jew first."

Section D surveys the blessings which will flow to both the Jews and the Church from restoring the Jewishness of the Gospel.

I have combined this appendix with portions of Chapters III, IV and V *of Messianic Judaism* to form a shorter book called *Restoring The Jewishness Of The Gospel,* whose intended readership is primarily Gentile Christians. Its purpose is to present some of the ideas to be found in this book in a briefer and less demanding form. Whoever has *Messianic Judaism* has no need to read *Restoring.* Anyone who reads *Restoring* and has unanswered questions, wishes to explore the issues further or watns to understand my point of view better ought to read *Messianic Judaism.*

---

1. See Chapter III, Footnote 9, on the use of the words "antisemitism" and "antisemitic" in this book.
2. The following table indicates where the material in *Restoring* can be found in *Messianic Judaism.*

Restoring	*Messianic Judaism.*
Introduction	Appendix, Section A
Chapter 1	Appendix, Sections B-l, B-2, B-3
Chapter II, Section A	Appendix, Section B-4
Chapter II, Section B	Chapter III, Sections B-3 (some), B-4

B. CONTEXTUALIZATION VERSUS RESTORATION

1. *Christianity And Culture*

a. "Transcultural Judaism"

Yeshua's "Great Commission" to the Church was to make disciples from every nation.[3] But as soon as the early Messianic Jews began reaching out to Gentiles, it was necessary to separate the Gospel from its cultural context, so that its essential message would not be encumbered with cultural baggage unnecessary for salvation.

Learning that the New Covenant did not require Gentiles to become Jews in order to be saved was a traumatic process for the Jewish believers in Yeshua [Jesus]. It began with Kefa's [Peter's] vision and Cornelius's coming to faith.[4] But it was Sha'ul, the emissary to the Gentiles, who worked out many of the details. Thus he was present at the Jerusalem Council when Ya'akov [James] announced the decision that Gentiles would not have to get circumcised and obey the *Torah* [the Law] as it had developed within traditional Judaism. Instead, the only entrance

Chapter II, Section C	Chapter IV, Section E-2
Chapter II, Section D	Chapter IV, Section E-3
Chapter II, Sections E-l, E-2, E-3	Chapter IV, Section E-4
Chapter II, Sections E-4, E-5, E-6	Chapter IV, Sections E-5, E-6, E-7
Chapter II, Sections F-l, F-2, F-3	Chapter V, Sections A-l, A-2, A-3
Chapter II, Section F-4	Chapter V, Sections C-2, B-7
Chapter II, Section F-5	Chapter V, Sections B-5, B-4
Chapter III, Section A	Appendix, Section C-l; Chapter III, Section D-3, paragraphs 2 and 3.
Chapter III, Section B	Appendix, Section C-2; Chapter III, Section E-2, paragraphs 3, 4, and 5.
Chapter III, Section C	Appendix, Section C-3
Chapter IV	Appendix, Section D

If a chapter or section of this book does not appear in the above table, it can be found only in *Messianic Judaism.*

3. Mattityahu [Matthew] 28:18-20.
4. Acts 10:1

requirement for them to be fully accepted as brothers in the Lord was obedience to the four *mitzvot* [commandments] outlined in Acts 15:20.

Later Sha'ul enunciated even more clearly the extent to which he was willing to go in order to win people—anyone, Jewish or Gentile—to the Lord. He wrote, in 1 Corinthians 9:19-22:

> "For although I am free from all men, I have enslaved myself to all, that I might win the more. To the Jews I became as a Jew, in order to win Jews; to those under law I became as one under law—though not being myself under law—in order to win those under law. To those apart from law I became as one apart from law—not being myself apart from law toward God but 'en-lawed' to the Messiah—in order to win those apart from law. To the weak I became weak, in order to win the weak. I have become all things to all men, that I might by all means save some."

In quoting this text I am compelled, because of criticisms commonly made, to note that in becoming "all things to all men" Sha'ul was not presenting himself as a chameleon or a hypocrite. Rather, in saying he "became" like others he meant that he put himself in their position, empathized with them, tried to understand their mindset, paid attention to "where they were coming from" and "where they were at." What motivated him was his desire to win the lost. He could have been lazy, he could have demanded that others adapt themselves to his culture rather than he empathize with theirs. But God's call on his life constrained him to go the extra mile, indeed to "enslave" himself to the needs of others.

In sum, Sha'ul did not compel Gentiles to adopt Jewish culture. He realized that the New Testament message for Gentiles was really, in Phil Goble's words, "transcultural Judaism," or, as it has come to be known, Christianity.

b. Non- Transcultural Christianity

But not everyone who has attempted to bring the Gospel message across cultural barriers has understood the principles of cross-cultural evangelism as Sha'ul taught them. Frequently the exact opposite happened: the Gospel was confused with culture, so that the message was not only to turn from sin to God through Yeshua, but also to abandon one's culture and become estranged from it.

In some parts of the world the missionaries lived (and still live) in a self-created ghetto, the "mission compound." When God touched a native and gave him a new spirit, the missionaries brought him into the compound and gave him a new culture (usually Western).

James Michener describes this approach graphically in his book, *Hawaii.* The book is historically inaccurate and filled with anti-Christian bias and prejudice, but we will adopt the author's perspective for a moment. He depicts missionaries from New England in the early 1800's requiring native Hawaiians to build wooden churches with steeples and dress like Puritans in order to become Christians. They had to become aliens in their own culture. True, the *kamaainas* often went about nude, and Christian discipleship entails modesty; nevertheless modesty does not necessarily entail adopting foreign dress. When people become Christians they need give up only their sin, not their culture, except the specific elements of it that violate scriptural norms.

c. "Now That You're Christian, Have A Ham Sandwich!"

As far as Jewish evangelism is concerned, it became standard practice by the fourth century *not* to follow Sha'ul's pattern of presenting the Gospel in the way most congenial to those for whom it was intended. On the contrary, it was not enough that a Jew should accept Yeshua as his Messiah, Savior and Lord; he had to "convert to Christianity,"[5] which usually meant

5. As used here, "converting to Christianity" is meant to be contrasted with "becoming

adopting an alien culture and sometimes required him to give up everything Jewish! The latter can be seen in the profession from the Church of Constantinople, cited above,[6] which Jews had to affirm if they wanted to join the holy Community of the Jewish Messiah, Yeshua.

I indicated earlier that sometimes Messianic Jews have been required to "prove their Christianity" by eating a ham sandwich;[7] and that my wife and I have on occasion experienced uneasiness emanating from Christian leaders when they discovered that we observe *kashrut* [the Jewish dietary laws].[8]

Another example: many Christians are offended when Messianic Jews celebrate the Jewish festivals instead of Christmas and Easter, even though the former are commanded in Scripture and the latter are human inventions. One of the Church's earliest expressions of anti-Jewishness was the second-century Quartodeciman Controversy, which led to the Gentile-oriented Nicene Council's decree that the date for celebrating Yeshua's death and resurrection should *not* be set by the Jewish calendar's date for Passover.

2. *Contextualizing The Gospel*

As modern-day missiologists—the scholars who help evangelists and missionaries in their work of obeying the Great Com-

---

a Messianic Jew." Jewish converts to Christianity and Messianic Jews both believe in Yeshua, but the latter retain their Jewish identity (which means Jewish practices as well as Jewish thoughts)—precisely what Jewish believers from the fourth century onward were often forbidden to do. See Chapter II, Sections A and B, and Chapter III, Section B-4. (In more recent times many Jewish converts to Christianity have voluntarily chosen to escape, ignore or limit their degree of Jewish identification.) Actually, in the New Testament the term "Christian" is not used by believers to refer to Messianic Jews but to Gentiles who came to know the one true God through Yeshua the Jewish Messiah. See Chapter II, Section C-4. Whether the term "Christian" should be applied to Messianic Jews today is discussed in Chapter III, Section H.

6. See Chapter III, Section B-4 and footnote 19 there.
7. This was discussed in Chapter V, Section B-3.
8. See Chapter III, Section E-4.

mission—began to look into the problem of people being alienated from their culture in order to become Christians, they developed the concept of *contextualization.* The word simply means presenting the Gospel within the context of the recipient's culture, rather than outside it. One could even say it's just a fancy way of talking about what Sha'ul did naturally.

When the Gospel is contextualized, new Christians remain within their culture and try to conform it as well as themselves to God's will.

a. Contextualizing The Gospel For Jews

The founding of what came to be called the Hebrew Christian movement in England and other European countries during the nineteenth century was essentially an effort at contextualizing the Gospel for Jews. Jewish believers were advised not to leave their people but to stay Jewish, so long as their Christian faith remained orthodox. They were encouraged to celebrate Passover, *Chanukah* and other festivals, and, generally, to express their Jewishness. They were also reminded that their observance of elements in the Mosaic Law did not enhance their salvation—that they, like Gentiles, were saved by faith and not by "works of law."

Clearly contextualization was an improvement over requiring Jews to renounce everything Jewish. But it dealt with Jewish believers as problem individuals—rather than with Judaism and the Jewish people as a corporate entity standing over against Christianity and the Church, and making conflicting claims concerning biblical truth.

b. Type I, Type II And Type III Evangelism

Missiologists have come up with a threefold classification of the cultural and linguistic barriers across which the Gospel must be proclaimed.

Type I Evangelism is sharing with nominal Christians in one's own culture. These are people who not only share one's language and cultural background but may have grown up going to church, hearing the Gospel and reading the Bible. In short, they are "Christianized" but not born again. In terms of ease of communication, this type of evangelism is the simplest. (Whether it is easiest in terms of getting people saved is another question.)

Type II Evangelism is with people who share one's language and perhaps live in the same or a similar society, but whose cultural and religious presuppositions may be very different. Suburbanite white Christians bringing the Gospel to unsaved inner-city blacks and middle-class blacks sharing the Messiah with white street people are both engaged in Type II Evangelism. So are Japanese Christians in Japan, where the religious milieu is Buddhist and Shinto.

Type III Evangelism brings the Gospel across cultural and linguistic barriers that at times can seem all but insuperable. The idea is conveyed well by the traditional picture of the missionary in a primitive jungle tribe learning the language, inventing an alphabet, translating the Bible, fighting the alien cultural and physical environment, all in order make God's grace known. Likewise, the on-fire Christians of Korea or Indonesia who preach to the blase youth of Europe may find themselves doing Type III Evangelism.

Each of these types requires its own approach to contextualization. To give one example, consider the verbal presentation of important theological concepts. In Type I Evangelism one can use "Christian language," with such terms as "sin," "born again" and "saved," the object being to deepen the hearer's spiritual understanding of what these mean, so that he will respond with faith. In Type II Evangelism such terminology seems peculiar and troublesome. These ideas must be conveyed differently to un-Christianized hearers, with examples from life, not jargon from church. In Type III Evangelism the language and culture may make it difficult to express the concepts at all.

c. Where Do The Jews Fit In?

Where do the Jews fit into this schema? If one regards Jewish people as candidates for Type II Evangelism, as un-Christianized members of the same society and language-group, then one is assuming that the Church is proclaiming the true Gospel, so that the task is only to contextualize it. Someone who takes this approach will argue that if a Samoan can be Christian and remain Samoan, why can't a Jew be Christian and stay Jewish?

Nevertheless, there is something strange, even wrong, in talking about contextualizing the Gospel for Jews; because the Gospel was completely Jewish in the first place! If Christianity's roots are Jewish, if the Gospel itself is Jewish in its very essence, why should it need to be contextualized for Jews?

The answer is that it doesn't need to be—provided the New Testament Gospel is actually being proclaimed! In fact, the Gospel had to be contextualized for Gentiles! That was Sha'ul's ministry. This was the victory of Acts 15, in which the Jerusalem Council decided that Gentiles did not have to become Jews in order to become Christians. This was the victory of Galatians 2, in which Sha'ul confronted Kefa [Peter] over Judaizing Gentile believers. The subsequent history leading to the outcome that *Jews* were required to be *Gentilized* in order to become Messianic shows how far practice strayed from the principles Sha'ul had set forth in the New Testament. It also signalled that something very strange had happened to the Jewish Gospel along the way!

And practice deviated not only from Sha'ul's principles, but from his practice as well. Sha'ul was a lifelong observant Jew. According to the Book of Acts, Sha'ul circumcised Timothy (Acts 16:3); regularly went to synagogue (17:2); took a Jewish vow (18:18); rushed up to Jerusalem to observe the Jewish pilgrim festival of *Shavu'ot* [Pentecost] (20:16); paid for other Jews to offer Jewish sacrifices at the Jewish Temple (21:23-27); stated before the Jewish *Sanhedrin* that he was then—as of that moment and not just formerly—a *Parush* [Pharisee] (23:7);

and declared to the Roman governor, Festus, that he had "done nothing against the *Torah* to which the Jews hold, nor against the Temple" (25:8, *Jewish New Testament* version). Finally, having fought the good fight, finished the race and kept the faith, he could tell an audience of Jews in Rome, "I have done nothing contrary to the people or to the ancestral customs" (28:17) and the phrase "ancestral customs" in eludes Jewish traditions as well asthe Written *Torah.* If this kind of life was good enough for Sha'ul, it is good enough for Jewish believers today. No ham sandwiches, please, for Messianic Jews who keep *kosher.*

3. *Not Contextualization But Type IV Evangelism*

Indeed any Jew can, like Sha'ul, be Messianic and remain Jewish. Nevertheless, to think this resolves all the issues is a great mistake because it misses the point. The reason is theological. From a sociological viewpoint, the Jews are just another culture, like the Samoans (actually it's not quite that simple, since there are many Jewish cultures).

But theologically, the Jews are unique because God chose them as the vehicle for bringing salvation to the world. The entire Hebrew Bible attests to that, as does the New Testament (see Yochanan [John] 4:22; Romans 3:2, 9:4-5). The Jews are God's people in a sense that applies to no other people on earth. Because of this, the New Testament abounds with theological Scyllas and Charybdises, rocky places that offer dangerous passage. What other people is faced with Galatians 3:28 ("there is neither Jew nor Greek") or Ephesians 2:11-22 ("the middle wall of partition")? If the French Christians Frenchify other believers, who raises any doctrinal question? But if Messianic Jews engage in Judaizing—watch out!

No, the Jewish people are more than a culture, they are the people of God. Therefore, the task in relation to Jews is not to contextualize the Gospel as it has come to non-Jews, with their pagan history, but rather to communicate a Gospel which is theologically correct vis-a-vis the Jewish people, whose history and role in communicating God's salvation is an eternal part of Holy Scripture. *Type IV Evangelism is needed to evangelize the people of God.*

To put it another way, contextualizing the Gentile form of the Gospel for the Jews is a double diversion. Originally its Jewish form was contextualized for Gentiles—this was Sha'ul's great contribution to evangelism. But then, as the early Messianic Jewish communities fell on hard times and disappeared, the Jewishness originally present in the Gospel also vanished, so that a Gentile-contextualized Gospel deprived of its Jewish substratum was the only Gospel there was, a Procrustean bed in which the Jewish believer was forced to lie. Recently this Gospel-at-one-remove (from a Jewish standpoint) has been reworked, "contextualized," to make it "seem more Jewish." But the double adaptation is not the same as the original. Looking at a person's mirror reflection reflected in a second mirror is not the same as looking at him.

What Type IV Evangelism requires is not a Gentilized Gospel contextualized for Jews, but a restoration of the Jewishness which is in fact present in the Gospel but which has become obscured. Moreover, Gentile Christians too need aspects of the Gospel which a restoration of its Jewishness will bring them.

But many believers feel uneasy about restoring Jewishness to the Gospel and encouragingMessianicJewsto express their Jewish identity. They fear an elitism will arise in which Gentile Christians will be made to feel like second-class citizens of the Kingdom. This is a real pitfall, and Scripture warns against division between Jew and Gentile in the Body of the Messiah. However, the New Testament also gives assurance that both are one in Yeshua, serving one God by one Spirit. Therefore, let all believers, both Jewish and Gentile, work together to avoid invidious comparisons, which only serve the Adversary. Let every Messianic Jew and every Gentile Christian demonstrate in his own life those elements of Jewishness which arise from his own spiritual consciousness and identity, without feeling condemned for expressing either too much or too little. And let each one remain open to God's leading, so that this aspect of his life, like all others, can be conformed more and more to the image of Yeshua, the Messiah of Jews and Gentiles alike.

Having warned against elitism and division, we ask what restoring the Jewishness of the Gospel actually entails. To this question we turn our attention now.

4. *What Is Meant By "Restoring"?*

Restoring the Jewishness of the Gospel means filling out the *content* of the Gospel in all its fullness as it pertains to Jews and to the relationship between the Jewish people and the Church. In other words, it means offering, in relation to these things, "the whole counsel of God," not just part.

It is important to understand what theologians mean when they talk about "restoration." We would all like to see the Church "restored" to what it was in the first century. Or so we say. Certainly it would be good to restore the zeal of the first believers, the righteousness of their lives, their willingness to follow Yeshua the Messiah no matter what the cost, their being filled with the Holy Spirit, their eagerness to pray, their assurance and experience that God performs miracles in response to faith. But are there external aspects of the first century believers' lifestyle that we should set out to restore? or aspects of doctrine that they would have accepted, but which later believers have ignored? And if so, which ones? and what should we do about them?

My view is that we ought to start by making every effort to *understand* the text of the New Testament as its first century hearers would have *understood* it and applied it to their situation in life. But I do not believe we are expected to *apply* the Gospel in the same way, because that would mean restoring the first-century situation in life, which, even were it desirable, is impossible—there is no turning back the clock. Rather, we must understand Scripture properly and then apply it to our own situation in the appropriate way.

The above paragraphs do not express a new philosophy. They express a familiar approach which normally leads to asking whether a given New Testament injunction is to be applied literally, or should one look for a general principle behind the written command. For example, in reference to 1 Corinthians 11:2-15, must a woman today cover her head in a congregation meeting? Or was this requirement related only to the first-century life situation, so that the modern application is to dress modestly by current standards?

I have not addressed matters of this kind in this book, although they will become important practically as Messianic Judaism develops. Rather, I have tried to call attention to aspects of the Gospel which would have been evident to first-century believers but which centuries of neglect have hidden from view.

Restoring the Jewishness of the Gospel will mean, first, allowing and encouraging Messianic Jews to develop Messianic Judaism, and second, having non-Jewish Christians learn from this process, so that they incorporate into their own Christian life those neglected aspects of the faith which a restored Messianic Judaism will make known.

C. PRESUPPOSITIONS TO RESTORING THE JEWISHNESS OF THE GOSPEL

In Section A, I wrote that I assume my readers will agree to the following three points, which are not themselves part of restoring Jewishness to the Gospel but are presupposed by it: (1) Christianity is Jewish, (2) antisemitism is un-Christian, and (3) refusing or neglectingto evangelizeJews is antisemitic.The time has come to discuss these matters, since some readers will not have agreed and need to be convinced. We will conclude by considering what Sha'ul meant when he wrote in Romans 1:16 that the Gospel is "for the Jew first."

1. *Christianity Is Jewish*

Edith Schaeffer, wife of the late Francis Schaeffer, wrote a book with the title, *Christianity is Jewish.*[9] Her point, and mine too, is that Christianity, no matter how un-Jewish some of its current forms of expression may be, has its roots in Judaism and in the Jewish people.

As we saw earlier, the basic facts cannot be disputed—the main characters and authors were Jewish, and the New Testament itself must be understood against its Jewish background.[10] Sha'ul makes the Jewishness of Christian faith most explicit in the book of Romans. He writes, "In the first place, theJews were entrusted with the very words of God,"" meaning the Hebrew Bible, and then expands on the theme, adding that the people of Israel

> "were made God's children, the *Sh 'khinah* [God's glory manifested] has been with them, the covenants are theirs, likewise the giving of the *Torah,* the Temple service and the promises; the Patriarchs are theirs; and from them, as far as his physical descent is concerned, came the Messiah."[12]

Thus the entire context of Messianic faith is nothing but Jewish. Even if one were to accept the false premise of Replacement Theology that the Jews are no longer God's people, this would not change the fact that Christianity is Jewish. To try to understand it differently can only distort God's message.

But Christianity is Jewish in yet another sense, namely, that it is in principle best assimilated by Jews. This is Sha'ul's very point in the quoted passages of Romans; his object is to show

9. Edith Schaeffer, *Christianity Is Jewish* (Wheaton, Illinois: Tyndale House Publishers, Inc., 1975).
10. See Chapter III, Section D-3, paragraphs 2 and 3.
11. Romans 3:2.
12. Romans 9:4-5.

that the Gospel is "for the Jew especially"—as we will see in Section C-4.

2. *Antisemitism Is Un-Christian*

In another context we spoke about how antisemitism is incompatible with biblical faith.[13] To say it very simply: any thoughts, words or deeds which damage Jewish individuals or the Jewish people as a whole merely because they are Jews violates everything Christian and must be regarded as sin.

In a slightly different category are unconscious forms of antisemitism (a rereading of this book will point at many of them[14]). There are well-meaning Christians who neither dislike nor wish to offend Jews but nevertheless absorb anti-Jewish attitudes from a culture steeped in centuries of anti-Jewish teaching. Replacing anti-Jewish interpretations of the New Testament with interpretations based on its Jewish background may be the one effective way of dealing with this phenomenon.

3. *Refusing Or Neglecting To Evangelize Jews Is Antisemitic*

Only bigots and boors would dispute the first two points in this section. But there are many who call themselves Christians who would disagree with this third point, who would insist that what is proper and appropriate is *not* to bring the Gospel to Jews, either as individuals or as a people. Others do not actually refuse to evangelize Jews on principle, but simply neglect to do so, considering it a relatively low priority in their Christian lives.

So our task here is to establish that evangelism of Jews should be a high priority for every Christian.

---

13. See Chapter III, Section E-2, paragraphs 3, 4, and 5.
14. See especially C.iapter III, Section E-4, and Chapter V, footnote 8.

a. Benign Neglect Of The Jews Is Antisemitic

There are Christians who justify their neglect of Jewish evangelism with remarks such as, '1 don't know any Jews; ""I Ve never thought about Judaism;" "God hasn't called me to concern myself with Jews."

All are unsatisfactory excuses, because Scripture does not allow the option of overlooking the Jews. Zechariah 1:15 is a very interesting verse. God tells the prophet, "I am highly displeased with the *goyim"*—the Hebrew word can mean Gentiles, pagans, or nations—"who are at ease; for I was only a little displeased, but they helped forward the affliction." How did the Gentiles help "forward the affliction" of the Jews? By being "at ease"—indifferent, not caring, ignoring the situation. Edmund Burke noted that the world's evil can be laid at the feet of good men who sit back and do nothing. Yeshua himself said, "Those who are not with me are against me, and those who do not gather with me are scattering."[15] There is no middle position, no *tertium quid.* Everyone must take a stand; taking no stand is taking a stand against by default.

If indifference to the Jewish people counts as opposition and is wrong, then what is right? What is right is to bring the Gospel to the Jewish people in a way that takes seriously their position as the people of God, whose gift and calling, Sha'ul wrote, are irrevocable. Or, to put it differently, what is right is to be a channel for God's love to the Jews.

b. Purposeful Neglect, Justified By History, Is Antisemitic

But there are also people who call themselves Christians who not only neglect Jews and refuse to evangelize them, but do so on purpose and believe that they are right.

Some are simply afraid of being rejected, since it is well known that many Jewish people are not open to considering the claims of Yeshua and the New Testament. If that is their only reason, they can be encouraged to drop their fear, pray

15. Luke 11:23.

that God will bless their efforts, and then obey the Great Commission by reaching out to the Jews with the offer of God's love and forgiveness through the Messiah.

Others feel they should respect the sensibilities of Jewish people who say they do not want to hear about Yeshua. For them the remedy is to give Scripture heavier weight than their feelings and to renew their efforts—tactfully, sensitively, as the Lord leads—at communicating the truth of the Gospel to Jews. I owe my own salvation in part to a young man who was quite unaware of my sensibilities but told me the truth about Yeshua anyway.

However, there are those who do not rely on emotions but attempt to rationalize steering clear of Jewish evangelism by marshalling facts. A common justification for not evangelizing Jews is the Holocaust. Six million Jews died at the hands of the Nazis. During Hitler's twelve-year rule the state churches were notoriously silent and weak in the face of visible evil; moreover, mainstream Christian theology, if not actually antisemitic, was sufficiently cold toward Jews and Judaism to allow virulent antisemitism to express itself unchecked. Many well-meaning Christians ask how, in the face of such sin by the Church, do we dare tell Jews they should believe in Jesus?

The answer is twofold. On the one hand, the answer to the question, "How?" is: "Humbly." A Christian should be willing to shoulder the burden of the Church in respect to the Jews. He should not say, "The bad Christian theology was done by liberals, and they weren't real Christians. The state churches were not run by real Christians." Instead, he should admit, "It is possible that people who are my brothers in Christ committed horrors against Jews. I don't know for certain that they really are my brothers, but I will not massage my own conscience by denying the possibility categorically."

Moreover, his stance toward Jews in regard to the Holocaust should be one of seeking forgiveness without expecting it. He should acknowledge that the Church sinned. And he should ask forgiveness. But why should a Jew grant it? What has the Church done to earn the Jewish people's forgiveness? An element in forgiveness is restitution. How can the Church, or anyone, make restitution for the death of six million people? Ultimately, the answer is that only God can make restitution. The Holocaust is too horrible to allow that any human act or combination of human acts could pay for it. Only God, in his miraculous way, through the healing that Yeshua the Messiah brings, can restore the hearts of the living to the point to where they can forgive. No Christian has a right to expect Jewish forgiveness for the Holocaust, and in fact he will probably not get such forgiveness from Jews whose hearts have not been healed by Yeshua the Messiah.

Nevertheless, a Christian should bring the Gospel to the Jews. Why? Because it is true, and because it is necessary—without Yeshua Jewish people, like Gentile people, are destined for eternal destruction; moreover, without Yeshua the true Messiah of the Jewish people, the Jewish people will not achieve its own glorious goals promised by Scripture. *Not to preach the Gospel to Jews is the worst antisemitic act of all.* Therefore, in spite of the Holocaust—and the Inquisition, and the pogroms, and all the other horrors—Christians must take up the Gospel and bring it to Jews. For without Yeshua, the Jewish people (and other peoples), individually and collectively, have no hope.

c. Purposeful Neglect, Justified By Theology, Is Antisemitic

Another way in which Christians who will not evangelize Jews justify themselves is through two-covenant theology. This says that Jesus brought the covenant through which Gentiles emerge from paganism to know the one true God; but that Jews already have the covenant through Moses, so that they do not need Yeshua the Messiah—in fact, it is both a diversion and an insult to tell Jews about him.

The first objection to this is simply a matter of logic. If Yeshua is not the Messiah of the Jews, then he is nobody's Messiah, and Gentiles don't need him either.

But for anyone who accepts the New Testament as God-given, one verse is enough to blow two-covenant theology out of the arena, Yochanan [John] 14:6: "Yeshua said, 'I am the way and the truth and the life; no one comes to the father except through me.'" This verse teaches that *no one*—neither Jew nor Gentile—comes to the Father except through Yeshua the Messiah. If that weren't sufficient, there is also Acts 4:12, where Kef a [Peter] says of Yeshua, "There is salvation in no one else! For there is no other name under heaven given to mankind by whom we must be saved!"—no other name but Yeshua given to mankind for salvation, not to Gentiles and not to Jews.

It is understandable that two-covenant theology began not in Christianity but in Judaism, since it provides a Jewish defense against the Gospel. The *Rambam,*[16] functioning in an environment wherein Christendom controlled the state and all major institutions, developed the theory that Christianity was right for Gentiles, since it enabled them to stop worshipping idols and to worship instead the God of Abraham, Isaac and Jacob. Their worship was imperfect because it was mixed with worshipping a man as well as God; but imperfect worship of God was better than idolatry. This was a relatively sanguine view of Christianity, compared with Jewish opinions which regarded Christianity itself as idolatry.

In the early twentieth century Franz Rozenzweig picked up this approach. In his book *The Star of Redemption*[11] he expressed the two-covenant theory in modern theological language. Yeshua is truly the Messiah for the Gentiles, he argued, even if he isn't for the Jews. Rosenzweig even came up with an answer to Yochanan 14:6. Yes, Jesus is the way, the truth and the life for Gentiles, and no one comes to the Father except through him. But Jews are *already* with the Father, because of the Mosaic and Abrahamic covenants; so they don't need to *come* to him. Reinhold Niebuhr, the theologian, and

---

16. "*Rambam*" is an acronym for Rabbi Moshe ben-Maimon, known as Maimonides (1135-1204).
17. Franz Rosenzweig, *The Star of Redemption* (Boston: Beacon Press, 1972).

James Parkes, the historian who wrote extensively about the relationship between the Church and the Synagogue, were among those who proposed the two-covenant theory within a Christian thought-framework. They were well-meaning, but they missed the essential point that according to the New Testament (e.g., Ephesians 2:11-16), Jews and Gentiles can be reconciled with God and with each other only when both accept Yeshua asMessiah, Savior and Lord.

For Yochanan 14:6 cannot be so easily disposed of. Yeshua was speaking to Jews when he said those words; moreover, when he spoke them, the Gospel had been presented only to Israel, so that there is no reason to suppose he was referring to Gentiles. Likewise, Mark tells us that only hours later his answer to the high priest's question, "Are you the *Mashiach, Ben-HaM'vorakh* [the Messiah, the Son of the Blessed One]?" was unmistakable: "I AM." Then, to make his answer crystal clear, he cited two verses from the *Tanakh* with Messianic overtones, Psalm 110:1 and Daniel 7:13: "Moreover, you will see 'the Son of Man' 'sitting at the right hand of *HaG'vurah* ["the Power," i.e., God] and 'coming on the clouds of heaven.'"[18] The very concept of a Messiah is Jewish, not Gentile. All four Gospels depict him coming from Jews, to Jews and for Jews (while not excluding others). The two-covenant theory is fantasy and wish, not truth and reality.

Yeshua himself longed to be accepted by the Jewish people as who he is. But he did not force people to receive him, nor would he allow others to use force to obtain for him what was his by right.[19] Rather, he wept, "Jerusalem! Jerusalem! . . . How often I wanted to gather your children, just as a hen gathers her chickens under her wings, but you refused! . . . For I tell you, from now on, you will not see me again until you say, 'Blessed is he who comes in the name of *Adonai.*'"[20]

18. Mark 14:61-62, *Jewish New Testament.*

19. Yochanan [John] 6:15.

20. Mattityahu [Matthew] 23:37, 39, *Jewish New Testament.*

In conclusion, Yeshua is the Messiah of both Jews and Gentiles. There is one New Covenant, made "with the house of Israel and the house of Judah," (Jeremiah 31:30-34) for both Jews and Gentiles. Jews need Yeshua and the New Covenant as much as Gentiles. It is up to Gentile Christians and Messianic Jews to make this known to unsaved Jews as well as unsaved Gentiles, not to find excuses for disobeying the Great Commission.

d. Romans 1:16—The Gospel Is "For The Jew Especially."

Romans 1:16 (in the *Jewish New Testament* version) says,

> "For I am not ashamed of the Good News, since it is God's powerful means of bringing salvation to everyone who keeps on trusting, to the Jew especially, but equally to the Gentile."

This rendering brings out the meaning of the phrase usually translated, "to the Jew first."

Mitch Glaser, president of Chosen People Ministries, in his 1984 Covenant Theological Seminary lecture trenchantly entitled, "To the Jew First: The Starting Point For The Great Commission,"[21] presented three options for understanding this phrase. He concluded that it does not only refer to "historical priority," to the fact that historically the Gospel was presented first to Jews and only later to Gentiles, although this is true.

Nor does it refer only to "covenant priority," the idea that, as John Murray put it in his commentary on Romans, "Salvation through faith has primary relevance to the Jew . . . aris[ing] from the fact that [he] had been chosen by God to be the recipient of the promise of the Gospel and that to him were committed the oracles of God," although this too is true.

21. Mitch Glaser, "To the Jew First: The Starting Point for the Great Commission," lecture presented at Covenant Theological Seminary, 1984.

Rather, "to the Jew first" means that there is a "present priority" in bringing the Gospel to Jews, and the Church should acknowledge it. This does not necessarily mean that every single believer should seek out the Jews in the community and witness to them before telling any Gentiles about Jesus—although that is exactly what Sha'ul did throughout the book of Acts. As Mitch Glaser puts it, believers today should have

> "a priority of Gospel concern for the Jewish people.... Perhaps the most lucid explanation of the Present Priority view of Romans 1:16 can be found in the statement of the Lausanne Consultation on Jewish Evangelism, Occasional Papers No. 7:
>
> > 'There is, therefore, a great responsibility laid upon the church to share Christ with the Jewish people. This is not to imply that Jewish evangelism is more important in the sight of God, or that those involved in Jewish evangelism have a higher calling. We observe that the practical application of the scriptural priority is difficult to understand and apply. We do not suggest that there should be a radical application of "to the Jew first" in calling on all the evangelists, missionaries, and Christians to seek out the Jews within their sphere of witness before speaking to non-Jews! Yet we do call the church to restore ministry among this covenanted people of God to its biblical place in the strategy of world evangelization.'"[22]

Christians pray in the Lord's Prayer, "Thy kingdom come, thy will be done on earth as it is in heaven." Jews pray in the *Kaddish,* "May he establish his kingdom in your lifetime and in your days, and within the life of the whole house of Israel, speedily and soon." 2 Kefa [2 Peter] 3:12 says believers in Yeshua should work to hasten the coming of the Day of God.

---

22. *Ibid.*

Could it be that one reason for the "present priority" of preaching the Gospel "to the Jew especially" is that neglecting Jewish evangelism delays the coming of the Kingdom of God on earth?

D. BLESSINGS

Why restore the Jewishness of the Gospel? In order to bless both the Church and the Jewish people.

1. *How Will The Church Be Blessed?*

How will the Church be blessed? We spoke already of Genesis 12:3, in which God tells Abraham, "I will bless those who bless my people." That is a blessing Christians can experience right now. Any blessing, either spiritual or material (see Romans 15:27) to the Jewish people will bring return blessings to the Church. "Cast your bread on the waters, for you will find it after many days."[23]

But there is a further blessing in store for the Church. Sha'ul tells Gentile Christians concerning the Jewish people:

> "For if their being cast aside means reconciliation for the world, what will their acceptance mean? It will be life from the dead!"[24]

It will be life from the dead both for Jews and for Christians. This is a powerful motive for successfully evangelizing the Jewish people. I emphasize "successfully," because Sha'ul here does not promise an "A" for effort. It is only when the Jews are actually "accepted" that "life from the dead" will come. And this "life from the dead" will not be merely what some Christians understand by "revival"—having a bit more energy and feeling good—but the Resurrection itself! The Resurrection will take place only when "all Israel shall be saved."

23. Ecclesiastes 11:1.
24. Romans 11:15.

2. *How Will The Jewish People Be Blessed?*

How will the Jewish people be blessed? By being able to realize its age-old goal of being a light to the nations, and also by receiving the deliverance for which it has waited so long. The deliverance will be both individual and corporate, as we have seen.

How will these blessings come to the Jewish people? From God, of course. But not directly! Rather, they will come through the Church, and specifically through Gentile Christians when they finally make Jews jealous![25]

Have Jews a reason to be jealous of the Church now? A Jewish bumper sticker from some years ago said it all. During a national evangelistic campaign in the 1970's Christians put stickers on their car bumpers with the slogan, "I found it," hoping to provoke, if not jealousy, at least interest. Jews answered with stickers that said, "We never lost it."

Three things here: First, Jewish people understood well what the "it" was that the bumper sticker people had "found," namely, a relationship with God through Jesus. In effect proclaiming two-covenant theology to the world, their bumper stickers said that they already had a relationship with God and therefore didn't need Jesus; moreover, by implication they questioned the Christian theology that supposes people go out of relationship with God, so that they need to be saved.[26]

Secondly, the stickers poked fun at the very idea that as serious a matter as being related to the living God could be dealt with so offhandedly. You want to talk about ultimate matters of universal significance with slogans on bumper stickers? You found it? "It"? We should be jealous? You've got to be kidding!

Thirdly, the sticker says a lot about the difference between Judaism and Christianity as currently purveyed: *I*, all by myself

---

25. Romans 10:19; 11:11, 14.
26. On this see Abba Hillel Silver, *Where Judaism Differed (op cit.*, Chapter IV, footnote 55), Chapter 10, entitled "That Men Need to be Saved."

in my little warm cocoon, found it; *WE,* the Jewish people, the people of God, never lost it. Corporate mentality—unfortunately Christianity, especially in most of its Protestant manifestations, lost it!

How will Christianity overcome its handicap? One way![27] By making Jewish people jealous. And how will Christians accomplish that? By showing God's mercy to Jewish people. This is what Sha'ul prescribes to Gentile Christians at the end of Romans 9-11:

> "Just as you yourselves were disobedient to God before but have received mercy now because of Israel's disobedience; so also Israel has been disobedient now, so that by your showing them the same mercy that God has shown you, they too may now receive God's mercy. For God has shut up all mankind together in disobedience, in order that he might show mercy to all.[28]

Some suppose this passage says only that God will show Jews the same mercy he has shown Gentiles. This is true, but it misses the point. After severely warning Gentile Christians in Romans 11:17-24 not to boast against the cut-off branches (unsaved Jews), Sha'ul concludes his exhortation by counseling them to do something very different, to show them mercy. It will indeed be the mercy which God has given them that they will channel to Jews. But Sha'ul is not calling for watching passively to see how God will show his mercy to Jews. Rather he adjures Gentile Christians to show mercy actively to Jews right now. God calls for active participation in his salvation program. This is the one thing that can melt hearts and make unsaved Jews jealous of Christians. Nothing else will! Too bad so few have tried it!

This remarkable plan of God's causes Sha'ul so to marvel that he breaks into song at the end of Romans 11, a song so

27. "One way!" was another evangelism slogan in the '70's, and not a bad one in the face of two-covenant theology and "new age" religions.

28. Romans 11:30-32, *Jewish New Testament.*

joyous and profound that there is nothing to match it in the entire New Testament—and with it I close the appendix as I did the body of the book:

> "O the depth of the riches
> and the wisdom and knowledge of God!
> How inscrutable are his judgments!
> How unsearchable are his ways!
>
> "For from him and through him
> and to him are all things.
> To him be the glory forever!
> Amen.[29]

29. Romans 11:33, 36, *Jewish New Testament.*

APPENDIX 2: *ALIYAH* UPDATE

As a result of the Beresford cases (see pages 18 and 229-230) the situation for Messianic Jewish *aliyah* is different from what it was when the first edition of this book was published in 1988. This epilogue is intended to bring the reader up to date. In a January 1988 public opinion survey conducted by the Dahaf Research Institute, Israel's equivalent of the Gallup Poll, 61% of the 1,189 Israeli Jews polled agreed that "a person born to a Jewish mother who believes that Yeshua is the Messiah" should be allowed to make *aliyah* as a Jew under the Law of Return (35% disagreed, 4% had no opinion). As for someone described as "born to a Jewish mother, faithful to the State of Israel, pays his taxes to the State, serves in the army, celebrates the Jewish holidays, keeps commandments from Israel's tradition, feels that he is a Jew, and believes that Yeshua is the Messiah, but was not baptized into Christianity," 78% agreed he should be allowed to make *aliyah* (17% disagreed, 5% had no opinion); surprisingly, a breakdown by religious self-identification showed that even 77% of the *dati 'im* (religious) agreed.

Nevertheless, on December 25, 1989, *Bagatz* (the High Court of Justice) rejected the petition of Messianic Jews Gary and Shirley Beresford to make *aliyah* as Jews. Two of the three judges hearing the case wrote opinions. Menahem Elon, who is *dati,* wrote in effect that no conceivable change could reverse the "historic decision of the Jewish people" centuries ago to deny rights as Jews to Jewish believers in Yeshua (except, I would suppose, legislation by the Knesset specifically defining Messianic Jews as Jews under the Law of Return). Aharon Barak, on the other hand, wrote that a liberal, secular criterion should be used; the Israeli Jewish public, in his judgment, was not ready *now* to accept Messianic Jewish *aliyah* (despite the poll!); but this could change, so that a future court might reverse the interpretation which the Court made in the Beresford verdict.[1]

The Beresfords, relying on the Barak reasoning, along with two other families, continued their fight for recognition under the Law of Return. They also applied to be admitted under the Law of Entry, the ordinary immigration law under which non-Jews apply for permanent residence in Israel. The *Misrad HaP'nim* (Interior Ministry) rejected these latter applications, and shortly afterwards, in September 1992, *Bagatz* turned down all three families' requests for admission under the Law of Return. At present, therefore, the legal status of Messianic Jews is that they are not allowed to make *aliyah* under the Law of Return, and the *Misrad Hap'nim* is not required to grant them permanent residence (although neither is it required to refuse such a request; they may choose to grant it).

I think these two court decisions brings to an end, for now, the possibilities for using the courts to obtain the goal of having Messianic Jews accepted for *aliyah* under the Law of Return. We and our supporters must now expand our campaign from the courts into the public arena, for at this point there can be redress only in a political solution. In 1993 we demonstrated for a week across from the Prime Minister's office, an event reported on national television and radio, but events leading to the Oslo Peace Accord and coalition problems with the *Shas* party soon crowded us off the stage. Neverthe-

1. For more on the Dahaf poll and the Beresford verdict see David H.Stern, "The Beresford Case and Israeli Public Opinion About Messianic Jewish Aliyah," pp. 4-11 in *LCJE Bulletin,* Issue No. 20 (Ellebaekvej 5, DK-8520 Lystrup, Denmark: Lausanne Consultation on Jewish Evangelism, May 1990).

less, it behooves us Messianic Jews to continue expressing our views and aims more publicly.

Essential to such an experiment in public relations is increasing the number of Messianic Jews wanting to make *aliyah.* Numbers count. For were the Law of Return interpreted or changed to allow Messianic Jewish *aliyah,* it would be a Pyrrhic victory if no Messianic Jews came! Also essential is insisting that we are, despite the bad theology delivered from the bench in the various court decisions, Jews—according to God, according to *halakhah,* and according to the content of our faith. Yet we must be careful not to focus primarily on ourselves as a social movement deserving rights but on Yeshua as God's anointed one, the Messiah of Israel. It would be not only a Pyrrhic victory but a dreadful tragedy if in the course of winning the right to make *aliyah* Messianic Jews somehow lost sight of why they are who they are.

One positive function of the Dahaf Survey should be to reassure us that in such a struggle we do have friends. In effect, the majority of Jewish Israelis believe our cause is just. I am sure that some will stand with us publicly, especially those who, without necessarily sharing our faith position, believe strongly in civil rights for everyone.

The Messianic Jewish Alliance of America took the lead in publicizing the issue of Messianic Jewish *aliyah* by sponsoring a full-page advertisement protesting the Beresford verdict in the May 5, 1990 issue of *The Jerusalem Post International Edition.* The Union of Messianic Jewish Congregations has also protested the Beresford decision in a letter to Israeli authorities. All this is to the good: the Jewish and Christian publics must be constantly challenged by the injustice being done to us. No other group of Jews is subject to such discrimination in Israel. Jewish Buddhists and Hindus can make *aliyah.* Jewish members of any "new age" sect, no matter how odd, can make *aliyah.* Jewish idol-worshippers can make *aliyah.* Jewish atheists can make *aliyah.* Even Jewish known criminals can make *aliyah*—in fact, we had one in the Knesset a few years ago.

We Messianic Jews would have died as Jews in Auschwitz, so why can't we live as Jews in Israel? Why are we the only Jews who must pass a confessional test to make *aliyah?* Why are we Israel's refuseniks?

In the meantime, I am often asked by Messianic Jews wanting to make *aliyah* if they should enter the country without stating on their applications that they are Messianic Jews. In the past, I would have said "Yes" without hesitation, on the ground that Messianic Jews are Jews, that the applicant is asked only to state his religion, and that the religion of a Messianic Jew is Judaism, just as the religion of a Reform, Conservative or even atheist Jew is, for the purposes of the application, Judaism without a clarifying adjective.

Now my "Yes" requires a defense. I have never believed that applicants for anything must answer unasked questions, and I know of very few cases where a Messianic Jew has been asked by the *Misrad Hap'nim* in Israel or the *shaliach (aliyah* emissary) abroad what he thought about Jesus (these few were all instances where the questioner had been informed in advance about the applicant's beliefs). So I would recommend not volunteering information.

More importantly, if a Messianic Jew is asked, he can refuse to answer. This is not "denying the Messiah," which consists in stating or agreeing that Yeshua is not the Messiah—there's a difference between saying "No" and saying nothing. Rather, it is defending one's privacy. One's private opinions are nobody else's business, not the *Misrad HaP'nim's* and not the courts'. It is not our responsibility to encourage clerks and judges in their role as thought-police. Moreover, although a believer is expected to regard the laws of his country and government as being "from God,"[2] he need not so regard the laws of countries of whom he is not a subject (except that tourists are expected to obey local regulations). Therefore, Messianic Jews

2. Romans 13:1-7.

in the Diaspora do not have to agree with, support or cooperate with Israel's current interpretation of its Law of Return. They are, of course, subject to the consequences of that interpretation—acceptance or rejection; if the latter, they may choose to fight in court or not. But we need not help the Israel authorities exclude us from the Land of our forefathers merely on the basis of our own statements. Let Israel enforce its own law. My view is that the authorities should be required to collect their own evidence and prove their case in court every time they want to turn back a Messianic Jew.

But for various reasons not every Messianic Jew will wish the burden of a court fight. And there are two sides to the question of whether it is ethical for a Messianic Jew to violate a law (by immigrating to Israel under the Law of Return in its current interpretation) for the sake of a higher goal (the right of Messianic Jews, like all other Jews, to return to the Land God has given them without discrimination or hindrance). Although I think all Messianic Jews can agree that a Messianic Jew is indeed a Jew, no matter what Israel's highest court says, the fact is that the Messianic Jewish movement, as such, has not yet taken a unified, public stand on whether individual Messianic Jews should continue to attempt *aliyah* under the Law of Return. Therefore the situation now is that each must act according to his own conscience.

My personal view is that Messianic Jews should continue to attempt *aliyah.* My model for this view is what is known in Israel as "*Aliyah Bet.*" After England, in the 1930's, passed laws prohibiting Jews from coming to Palestine and began turning back ships, such as the Exodus, that were bringing Jews to Israel and incarcerating their passengers in Cyprus, Jewish underground movements began organizing clandestine voyages. These voyages brought Jewish passengers ashore by night, spiriting them off to *kibbutzim,* where they appeared to English investigators no different from *kibbutzniks* who had been there ten years or more. Today these people and those who smuggled them into the Land are heroes. I regard Messianic Jews who make *aliyah* today as heroes, and I, for one, am prepared to help them do it. Of course, like the Jews in the 1940's, we must work to make Messianic Jewish *aliyah* legal in every respect.

APPENDIX 3: SOME THOUGHTS ON THE FUTURE OF MESSIANIC JUDAISM

SUCCESS STORY?

Forecasting the future of Messianic Judaism is a daunting challenge. Forecasters must base their predictions on available relevant data, so here are some: In 1988 I wrote in Messianic Jewish Manifesto that there were in the United States 50,000-100,000 Jewish believers in Yeshua and over 120 Messianic Jewish congregations. I wrote that in Israel there might be 1,000-3,000 Jewish believers in 25-30 congregations. Today in America there must be 200,000 Jewish believers and at least 300 Messianic Jewish congregations, whereas in Israel, as of 2003, there were between 2,500 and 10,000 Jewish believers in some 90 congregations." In 1988 institutional Messianic Jewish education in the USA was just getting started, and there was virtually nothing in Israel. Today the Messianic Jewish Alliance of America and the Union of Messianic Jewish Congregations both run educational programs to prepare congregational leaders, and the Messianic Jewish Theological Institute is functioning in a manner intended to bring it to the academic level of a seminary. In Israel we now have the Israel College of the Bible, the Caspar! Center and the Messianic Midrashah. The Messianic Jewish Bible Institute has branches in Brazil, Argentina, Ukraine, Russia, Korea and the USA.

The congregational movement has also grown geographically. Since the Iron Curtain fell, close to 100 Messianic Jewish congregations, as well as schools, have developed in the former

---

This appendix is a modified version of my article, "The Future of Messianic Judaism," published in Stanley N. Gundry and Louis Goldberg, editors, How Jewish Is Christianity? - Two Views on the Messianic Movement (Grand Rapids, Michigan, Zondervan, 2003). The book includes contributions by William Varner, Arnold G. Fruchtenbaum, John Fischer and Gershon Nerel; my article was presented as the "Summary Essay." It is used here with permission.

Soviet Union and Eastern Europe. In Kiev, Ukraine, is the largest Messianic Jewish congregation in the world, with more than a thousand members,60-70% of them Jewish. The movement has also begun to take hold in Latin America, with congregations in Argentina, Brazil, Mexico, Peru and other countries. Not bad growth for eighteen years!

Data concerning the Jewish aspects of the Messianic Jewish congregations are harder to come by. I would guess that 10-20% of them have Torah scrolls. A much larger percentage celebrates the major Jewish holidays in some fashion. A significant number of their members light Shabbat candles. Observance of kashrut varies from "not at all" to the careful separation of meat and milk along the lines of the halakhah.

I could try to find more statistics documenting our institutions and other physical signs of our success as a movement, but it would be a mistake. First, our movement's "success," if such a word is even appropriate, should be measured by spiritual and not physical criteria. Second, in my opinion, we have a history of triumphalism, by which I mean, declaring victory before it has happened. It's too easy to become unduly proud of our achievements, and this gets in the way of further achievement! An experience of mine will explain what I mean.

When I was nineteen I led a group of Boy Scouts up a mountain in the High Sierras. It wasn't a complicated climb - just keep putting one foot in front of the other, and follow the trail to the summit. The older boys took off like a shot, but I stayed with Don, the youngest and slowest. He was a chubby, un-athletic kid, who was huffing and puffing within minutes. After walking through the scrawny pines for a few hundred yards he asked an astonishing question: "Have we reached the summit?" After a moment's thought I simply said, "No, not yet, let's keep going." But ten minutes later he asked again, "Is this the summit?" "No," I explained, "the summit is the top, where you can look down in every direction. As you see, the trail continues uphill. Keep climbing, don't give up!" Fifteen minutes later: "Is this the top?" "No, but you'll get there. You can do it!" And so on, every few minutes, the same question. But finally, nearly an hour after the next slowest hiker, we arrived at the top of the mountain. And he was so happy! He had accomplished what he had set out to do.

But if at any point I had answered him, "Yes, this is the top," he would have been just as happy. And he would have felt the same pride of accomplishment. The only trouble is that my answer wouldn't have been true. So his pride would have been false and unjustified, but he wouldn't have known it.

I don't want us Messianic Jews to think we have "arrived at the top" when we haven't. Achievements in our movement are real, yet not a reason to settle into our "comfort zone." We have accomplished much, yet we must brace for lengthy and continuing effort in order to reach our goals. Nevertheless, like Don, we will get there. We can do it because God is with us and gives us strength![4]

CRISIS AND GOALS

It might seem that we need only remind ourselves of what our goals are and then set out to reach them. This is the world's way, but it can't be ours. The faith we have implies doing everything in the presence of God. Both choosing our goals and reaching them must be done in an intimate relationship with him. And in this regard the American Messianic Jewish movement at present faces a crisis, a crisis of faith. This crisis has a generational aspect common to many movements: the children of the founders have to find their own way of leading. Like Yochanan (John) I want to speak directly to both the parents and the children.[5]

You parents, you who came to faith in the exciting period of the Jesus Movement in the late 1960's and 1970's, your love and ardor for Yeshua, together with your excitement at the idea that you could believe in him and still stay Jewish, worked to make you a generation of zealous, enthusiastic leaders. With the rest of the Boomers you were tired of materialism and sought a

4. Isaiah 8:10, Philippians 4:13
5. 1 Yochanan (1 John) 2:12-14

more spiritual path, and in Yeshua you found the right answer to your quest. With your pioneering spirit you created the Messianic Jewish movement as it is now. But many of you have allowed yourselves to become entangled in its institutionalism and bureaucracy, refining its theology and practices and generating finances. In the process you have left your first love. You have retreated into your heads, and your hearts are dying. Like Yochanan in the book of Revelation, I call you to return to your first love, Yeshua, the Messiah of Jews and Gentiles alike. Without him your great talents will dry up the movement. "Therefore, remember where you were before you fell, and turn from this sin, and do what you used to do before."[6]

But you children, the children of these leaders, you were born into believing families and don't remember having had the experience of coming from unbelief to faith. I see you as struggling to find out who you are and what will give purpose and meaning to your life. A few years ago the Union of Messianic Jewish Congregations conference called you the "Joshua Generation," ready, like him, to receive the scepter of authority in the movement from your aging "Moses" parents. But they failed to see that except for Joshua and Caleb, that entire generation died in the wilderness! Don't die! There is life in Yeshua, eternal life, and he will give new life to you and to the Messianic Jewish movement if you will only seize the opportunity and not settle for the easy existence you could readily choose. Find the challenges and meet them! If you are lukewarm, Yeshua will spew you out of his mouth![7]

Genesis 18:17–19 teaches the Messianic Jewish "parents" how to help "their children" find and meet those challenges. They should relate to them in the same way as God related to Avraham—and for the same reasons. ADONAI said, "Should I hide from Avraham what I am about to do [to Sodom and Gomorrah], inasmuch as Avraham is sure to become a great and strong nation, and all the nations of the earth will be blessed by him? For I have made myself known to him, so that

6. Revelation 2:4, 5
7. Revelation 3:15ff

he will give orders to his children and to his household after him to keep the way of ADONAI and to do what is right and just, so that ADONAI may bring about for Avraham what he has promised him."

There is one piece of unfinished business that could affect negatively the relationship between the two generations, and that is the way in which the Messianic Jewish "parents," when they were younger, related to the Hebrew Christian "grandparents." In the early 1970's, when the present "parents," in their excitement for Messianic Judaism, were instrumental in changing the name of the Hebrew Christian Alliance of America to the Messianic Jewish Alliance of America, some did not honor the older Hebrew Christians who had been the earlier pioneers. They had laid the foundation for the present movement, and then these worthies were alienated by the young folks' rudeness. Many of them left the Alliance altogether, depriving the young movement of their seasoned wisdom. I would not like to see the younger generation today make the same mistake, but the initiative really belongs with today's "parents" to correct their own earlier mistake—to admit their sin, repent, and take responsibility for it. The "grandparents'" generation is gone, so they can no longer grant forgiveness. But I believe that if the "parents" acknowledge their wrong, they and the "children" will both be blessed, the inter-generational tension will be reduced, and our own young generation will be empowered to move forward, building on what Messianic Judaism has already accomplished.

So there is urgency to my message. The American Messianic Jewish movement can either fall back, becoming just another religious denomination, or it can spring ahead, determining what Yeshua's goals for our community are and looking to him for the wisdom and energy to reach them. (The situation in Israel for Messianic Jews is different, because here the movement is still in its pioneering phase; I will have more to say about it below.)

Here are six goals I would like to see the Messianic Jewish movement and every one of its congregations actively pursuing. There are other worthwhile goals, some perhaps more important than these, but the ones I want to look at now are: emotional healing, community, Jewishness, evangelism, preparing for the Land of Israel to become Messianic Judaism's center of gravity, and working with Gentile believers to end the schism between the Body of the Messiah and the Jewish people.

EMOTIONAL HEALING

We can achieve our goals. Yes, we can do it! But the doing our movement requires is not our first priority. Our first priority is being, not doing, and this being is primarily an individual experience, not a communal one. Developing Messianic Judaism is a communal task, but before we can function effectively as a community, most of us need emotional healing as individuals. Thus the being that we need is individually being in the presence of God and receiving his love, so that we can give love to God and to others. Love is our first and final spiritual criterion. Yeshua said that the two most important mitzvot were to love God and to love other people; moreover, his "new commandment" to us as his disciples was to love one another as he himself loves us. The Bible's "love chapter"[8] teaches that anything we do which is not motivated by love has no value for us, even if our deeds help others.[9]

This is something we all know in our heads. But between 1998 and 2003, after publishing the Complete Jewish Bible, I stopped writing, and when I was asked, "What book are you working on now?" I answered, "None. I'm working on personal issues." I felt compelled to do this because until then I had been so much a "head person" that I had put matters of the heart aside. I was thus unaware of deep inner needs and una- ware of my pain in not having them met, and for this reason I tolerated in myself sin that should have been confessed and not allowed to continue. During those five years God gave me much healing, so that I was able to turn from that sin. In the process I came to experience how important it is for all of

8. 1 Corinthians 13:l-14:la

9. See Mark 12:28-31, Deut. 6:5, Lev. 19:18, Yochanan [John] 13:34-35

us to get emotional and spiritual healing—for our own individual sakes, for the sake of the movement, and for the sake of the Messiah's Body.

There are believers, some of them pastors and leaders, who win unbelievers to the Lord (good deeds), but their own marriages, families and other relationships are a shambles (lack of love). They can give wonderful sermons and teachings but are secretly addicted to pornography or other sexual sins, or to substance abuse. They are violent physically or verbally. They have ethical lapses in their use of money. Or they have other serious sins in their lives. By God's grace they manage to function and do some good in the world, even though their "holiness" is a facade. But their functioning is truly dysfunctional—they are not operating at God's optimal level, and they do damage along with the good they accomplish. Usually the poor quality of their prayer life and devotions in the Word of God are an indicator of this sort of difficulty. What is required in such situations is less doing and more being, more being open to letting God work in their life. I call this receiving of God's love being open-hearted or seeking truth in the inner person.[10] Our movement, as well as the Church at large, is in drastic need of narrowing the gap between what we say we believe and what we really are, of being truly godly instead of putting on a show, of shining forth Yeshua from within instead of being hypocrites.

How do we become openhearted? Two requirements are honesty and trust, because only with these can we take down the walls that separate us from God and from our fellow humans. Six emotions block the way to being honest and exercising trust: anger, fear, pain, despair, confusion and shame. While psychological therapies can be helpful, each of these obstacles deserves deep devotional Bible study in order to grasp the spiritual factors at work in them. Anyone who experiences his life as dominated by one or more of these negative feelings knows how distressing they are. But others avoid this distress by suppressing their feelings—they are "in denial," or they dis-

10. Psalm 51:8 in the Hebrew Bible, 51:6 in Christian translations

sociate ("space out"), or they cover up. These make healing more difficult—yet God can heal even these.

The Gentile branch of the Body of Messiah has pioneered in his area, commonly called inner healing or emotional healing; our movement has lagged behind. This may be due to our fewer numbers, but I think we also have a tendency toward "head orientation" rather than "heart orientation." There is nothing wrong with intellectual clarity—my own life work has depended on it. Yet the essence of the Gospel must touch the heart; no amount of head knowledge can produce or substitute for a genuine change of heart. Among the helpful Christian writers I have encountered are Henry Cloud, on emotional boundaries; Paul Meier, on codependency; Larry Crabb, on the role of a believing community in healing; John Smeltzer, on the importance of being "ordinary"; Jack Frost, on our need for "father-love," and Leanne Payne, on sexuality and gender roles. Others have pointed out how the lies we believe can generate the sins we commit. Moreover, secular writers can be helpful, provided that we set their truths in a biblical context: Merle Possum and Marilyn Mason, on shame; and Alexander Lowen, on narcissism (which can also be called image management).

The point is that our movement and the individuals comprising it urgently need to face up to the emotional pain from which nearly all of us suffer. Some think it's selfish to seek one's own emotional healing. It isn't, because unhealed believers can't serve God as effectively as they would like. To the degree that believers get healed emotionally they will be able to serve God better, because they will use less energy to suppress pain, fear, anger, shame, confusion and despair and have more energy available for service.

I hope that this will become a major focus in the Messianic Jewish movement and its congregations, and I especially urge and exhort the leaders to seek emotional and psychological healing for themselves. I also believe that as we proclaim the Gospel to our own people, among the most effective of the "signs" Jews ask for[11] will be the dramatic changes at the psy-

11. I Corinthians. 1:2

chological and spiritual levels that will result from Messianic Jews getting emotional healing through Yeshua the Messiah. Healed believers are superb witnesses to Yeshua, because their transparency and genuineness proclaim his work and his love.

COMMUNITY

Congregational community grows naturally from emotional healing. A congregation has developed a measure of community if it is a safe place where people can be open and transparent without having to put on a show, if its members are friendly and open with each other and toward outsiders, if they are interested in understanding how others' God-given goals fit into God's larger plan, if they are willing to sacrifice pursuit of their own goals in order to help others attain theirs, if they pray for each other and if the congregation has goals for itself as a congregation. A congregation in which the main activity is sitting at meetings that are half music and half sermon is not a community. It lacks the intimacy community requires. I'm sure there are better descriptions of community than mine; all I want to do here is point out that community is a goal to be consciously defined and pursued, for its presence cannot be merely assumed. The Jewish world has developed a deep sense of community; we Messianic Jews should participate in it and learn from it.[12]

JEWISHNESS

Messianic Jewish congregations have put a great deal of energy into developing and refining theological, ceremonial and practical ways to express Jewishness. This is to be expected, especially in the Diaspora, where Messianic Judaism is a double minority—a tiny percentage of Jews and an even tinier percentage of believers in Yeshua. So we find ourselves con-

12. See pp. 102-105

stantly wanting to prove to Jews that we too are Jews, generally by showing that our practices and ceremonies are Jewish in character even though they honor Yeshua, and prove to Christians that we too believe in Yeshua, generally by showing that our theological positions are sound, even though expressed in Jewish terms.

But this effort spent proving ourselves to others—and to ourselves—distorts our lives, our congregations and our movement! We should not overemphasize the goal of becoming acceptable within the non-Messianic Jewish community. Instead, our Jewish practices and ceremonies should be chosen to meet our own needs in expressing our faith, with an eye to what is Jewish and what isn't, and the other eye to what is biblical and what is anti-biblical. If we do this, our congregation meetings will be comfortable places for us to express our faith, both the Jewish and the Messianic aspects, and also places where interested non-Messianic Jews too can feel comfortable as they experience what it means to be Messianic.

In the last eighteen years the movement and its congregations have developed Messianic Jewish ceremonial and liturgical aspects of Shab-bat and the biblical festivals. But in many cases the ceremonies and liturgies have settled into a rut and become ritualized, automatic and boring. People recite the prayers in rote fashion, as a matter of duty. This is legalism! Often the leaders aren't sure what they can do to solve the problem. My solution is to let God's Spirit work within the liturgy. When God's Spirit is absent, Messianic Jewish liturgies, ceremonies and customs are performed in the letter and not in the Spirit, so that they bring death instead of life. I have not the slightest doubt that nearly all the prayers of the Jewish prayer books (the Siddur and the Machzor) can be prayed with joy and wholeheartedness when the people praying are filled with spiritual life by the Holy Spirit. But for this to happen, we must educate ourselves in depth. We must become more familiar with the content of the traditional prayers. Then the Holy Spirit will show, within this framework, when to use particular prayers, and when to stop reciting the traditional ones and begin praying spontaneously. Focus on God, and let the Holy Spirit guide experimentation and adventure with the liturgy.

While examining how the congregations express Jewishness, I would like to explain what I consider the proper place of the Oral Torah (i.e., the Talmud and other rabbinic writings) in Messianic Judaism, because this is still a matter of controversy in the movement. To start with, however, I should say that I regard the New Testament as Written Torah. It modifies, explains, and adds to the Written Torah, as it existed prior to Yeshua's coming. I have discussed this and other aspects of how the Torah applies today in Chapter V.

I compare the Written Torah with the American constitution. The constitution does not tell in detail how to run the country, but it does set up the legislative, executive and judicial branches of the government, along with the limits they must observe. Likewise, the Written Torah is inadequate for governing the Jewish nation under all circumstances, but in Deuteronomy 17:8–13 it establishes a method for determining God's will in situations not specifically foreseen in the Written Torah. Cases are to be brought before the court at the city gate, with difficult ones referred to the cohanim (priests) and the shofet (judge) in office at the time; they declare what the Torah requires in the particular circumstances.

I think this was meant to be a flexible system, allowing two similar cases to yield different verdicts if times and conditions changed. Precedents would be noted but could be overridden. The rabbis' takeover of the role of the cohanim and shofet is not biblically sanctioned, but in this discussion I am not going to take up time disputing their usurpation of authority. The problem we are left with is that ossification set in as the precedents of the Oral Torah came to be regarded as decreed by God for all time and just as binding as the Written Torah. While the U.S. Congress can pass any law that doesn't violate the constitution and can decide later to revoke all or part of that law, the Oral Torah has been "set in stone," so that its decisions cannot be revoked. The Jewish system of halakhah (law) has had to devise ways to get around previous decisions without revoking them, and sometimes it seems unable to do so. If the Oral Torah, that is, the system for determining how to apply the Written Torah in real life, were as flexible as I believe it was meant to be, it could work. If its rulings had been easier to change, Yeshua might not have had to scold the scribes and Pharisees, "With your tradition you nullify the word of God."[13]

The reason I am devoting space to this subject is that there are Messianic Jews who reject as unbiblical everything added to the Written Torah by the rabbis. They believe that by doing so they will arrive at truly biblical Judaism. I believe this approach fails. Because the Written Torah does not completely specify the behavior God wants, it still has to be applied in particular settings. Therefore, such a supposedly "biblical Judaism" will end by creating its own Oral Torah. The Roman Catholic Church, with its canon law, and numerous Protestant denominations with their various rules and regulations, do precisely this, but it obviously doesn't mean that they have thereby created "biblical Judaism." I believe that the right way to relate to the existing Oral Torah is not as divine command but as religious and cultural tradition. Its purpose is to guide us toward holiness and toward making congregational life satisfying for ourselves and useful for showing non-Messianic Jews the Gospel in the context of who and what we are. Also relating to the Oral Torah will better prepare us to dialogue with the Jewish religious world when the opportunity arises.

EVANGELISM

Let me say at the outset that, scripturally, evangelism is a command, not an option. Moreover, no congregation can be healthy if it is not doing evangelism. Just as the human body, in order to be healthy, must interact with the outside world, so that through breathing and eating it makes some of its environment a part of itself, likewise a congregation must act to make some of the people outside part of itself. Outreach ministries ("missions to the Jews") do make the Gospel known to Jewish people, but the normal way for the Body of the Messiah to grow is to have its members sharing the individual and communal life of Yeshua with the people around them.

13. Mark 7:13

By the sixteenth century, it had been over a thousand years since an identifiable community of Jewish believers had existed, so evangelism of Jewish people in modern times began within the Church. It was wonderful that Jewish people were once again being told about Yeshua, but an undesirable side-effect was that the essential Gospel message was mixed with the prevailing Gentile culture—which was not essential. Messianic Judaism has yet to free itself from this to the point where we routinely function in normal Jewish ways. For the sake of the Gospel we need to embrace every aspect of our Jewishness (unless it directly conflicts with the Bible)—which does not mean that we are to all become imitation Orthodox Jews. When we draw away from the Christian cultural habits to which we have assimilated and instead behave like ordinary Jews, our testimony to Yeshua becomes more meaningful to Jewish people.

For example, when our congregation in Jerusalem had its first Shabbat service making use of the traditional prayers from the Siddur, back in 1987, my wife Martha sensed that we were changing things in spiritual realms. She understood that the service itself was a form of spiritual intercession. By making our congregation's meeting into a "Jewish space," an observant Jew could feel comfortable and therefore safely able to inquire into who we are and what we believe. Her intuition was quickly confirmed: within a week, out of the blue, two Orthodox Jews did exactly that, phoning to talk with our congregation leader about believing in Yeshua.

We must also not forget that the Gospel speaks to the heart as well as to the head. For two hundred years evangelists have been taught that to win Jews to Yeshua, one must prove that Yeshua fulfills the Messianic prophecies found in the Old Testament and denigrate rabbinic Judaism as a human creation not from God. This has been thought to be the best way to convince Orthodox Jews, traditional Jews, Jewishly educated Jews, to believe in Yeshua. It is not.

What all people need, and at some level want, is a genuine heart connection with God. They want to receive his love, and they want their sins forgiven! They receive this in their spirits through our expressing Yeshua's love, and for us to express

Yeshua's love requires that we receive the emotional healing that we need.

A second thing we must do is eliminate negative attitudes toward "rabbinism." The fact is that rabbinic Judaism, even without Yeshua, has preserved a wealth of godly truth, especially in the area of ethics. Rather than deprecate religious Judaism, as some do, we would do better to assume that an observant Jew is not disenchanted with his tradition, but that he still has not found in it what his soul seeks. So, being affirmative about his lifestyle and negative about nothing, we should show him that Yeshua can supply his need.

To be sure, there are strangenesses in religious Judaism—as in every religion, including Christianity and Messianic Judaism. If this weren't true, none of us would ever feel embarrassed at presenting the Gospel in a Messianic Jewish way. But most of us do, at one time or another, because we recognize how imperfect our congregations and we are. Yeshua is perfect, but we are clay vessels,[14] and most of us are broken clay vessels. So our strategy must be not to pretend we're perfect, but to admit that in us, that is, in our flesh, dwells no good thing,[15] and that to the extent that there is anything good about us at all, it is God's grace, not our own accomplishments.[16]

In explaining the Gospel to Orthodox Jews, I have found it helpful to point out that the main topic of the Torah is the sacrificial system, and that the reason it is central is that the punishment for sin is death.[17] Thus the Torah introduces vicarious atonement in the form of animal sacrifices. But without a Temple there are no sacrifices today, so how is sin atoned for in modern Judaism? The rabbinic substitution of "repentance, prayer and charity," in place of the biblical sacrifices,[18] is not

14. 2 Corinthians 4:7
15. Romans 7:18
16. Ephesians 2:10
17. Genesis 2:18
18. As stated in the Unetanneh tokef prayer in the Machzor for the High Holidays; see above, Chapter V, Section D-3 and footnote 16

authorized by God. An Orthodox Jew will usually acknowledge this, thereby laying the groundwork for his understanding why Yeshua's sacrificial death on the execution-stake is effective as atonement for sin. In this context the Messianic prophecies play an indispensable supporting role.

In the past two or three years I have both received reports and seen for myself that a number of Orthodox Jews have become believers, more than in the past. Is this a trend? I hope so.

Another opportunity for evangelism in Israel is the New Age festivals, a phenomenon that draws mostly young secular Jews. Since 1998 these festivals have been timed to coincide with the holidays—the *Boom/bamela* Festival at Passover, the *Shantipi* Festival at Shavu'ot, and the *Beresheet* Festival at Sukkot. Thousands of young people camp out at these three or four-day events for the trance music, the eastern religion booths and simply for fun and freedom. *Boom/bamela* is the largest one, drawing 30,000 to 40,000 Israelis mostly between ages 12 and 30. Compared with the population of the United States Israel that's the equivalent of 1,500,000–2,000,000 people in one place at one time! These young folks remind me of the people of Nineveh, who didn't know their right hand from their left. They're looking for spiritual truth and reality but haven't a clue where to find it.

So two or three groups of believers totaling up to 200 people do outreach at these festivals. They set up base camps, book booths, chai shops, seminars and stages for dramatic and musical performances, all centered on Yeshua. Attendees at one festival accepted nearly 2,000 Hebrew New Testaments and thousands of other books about our faith and about Jews who believe it. More than a few have become believers and joined Israeli Messianic Jewish congregations.[19]

---

19. For more on Jewish evangelism in Israel see David H. Stern, "Evangelism in Israel. 1979-2005," pp. 6-17 in Issue #46 of Mishkan. This issue is subtitled "The Messianic Movement in Israel Today."

Already, Messianic Jews are going out to nations around the world with the Gospel, following the examples of Isidor Loewenthal (1826–1864), who evangelized in Afghanistan, and Samuel Schereschewsky (1831–1906), who evangelized in China. Since the Iron Curtain fell in Eastern Europe (1989) and the Soviet Union (1991), Messianic Jews such as Jonathan Bernis, Richard Glickstein and Jeff Bernstein have discovered an unprecedented degree of openness to the Gospel among the Jews in these countries. This is partly in reaction to the suppression of religion for over seventy years under the Communists. Thousands have come to faith, and Jews who have emigrated from these countries to the West and Israel are equally receptive. Messianic Jews who want to recapture the pioneering spirit should seize some of these opportunities.

In addition to evangelism there is pre-evangelism—preparing the emotional, mental and social ground for the Gospel. In this connection my friend Joseph Shulam, here in Jerusalem, has coined a phrase I like: "We have to bring Yeshua home"—back to his own people and land. After two thousand years of being a wandering Jew rejected by the Jewish people and accepted by Gentiles, the image everyone has of Yeshua has become gentilized. I'm speaking not only of how he is portrayed in paintings but also of how he is described, imagined, understood and even theologized about by Jews and Christians alike. Consequently his reality, character, teachings and life work are misrepresented. Nearly everyone acknowledges the fact that he was a Jew (an exception: Yasser Arafat, who called him a "great Palestinian"), but few have explored what that really means. We—Joe and I and others—think it's high time to bring Yeshua back home where he belongs, where Jewish people can see him as a fellow Jew able to meet the need of every Jewish heart. This process has begun, but it still requires much historical and theological work, and it is one of the tasks the Messianic Jewish movement should pursue diligently.

ERETZ-ISRAEL, THE FUTURE CENTER OF MESSIANIC JUDAISM

The center of the Jewish world shifted from Europe to Israel when the State of Israel was created in 1948. But the world center of Messianic Judaism has remained the United States. Nevertheless I believe that God's promise, "All Israel shall be saved,"[20] will increasingly find fulfillment in Eretz-Israel, the Land of Israel. One reason for this is simply demographic—in 1948 only 6% of world Jewry lived here, whereas now close to 40% do, and the percentage is growing annually.

A more fundamental reason is that Israelis rarely have a problem with their Jewish identity, because they don't have to define it in relation to a non-Jewish majority, as in the rest of the world. In other words, being and feeling Jewish in Israel is the norm, not the exception. It does not depend on doing Jewish religious things or on consciously developing Jewish culture. In the Diaspora, emphasizing Jewish identity in evangelism diverts attention from Yeshua to Jewishness.

A major reason believers have found it hard to reach Israelis with the Gospel is because most of them are either Gentiles or Jewish immigrants; therefore they have had to learn about and adapt to Israeli society as outsiders. But now we have raised a generation of believers born here; and they know the Israeli mindset through and through, because it is their own mindset. These are the ones who will revolutionize Israeli society with the Gospel. This is just beginning, a few raindrops, but I predict that it will become a downpour! Moreover, when that happens, it will revolutionize the Messianic Jewish movement. I can't tell you how, but it will.

I urge the Messianic Jews of the Diaspora to prepare for Israel's becoming the center of Messianic Judaism by joining the

20. Romans 11:26

rest of the Jewish community in supporting Israel, by supporting specifically Israel's Messianic Jewish community, by visiting Israel and, at least in some cases, by making aliyah. Yes, it is still possible to immigrate, even after the Beresford decision of 1989, in which Israel's High Court of Justice ruled that Messianic Jews are not eligible to do so under the State's Law of Return (which states that every Jew "who has not changed his religion" can become a citizen of Israel) The Beresford decision says that for purposes of the Law of Return, Messianic Jews have "changed their religion." However, you must be careful how you go about it, because you only have one chance to do things right the first time.[21]

ECCLESIOLOGY AND OUR MESSAGE TO THE CHURCH

I have always felt that the major task of Messianic Jews within the Body of Messiah is to help heal what I called in Chapter I the greatest schism in history, the breach between the Church and the Jewish people. I think the best way to do this is to help Christians feel comfortable thinking of the Jews as their own people, as "us" not "them," because that is what Scripture teaches. This requires developing an appropriate ecclesiology. Ecclesiology is the branch of theology that deals with who constitutes the People of God and what their role is in his plan for the human race. Before Yeshua came—and in non-Messianic Judaism today—ecclesiology (a term Judaism does not use) was simple: the Jews are the People of God, period. After Yeshua it became clear that believing Gentiles had joined the People of God. The operative word here is "joined," not "replaced." For at Ephesians 2:11–13 Paul tells non-Jewish Christians to remember your former state: you Gentiles by birth . . . at that time had no Messiah. You were

21. See Appendix 2, "Update 1993—Messianic Jewish Aliyah" and Linda Alexander. The UnPromised Land, The Struggle of Messianic Jews, Gary and Shirley Beresford, Lederer/Messianic Jewish Publishers, Clarksville, MD 21029, 1994.

estranged from the national life of Israel. You were foreigners to the covenants embodying God's promise. You were in this world without hope and without God. But now, you who were once far off have been brought near through [the shedding of] the Messiah's blood.

Before having faith in Yeshua the Jewish Messiah, Gentiles were "estranged from the national life of Israel," but now Gentile believers, through all that Yeshua did (encapsulated in the phrase, "the Messiah's blood"), have been "brought near" to the national life of Israel. The term "brought near" doesn't mean "brought close, but still outside"; rather it means that they have been "brought all the way into the national life of Israel." This is evident from the following verse, which states that Yeshua "himself is our shalom—he has made us both one and has broken down the m'chitzah [wall of separation] which divided us."

But the Church, reacting to Jewish non-acceptance of the Gospel, instead of thinking of themselves as having joined the national life of Israel and thus become "joint heirs, a joint body and joint sharers with the Jews in what God had promised,"[22] developed Replacement Theology. Here the Church replaces the Jews as the People of God, and God's promises to the Jews are cancelled. This theology held sway without significant competition from the fourth century onward, and it remains dominant in Christianity today.

In recent centuries Protestants developed several less anti-Jewish forms of ecclesiology, but none of them gives any significance to the current activity of the Jewish people. Dispensationalism, for example, says that God is indeed "not finished with the Jews," but he will not be actively dealing with them again until "Daniel's seventieth week," which will not come until the Church is "raptured" (suddenly removed from the earth and taken to heaven).

I wrote in Chapter III above that it was necessary to develop an ecclesiology that takes into account three groups of people corresponding to the olive tree analogy of Romans

22. Ephesians 3:6.2

11:17–26: the cut-off natural branches grafted back into their own cultivated olive tree (Messianic Jews); the branches of the wild olive tree grafted into the cultivated tree (Christians); and the cut-off natural branches that have not yet been grafted back in (non-Messianic Jews).[23] What does the olive tree teach us about these three groups of people in relation to the Body of the Messiah? What impact does this have on relationships, both theological and practical, between Gentile believers, Jewish believers and the rest of the Jewish people? What is the current role of Gentile believers, Messianic Jews and non-Messianic Jews in God's plan? Messianic Jews should be in the forefront in developing further these aspects of theology for the sake of repairing the breach between the Body of the Messiah and the Jewish people.

Since 2003, when I wrote the material in the above two paragraphs, two books have appeared which embody some worthwhile thinking. Daniel Gruber's Copernicus and the Jews[24] argues that, like astronomy in the sixteenth century, ecclesiology needs a paradigm shift. Copernicus theorized that to explain the motion of the heavenly bodies, especially the planets (Greek planetoi, "wanderers"), which usually move forward in the sky but sometimes backward in "retrograde motion," a model was needed that put the sun, not the earth, at the center of the solar system. Likewise, says Gruber, ecclesiology must have a model, which puts the Jews, not the Church, at the center. It will be very different— and more true to the biblical and historical facts—than Church-centered ecclesiology has been; and at last it will explain the real role of the Jews, including the wandering ones.

Mark Kinzer's Postmissionary Messianic Judaism[25] develops this concept in considerable detail, and I urge people to read it. He describes the ekklesia (usually translated

23. See above, p. 56.3

24. Daniel Gruber, The Separation of Church and Faith, Volume 1: Copernicus and the Jews (Elijah Publishing, PO Box 776, Hanover, NH 03755; 2005)

25. Mark Kinzer, Postmissionary Messianic Judaism: Redefining Christian Engagement with the Jewish People (Grand Rapids, MI: Brazos Press, 2005)

"church" but more accurately rendered "assembly" of believers in Yeshua) as being "bilateral," consisting of a Jewish branch and a Gentile branch, and as being "in solidarity with Israel," which is defined as including both Jews who believe in Yeshua and Jews who don't. He sees God as having worked behind the scenes throughout the last two thousand years among Jews who don't believe in Yeshua; and that one of the ways he has done this is in overseeing the development of rabbinic Judaism, which, although it rejects Yeshua and the New Testament, nevertheless has preserved among the Jewish people a certain faithfulness to God (even if, as I would say, it isn't a saving faithfulness for individual Jews). His ideas may be controversial, but they are well worth studying, because they take into account Messianic Jews as well as Christians and non-Messianic Jews, the three components of the olive tree.

OTHER THINGS

I expect our infrastructure and our culture to grow in size, quality and depth. There will be more, larger and better congregations and schools, more and better discipleship, more development of the arts, more involvement in social, moral and political issues. These trends continue to be observed in our movement, as they have been for the last forty years.

I expect continued progress in developing Messianic Jewish theology, and not only in the areas of ecclesiology and Torah. We will express with increasing clarity our theology of 52 what Christians mean when they talk about the "Trinity" and the "deity of Jesus." And we will explore more deeply and practically the relationship between heart and head, and the relationship between sinning and having been emotionally wounded. One area of theology we can take pride in is apologetics: Dr. Michael Brown's four-volume Answering Jewish Objections to Jesus,[26]

26. Michael Brown, Answering Jewish Objections to Jesus, Volumes 1-4 (Grand Rapids: Baker Book House, 2000-2006).

which offers a systematic Messianic Jewish approach to this subject, is one of the most exciting, thorough and useful products our movement has produced.

Finally, here are some things I would like to see in the movement: (1) a Messianic Jewish systematic theology; (2) continued progress in proclaiming the Gospel to an increasingly broad spectrum of the Jewish public, notably intellectuals and "establishment" people, as well as the Orthodox; (3) greater efforts to deal with the Holocaust, which is still an open wound for our people; and (4) increased aliyah. The movement in Israel needs (1) a systematic theology book in Hebrew—whether Messianic Jewish or not; (2) counseling centers to help Messianic Jews work through personal issues and emotional pain; and (3) increased contact and genuine love between Israeli Jewish believers and Arab Christians, thus demonstrating the Gospel in action.

As I edit what I have written for this Appendix, Israel has just fought the Second Lebanese War. Hundreds have been killed. The West is under continuous pressure from extremist Muslims to unite against Israel, and many have succumbed to it. I see Satan at work in this, as we move toward Zechariah 12, when the whole world will come against Jerusalem. But with our message of salvation for everyone, Jew and Gentile alike, we were born "for such a time as this."[27] As Messianic Jews, let us connect intimately with our God, be true disciples who can transmit his love through Yeshua to others, and rise to the challenge of doing the works God has prepared for us to do[28] in these momentous days.

27. Esther 2:14
28. Ephesians 2:8-10

GLOSSARY OF HEBREW WORDS AND NAMES

Italicized vowels are pronounced as in the following words: Father, aisle, *bed,* neighbor, invest (usually when not accented) or marine (usually when accented), obey, rule; "ch" is pronounced as in Johann Sebastian *Bach,* and so is "kh"; "g" is always hard (game); other consonants are more or less as in English. Accented syllables are printed in **boldface**. Israeli pronunciation is shown generally; "Ashk" indicates certain Ashkenazic (German and eastern European) pronunciations common in English-speaking countries.

a • cha • **rit**-ha • ya • **mim**—the last times (literally, "the end of days").

A • cha • ro • **nim**—rabbinic sages of the last three centuries (literally, "last ones").

A • do • **nai**—my Lord, Lord of all; spoken by Jewish people instead of God's personal name *Y-H-V-H* ("Jehovah.").

a • fi • ko • **man** (Ashk: a • fi • **ko** • men)—the half of the middle *matzah* which is hidden at the beginning of the *Seder* and recovered at the end to be the final food eaten before after-dinner prayers. Messianic Jews regard it as symbolizing Yeshua the Messiah, who appeared two thousand years ago and will appear again in the *acharit-hayamim* but is hidden now.

ag • ga • **dah** (Ashk: ag • **ga** • dah)—literally, "narration;" hence everything in rabbinic literature which is not legal (halakhic) in character. Adjective: "aggadic."

a • gu • **nah**—a woman whose husband has disappeared, and his whereabouts is unknown.

a • li • **yah**—(1) immigration to Israel, (2) a call-up to read from the *sefer-Torah* in the synagogue service (literally, "going up").

A • **men**—so be it; yes, indeed.

am-ha • '**a** • retz—uneducated Jew (or Jews), ignorant of *Torah* (literally "people of the land," *i.e.,* rustics, "hicks").

a-ro • **not** To • **rah** (sing. a • **ron**-To • **rah**)—*Torah* arks, in which *sifrei-Torah* are kept.

Av • ra • **ham**—Abraham.

'**a** • yin ra • '**ah**—literally, "evil eye;" having an *'ayin ra'ah* means "being stingy."

'**a** • yin to • **vah**—literally, "good eye;" having an *'ayin tovah* means "being generous."

bar • mitz • **vah** (Ashk: bar-**mitz** • vah)—rite of passage for a boy at his 13th birthday, when he takes on himself the responsibility of observing the Jewish commandments (literally, "son of commandment," in Aramaic).

"Ba • **rukh** ha-**ba** ba-**shem** A • do • **nai**"—"Blessed is he who comes in the name of the Lord." (Psalm 118:26)

Ben-Ham'• vo • **rakh**—son of the Blessed One (i.e., of God).

Bir • **kat**-Ha • Mi • **nim**—blessing against the sectarians, probably the early Jewish Christians, added to the main synagogue liturgy around 90 C.E.

b'ra-**khah**—blessing, benediction.

b'rit-mi • **lah** (Ashk: bris-**mil** • lah)—covenant of circumcision; circumcision ceremony.

chal • **lah**—loaf or cake, and as such a special loaf of white flour bread made for *Shabbat;* but in Romans 11:16 it refers to the share of the dough set aside for the *cohanim* in accordance with Numbers 15:20 (where the word appears) and *Mishna* tractate *Challah.*

chalu • **tzim**—pioneers.

Cha • nu • **kah** (Ashk: **Cha** • nu • kah)—Jewish festival, the Feast of Dedication, celebrating the rededication of the Temple by the Maccabees in 164 B.C.E.; the first historical reference to it is in the New Testament, at Yochanan [John] 10:22.

che • sed—lovingkindness, grace, love, kindness.

co • ha-rum, sing, co-hen (Ashk: co-hen)—priests.

co • **hen** ga • **dol**—high priest.

da • **ti** (pi. da • ti • '**im**)—Orthodox Jewish (literally, "religious").

de • rekh-e • retz—proper behavior towards others (literally, the "way of the Land").

din-to • **rah** (pl. di • **ney**-to • **rah**)—Legal decision concerning the *Torah.*

drash or mi • **drash** (Ashk: **mid** • rash)—one of the four modes of rabbinic interpretation of a text: allegorical or homiletical application of it (literally, "searching").

E • retz-Yis • ra • **el**—the Land of Israel.

e • mu • **nah**—faithfulness, faith, trust, faithful trusting.

E • shet **cha** • yil a • **ni** ma • **tza** • ti!—"A woman of valor 1 have found." Takeoff on Proverbs 31:10-31, which commences: *Eshet chayil mi yimtza,* "A woman of valor who can find? (For her value is far above rubies.)" In observant Jewish homes the husband recites the passage in the presence of his wife every *Shabbat.*

ga • **lut**—exile. "The *Galut"* is the Diaspora, the dispersion of Jews from *Eretz Yisrael* to all parts of the world.

Gema • **ra** (Ashk. Ge • **mor** • ra)—Aramaic, literally, "completion;" commentary on the Mishna which completes the *Talmud.* See *Talmud.*

get—document which, according to *halakhah,* a Jewish husband must present to his wife in order to divorce her; "bill of divorcement" (Deuteronomy 21 :M, Mattityahu [Matthew] 19:3-9).

go • **yim** (Ashk. goy • **im**), sing, goy—nations, pagans, heathen, Gentiles.

Hag • ga • **dah** (Ashk. Hag • **ga** • dah)—The liturgy for the Passover *Seder* service.

Ha • G'vu • **rah**—the Power, the Majesty (i.e., God).

ha • la • **khah** (Ashk. ha • **la** • khah), pi. ha • la • **khot**—(1) the system of statutes which is determinative in traditional Judaism (literally, "way of walking"), (2) a particular statute or legal decision. For more, see Chapter V, footnote 9. Adjective: "halakhic."

Ha • **la** • khic Mi • dra • **shim**—Collection of rabbinic commentaries on the legal portion of the Pentateuch, that is, Exodus 12 through Deuteronomy 34, compiled in the 4th and 5th centuries C. E., but containing materials dating back to two or more centuries before Yeshua. Much of the material is not legal in character.

Ha • Sha • **nah** Ha • Ba' • **ah** Bi • Ye • ru • sha • **la** • yim—"Next year in Jerusalem!" The phrase ends the Passover *Seder* service recited in Jewish homes all over the world.

Ha • si • **dim**—Orthodox Jews who emphasize the devotional over the intellectual aspects of Judaism.

Kad • **dish** (Ashk. **Kad** • dish)—ancient prayer blessing God; resembles the Lord's Prayer; recited (1) in the synagogue to end a section of the service, (2) by mourners.

kal v' • **cho** • mer—argument *a fortiori,* signalled by the phrase, "how much more:" "If X is true, how much more so must Y be true!"

kap • pa • **rot**—custom among some Orthodox Jews of sacrificing a chicken at *Yom Kippur* to atone for sins (literally, "atonements").

kash • **rut**—the Jewish system of dietary laws.

Ke • **fa**—Peter's name in Aramaic (it means "rock").

ke • hil • **lah**—congregation.

ke • tu • hot, sing, ke • tu • **bah**—wedding contracts.

kip • **pah**, pi. kip • **pot**—skullcap, *yarmulke* (Yiddish), kol—all.

Kol Ni • **dre** (Ashk. Kol **Nid** • re)—Prayer which commences the *Yom Kippur* evening service, in which congregants ask forgiveness for vows they have not kept (or, in some versions, which they expect not to keep in the coming year). See text, Chapter V, Section D-4.

ko • sher (this is the Ashk. pronunciation, which is all but universal in America; the Israeli pronunciation is ka • **sher**)—fit [to be eaten, according to Jewish dietary law]. *Kashrut* is the noun meaning "the system of Jewish dietary laws." To "keep *kosher"* is to observe *kashrut.*

Ko • tel—the Western or "Wailing" Wall, the only portion of the Second Temple compound left standing after the destruction of Jerusalem in 70 C. E. (in fulfillment of Luke *21:6).* It is regarded as the holiest site in Judaism.

la • med-**vav** • nik—one of the supposedly 36 righteous men for whose sake God preserves the world. (The numerical value of the Hebrew letter *lamed* is 30, the value of *vav* is 6.)

Mach • **zor**—Collection of liturgical material to be used during a repeating cycle of religious holidays. If no further specification is made, it usually refers to the prayers for the High Holydays *(Rosh HaShanah* and *Yom Kippur).* Otherwise, it may refer to the cycle of Pilgrim Festivals *(Pesach, Shavu'ot, Sukkot)* or other cycles.

Ma • **shi** • ach—Messiah (literally, "anointed one"); translated into Greek as *Christos,* which comes over into English as "Christ." The expected king, foreseen by dozens of prophecies in the *Tanakh,* who would deliver the Jewish people from oppressors and bring peace to the world. The New Testament showed that Yeshua is this promised Messiah, and that his means for bringing peace included dying as the final sin-offering to atone for the sins of the world and rising from the dead to intercede for those who put their trust in him. At his second coming he will fulfill the national aspirations of the Jewish people, judge mankind and bring world peace.

Mat • tit • ya • hu —Matthew, a Jewish tax-collector for the Roman government who becabe one of the twelve emissaries (apostles) of Yeshua and wrote one of the four gospels.

ma • **tzot**, sing. ma • **tzah** (Ashk. **mat** • zah)—unleavened bread used at *Pesach.*

mentsh (Yiddish)—a good, reliable person; a real human being.

me • zu • **zah** (Ashk. me • **zu** • zah)—scroll containing four passages from the Bible, including two from the *Sh'ma,* affixed to gates and doorframes of Jewish homes and buildings in obedience to Deuter-nomy 6:9.

mi • **drash** (Ashk. **mid** • rash)—see *drash.*

Mi • **drash** Rab • **bah**—literally, "Great Midrash," collection of ancient homilies on the Five Books of Moses and the Scrolls (Lamentations, Ruth, Esther, Song of Songs, Ecclesiastes), mostly edited around the 4th and 5th centuries, but including some material predating Yeshua.

mik • **veh** (Ashk. **mik** • veh)—the ritual bath used for immersion in accordance with the purification laws of Judaism.

min • **yan** (Ashk. **min** • yan)—quorum of ten men needed for public worship in Judaism.

Mish • **na** (Ashk. **Mish** • na)—codification of the Oral *Torah* edited by Y'hiudah Ha Nasi, c. 220 C. E. See *Talmud.*

mitz • **vah** (Ashk. **mitz** • vah), pi. mitz • **vot**—commandment.

Motz • a • '**ey**-Shab • **bat**—Saturday night; in the Jewish calendar this is the beginning of the first day of the week (literally, "going-out of Sabbath").

mu • **sar**—ethics.

nid • **dah** (Ashk. **nid** • dah)—separation of husband and wife during and after her menstrual period.

no • **ten** ha • To • **rah**—*b'rakhah* recited before and after the public reading of the *Torah* in the synagogue.

n' • ti • **lat**-ya • **da** • yim—ritual hand washing required before eating, according to *halakhah* (the Oral *Torah),* but not according to Scripture.

nud • nik (Yiddish)—(1) a bore, (2) a bother, (3) both.

O • **lim** (sing, o • **leh**, m., o • **lah**, f.)—immigrants to Israel; see *aliyah.*

Pey • **lim**—see *Yad L'Achim.*

Pe • sach—Passover, one of the three Pilgrim Festivals.

pid • **yon**-ha • **ben**—redemption of the firstborn son, ceremony based on the biblical fact that the tribe of Levi was substituted for the firstborn sons of each family to serve God in the Tabernacle and in the Temple.

Pos • **kim**—rabbinic sages of the Middle Ages (10th to 13th centuries).

P'ru • **shim,** sing. Pa • **rush—**Pharisees, one of the two major religious parties in the time of Yeshua.

p'shat—one of the four modes of rabbinic interpretation of a text: its plain sense, what modern interpreters call grammatical-historical exegesis (literally, "simple").

Pu • **rim** (Ashk. **Pu** • rim)—festival celebrating the Jewish people's escape from the wicked Haman in Shushan, as recorded in the book of Esther.

rav—rabbi.

Ram • **bam**—acronym for Rabbi Moshe ben Maimon, "Maimonides"(l 135-1204), the best-known Jewish scholar of the Middle Ages.

re • mez—one of the four modes of rabbinic interpretation of a text: peculiarities in the text are regarded as hinting at a deeper truth than that conveyed by its plain sense (literally, "hint").

Ri • sho • **nim**—rabbinic sages of the 14th to 17th centuries.

Rosh-Ha • Sha • **nah** (Ashk. Rosh Ha • **Sho** • nah)—the Jewish New Year, celebrated as a time of taking stock, repenting, setting things right in preparation for *Yom Kippur* nine days later. The Bible specifies at this time (September or early Octobei) the Feast of *Shofars* ("ram's horns" or "trumpets").

Ru • ach Ha • **Ko** • desh—the Holy Spirit.

sab • ras—native-born Israelis.

San • he • **drin—**Jewish tribunal during the period of the Second Temple.

Sa • vo • ra • **im**—rabbinic sages of the 5th to 7th centuries.

Se • der—the service to be conducted in Jewish homes on Passover eve.

se • fer-To • **rah**, pi. sif • **rei** • To • **rah**—*Torah* scroll for public reading.

Shab • **bat** (Ashk. **Shab** • bos)—Sabbath, the seventh day of the week (Saturday).

sha • **li** • ach—literally, "emissary". The *aliyah* representative sent by Israel to the Diaspora to promote and administer *aliyah* under the Law of Return. (The word also is used in Hebrew to translate "apostle.")

Sha • **'ul**—Hebrew form of the name "Saul." In this book it refers to Saul of Tarsus, also known as Paul (see Acts 13:9).

Sha • vu • **'ot** (Ashk. Sha • **vu** • os)—Feast of Weeks, Pentecost, one of the three Pilgrim Festivals.

shit • **tuf**—Jewish theological concept describing the Christian doctrine of the Trinity as Jesus' "participation" or "association" with the Father in divinity.

Sh'khi • **nah**—the manifest glory of God.

Sh'ma—the most important affirmation in Judaism, consisting of three Bible passages (Deuteronomy 6:4-9, 11:13-21; Numbers 15:37-41), and commencing with the phrase, *Sh'ma Yisrael, Adonai Eloheynu, Adonai echad* ("Hear, O Israel, the LORD our God, the LORD is one."

Shul • **chan** A • **rukh—**16th century codification of *halakhah* by Joseph Karo and Moses Isserles (literally, "set table.")

Sid • **dur**—the Jewish prayerbook for daily and *Shabbat* use; along with the Hebrew Bible and the *Talmud* one of the three most important books in Judaism.

smi • **khah** (Ashk. **smi** • khah)—ordination.

sod—one of the four modes of rabbinic interpretation of a text: using the numerical values of the Hebrew letters to reveal "secrets" that would otherwise not be noticed (literally, "secret").

Suk • **kot** (Ashk. **Suk** • kos)—the Feast of Tabernacles, one of the three Pilgrim Festivals.

Ta • 'a • **mey**-ha • Mitz • **vot**—reasons for the commandments.

tal • **lit** (Ashk. **tal** • lis), pi. tal • li • **tot**—four-cornered ceremonial garment with *tzitziyot* at the corners worn by men in synagogue in obedience to Numbers 15:37-41. A *tallit katan* ("small *tallit")* may be worn under the shirt throughout the day.

tal • **mid,** pi. tal • mi • **dim**—disciple, student.

tal • **mid** cha • **cham**—"scholar, wise man"

Tal • **mud** (Ashk. **Tal** • mud)—Compilation of the Jewish Oral *Torah* made between the second and fifth centuries of the Common Era, comprised of the *Mishna* and the *Gemara.* The Soncino English version occupies about two feet of bookshelf space. Orthodox Judaism considers that the Oral Law (correrponding to what the New Testament calls the "tradition of the elders") was given by God to Moses on Mount Sinai along with the Pentateuch or Written *Torah.*

Ta • **nakh—**acronym made of the words *Torah* (Pentateuch), *Nevi'im* (Prophets), and *K'tuvim* (writings), which are the three main sections of the Hebrew Bible. Hence, the Old Testament.

tefil • **lin** (Ashk. te • **fil** • lin)—black leather boxes containing scrolls with Bible passages on them, one affixed to hand and arm, the other to forehead, by men during synagogue prayers, in obedience to Deuteronomy 6:8. Called "phylacteries" in most translations of the New Testament. To "lay" *tefillin* is to use them, to put them in place.

tik • **kun**-ha • '**olam**—correcting, repairing, fixing the world.

To • **rah** (Ashk. **To** • rah)—Law (literally, "teaching"). For more, see Chapter V, Section B-2.

To • **sef** • ta—rabbinic materials not included in the *Mishna* which were codified and preserved alongside it.

Tractates A • vo • **dah** Za • **rah** ("Idolatry"), B'ra • **khot** ("Blessings"), San • hed • **rin** ("Court"), Shab • **bat** ("Sabbath"), Ye • va**mot** ("Widows marrying their deceased husband's brother")—Tractates of the *Talmud.*

treif—unfit to be eaten, according to Jewish dietary law (literally "torn").

tzi • tzi • **yot**, sing. tzi • **tzit** (Ashk. **tzi** • tzis)—fringes worn on the corners of a man's garment, notably on his *tallit,* fulfilling the command in Numbers 15:37-41.

ul • pa • **nim**, sing. ul • **pan**)—Hebrew-language training programs.

Un' • **tan** • neh **to** • kef—prayer from the *Machzor* expressing the awesome holiness of the High Holydays.

Ya • 'a • **kov**—James, Jacob. In this book the reference is to the brother of Yeshua the Messiah who became leader of the Jerusalem Messianic Community and who wrote the book of Ya'akov [James] in the New Testament.

Yad L' • A • **chim**—an anti-missionary organization active in Israel. Also known as the *Peylim* ("activists").

ye • **shi** • va **bo** • chers (Yiddish English)—students at a *yeshiva,* a Jewish school in which *Torah* (chiefly the Oral *Torah) is* the main, if not the only, subject.

Ye • **shu** • a—the Messiah's name, given him in obedience to Mattityahu [Matthew] 1:21. This name found some 30 times in the *Tanakh,* is a contraction of *Yehoshua* [Joshua]; it means "God saves" or "salvation." The name *Yeshua* was rendered in Greek as *Iêsous,* which in turn was brought over into English as "Jesus."

ye • shu • **'ah**—salvation, deliverance.

Y-H-V-H—conventional English way of representing the four Hebrew letters *yud-heh-vav-heh* which are the consonants in God's personal name, usually given in English as "Jehovah" or "Yahweh."

yi • **rat**-Ha • **Shem**—fear of God (literally, "fear of The Name").

Yitz • **chak**—Isaac.

Yo • cha • **nan**—John, one of Yeshua's twelve emissaries (apostles), author of one of the four Gospels and of the three Letters of Yochanan [John]; it is also generally understood that he is the author of the book of Revelation.

Yom **Kip** • pur (Ashk. Yom **Kip** • pur)—Day of Atonement.

yud —the smallest Hebrew letter.

INDEX OF SCRIPTURE VERSES AND OTHER EARLY LITERATURE

TANAKH (OLD TESTAMENT)

NEW TESTAMENT

OTHER EARLY LITERATURE

GENERAL INDEX

An asterisk (*) follows the names of Messianic Jews.

DAVID H. STERN was born in Los Angeles in 1935, the great-grandson of two of the city's first twenty Jews. He earned a Ph.D. in economics at Princeton University and was a professor at UCLA, mountain-climber, co-author of a book on surfing,and owner of health food stores. In 1972 he came to faith in Yeshua; he then received a Master of Divinity degree from Fuller Theological Seminary and did graduate work at the University of Judaism. He was married in 1976 to Martha Frankel, also a Messianic Jew, and together they served one year on the staff of Jews for Jesus. Dr. Stern taught Fuller Seminary's first course in "Judaism and Christianity," organized Messianic Jewish conferences and leaders' meetings, and served as an officer of the Messianic Jewish Alliance of America. In 1979 the Stern family made *aliyah* (immigrated to Israel); they now live in Jerusalem. Their two children are married and living in the Land; they have three grandchildren (as of 2006).

Dr. Stern has written an abridgement of this book called *Restoring The Jewishness Of The Gospel: A Message For Christians* and is translator of the *Jewish New Testament,* a version of the New Testament that expresses its essential Jewishness. He has also written a companion volume, the *Jewish New Testament Commentary,* which deals with Jewish issues raised in the New Testament, and the *Complete Jewish Bible,* which combines his version of the *Tanakh* (Old Testament) with the *Jewish New Testament.*